QUEENS
IN THE KINGDOM

The Ultimate Gay and Lesbian
Guide to the Disney Theme Parks

By Jeffrey Epstein and Eddie Shapiro

alyson books
los angeles

Manufactured in the United States of America.

This trade paperback original is published by Alyson Publications,
P.O. Box 4371, Los Angeles, California 90078-4371.
Distribution in the United Kingdom by Turnaround Publisher Services Ltd.,
Unit 3, Olympia Trading Estate, Coburg Road, Wood Green,
London N22 6TZ England.

First edition: April 2003

03 04 05 06 07 a 10 9 8 7 6 5 4 3 2 1

ISBN 1-55583-745-X

Library of Congress Cataloging-in-Publication Data

Epstein, Jeffrey.

Queens in the kingdom : the ultimate gay and lesbian guide to the Disney theme parks / by Jeffrey Epstein and Eddie Shapiro.—1st ed.

Includes bibliographical references and index.

ISBN 1-55583-745-X

1. Disneyland (Calif.)—Guidebooks. 2. Walt Disney World (Fla.)—Guidebooks. 3. Gays—Recreation—California—Disneyland. 4. Gays—Recreation—Florida—Walt Disney World. I. Shapiro, Eddie, 1969– II. Title.

GV1853.3.C22D57315 2003

791'.06'8—DC21   2002043776

CREDITS

- Back cover photo used by permission from Disney Enterprises, Inc.

- Tower of Terror photo on page 198 used by permission from Disney Enterprises, Inc.

- All other photos © Disney Enterprises, Inc.

Table of Contents

Acknowledgments • xi
Key to Icons Used • xv
Introduction • 1

Part One: Stuff You Need to Plan

Chapter One: Gays 'n' Disney • 7

Chapter Two: The Preliminaries • 13
    How Much Time You'll Need • 13
    When to Go • 13
    Additional Information • 14
    Ticketing • 15
    Where to Stay • 17
    Should You Rent a Car? • 17
    Dining Overview • 18
    Gettin' There • 19
    Guided Tours • 19
    Disabled in the Park • 22

Chapter Three: The Disney Parks With Kids • 25

Chapter Four: Characters • 27

Chapter Five: Negotiating the Parks • 29

Chapter Six: Where to Sleep...Or at Least Check In • 33
    Disneyland Resort Hotels • 33
    Walt Disney World Resort Hotels • 37

Part Two: Disneyland Resort

Chapter Seven: Disneyland Park • 65
    Main Street, U.S.A. • 65
    Adventureland • 70
    New Orleans Square • 74
    Critter Country • 77
    Frontierland • 79
    Fantasyland • 83
    Mickey's Toontown • 93
    Tomorrowland • 97

Chapter Eight: Disney's California Adventure Park • 105
    Sunshine Plaza • 108
    Golden State • 108
    Hollywood Pictures Backlot • 115
    Paradise Pier • 119

Chapter Nine: Downtown Disney, Anaheim, and
    Other Area Parks • 125
    Nighttime at Disneyland Resort • 125
    Anaheim Gay Life • 127
    Surrounding Theme Parks—California • 128

Part Three: Walt Disney World Resort

Chapter Ten: Magic Kingdom • 139
    Main Street, U.S.A. • 139
    Adventureland • 143
    Frontierland • 146
    Liberty Square • 147
    Fantasyland • 149
    Mickey's Toontown Fair • 155
    Tomorrowland • 157
Chapter Eleven: Epcot • 163

Future World • 166
World Showcase • 180

Chapter Twelve: Disney-MGM Studios • 193

Chapter Thirteen: Disney's Animal Kingdom • 211
The Oasis • 214
Discovery Island • 214
Camp Minnie-Mickey • 215
Africa • 218
Asia • 220
Dinoland U.S.A. • 221

Chapter Fourteen: The Rest of the Resort • 225
Nighttime at Walt Disney World Resort • 225
Downtown Disney • 221
Water Parks • 236
Other Activities • 239

Chapter Fifteen: Orlando and Other Area Parks • 243
Orlando Gay Life • 243
Surrounding Theme Parks—Florida • 244

Part Four: Odds 'n' Ends

Chapter Sixteen: Lists and Charts and
Ratings—Oh, My! • 253
Compare and Contrast: Disneyland Resort Versus
Walt Disney World Resort • 253
Top Fives • 258
The Disney Parks' Top 10 Spots to Share a
Gay Moment • 264
Ride Ratings Chart • 265
Glossary • 278
Bibliography • 279

Index • 280
Contact Us • 284
About the Authors • 285

Acknowledgments

Though we'd like to pretend we did this whole thing ourselves, we have to thank the following individuals, without whom things would have been a lot harder than they were.

When we first began writing articles about the parks, the following people provided us invaluable information and access, sending us down the stony end: Doug Swallow of Gay Day at Walt Disney World Resort; Keith Peterson, Scott Smith, and Tom Dyer of Watermark and the Beach Ball; Audrey Eig and Michael McLane from Universal Hollywood and Orlando respectively; and especially Diane Ledder, Bill Warren, and Rena Callahan at Walt Disney World Resort.

In 1998, Gabriel Goldberg published our first piece on the parks, planting the seed that would become this book (so he's really to blame).

Thanks to Greg Constante, Alyson publisher, for taking on this project; Angela Brown for slaving over the pages; Matt Sams for mapping and charting himself to death; marketing whiz Dan Cullinane; and the entire Alyson staff.

We also must thank the tireless folks at the Walt Disney Company who have been instrumental in the creation of this book, providing us with a dizzying array of facts and figures. Charles Stovall, photographer Adrienne D. Helitzer (who's not really a cast member, but we won't hold it against her), Janelle Sowersby, Rick Sylvain, and Margaret Adamic, our mouse ears are off to you. And a special bundle of gratitude goes out to Bob Deuel at Disneyland, who has been both our Prince Charming and fairy godmother.

There are other Disney cast members past and present whose knowledge and friendship have also been instrumental in this book's creation: Nick Anderson, Vince Koehl, Jeff Kurtti, Denise Sparacio, James Starbuck, and Garth Steever.

And of course, a very special thanks to our interview subjects, all of whom were generous enough with their time and wisdom to offer us different perspectives.

We'd also like to thank all of our friends and relatives who've suffered the agony and the ecstasy, the joy and the trauma of spending time with us in the parks and providing the raw material that became this book (they also always listened as we complained about each other). They are valiant adventurers all: Melinda Berk, Austyn Biggers, Jessie Campbell, Paula Chudd, Kenny Davis, Jeffrey Dersh, Claudia Falk, David Franklin, Jeff Gurner, Stephen Hamblin, Dennis Hensley, Collin Jones, Lindsey Jones, Eric Kops, John-Michael Lander, Ron Lasko, Worthie Meacham, Clinton Meyer, David Miller, Michelle Milzow, Michael Paternastro, Deborah Praver, Erin Quill, Gregg Rainwater, Steven Rosso, Bob Smith, David Spiro, Tony Tripoli, Greg Wegweiser, and Keith Wilson.

Eddie wants to thank a few others who, for their own sanity, avoided going to the parks with him but provided invaluable and constant support nonetheless: Scott Cameron, Gregg Gettas, Erin Harkins, Cheryl Keller, Joe Quenqua, Arlene Shapiro, Gilles Wheeler, and Tom Young. Most especially he thanks Jen Keller, without whom he imagines he'd be a blithering idiot sucking his thumb in a corner.

Jeffrey thanks Bruce Steele for constantly lending an ear and an open mind, Chris Oakley for his indispensable knowledge, and Jeff Bader for always being there to give his support. And of course he thanks Eddie for always listening, always being supportive, and always putting their friendship above their writing partnership.

And finally, we need to thank the people who are really

responsible, the clan who took us to the parks to begin with and began this obsession we share. They also gave us the education that enabled us to write. (Of course, there are those who might argue that they made us gay as well, so they get thanks for that too.) Our families, who frequently believed in us more than we did ourselves: Sue, Julian, and Jennifer Epstein; Ann, Donald, and Rona Shapiro; and Emma Morgan.

Key to Icons Used

🍴 Sit-Down Restaurant

☕ Cafeteria

🏋 Spa/Fitness Center

ℂ Business Center

😊 Character Dining

⚡ FASTPASS

🚌 Bus Transportation

⚓ Water Transportation

🚶 Within Walking Distance of One or
      More Parks

🚆 Monorail Access

B=breakfast, L=lunch, D=dinner

Attraction Ratings

✪ Cruella De Vil

✪✪ Give a Little Whistle

✪✪✪ Zip-A-Dee-Doo-Dah

✪✪✪✪ You Can Fly! You Can Fly! You Can Fly!

✪✪✪✪✪ Supercalifragilisticexpialidocious

Introduction

Why We Wrote This Book

Since we began work on this book, the question most frequently asked of us has been "Why?" Why would anyone need a gay and lesbian guide to the Disney theme parks? Why, for that matter, does anyone need a guide at all? It's a friggin' theme park! Well, yes. And no. The Disney parks are, without question, America's most popular tourist destination. They are massive worlds with their own cultures. While one could navigate the parks without a guide, there is simply too much information and too many variables to leave your trip to chance. You should know as much as possible so you can plan your days wisely. Otherwise, you're bound to find yourself stuck in long lines and paying through the nose for substandard food. We're here to help.

But there are other guides that do that too. We wrote this guide because, as gay people, we look for something else in a vacation. Something a little less common, a little less obvious. We look for *fabulous*! And you can find it at the Disney parks, if you know where to look. So first and foremost, our goal is to point out some of the parks' attributes that may or may not resonate with breeders but definitely ring bells for us.

Then there are the more base reasons. Specifically, in parks populated predominantly by straight couples and their spawn, where can gay people cruise, hold hands, or grab a kiss without feeling stared at? We provide that information, making our recommendations somewhat different from those of your Aunt Peg from Sheboygan.

And finally, we're here to offer you our opinions. So instead of the Disney-produced official guides, which lead you to believe that everything in the parks is amazing and wondrous, we're here to tell it like it is. If a ride sucks, we're not afraid to say so (in fact, we're chomping at the bit to tell you about it). And unlike the authors of any other guide, we'll do so between sips of apple martinis. Consider us the Edina and Patsy of guidebooks (if that's not a reference you understand, you should put this book down now—we're not for you).

A Word About Us

All of the above really doesn't answer why *we* wrote this book—why two seemingly sane young men would dedicate hours of their lives to half a dozen theme parks. The truth is, ever since we were kids growing up in Manhattan (Eddie) and outside Boston (Jeffrey), our parents brought us to these magic places where everything was perfect. We've been hooked ever since. It's like heroin without the chic.

Every time we went to the parks with friends, we delighted in showing the subtle (and not-so-subtle) gay side of things. Friends who didn't even like the parks enjoyed going with us because they knew we'd show them things they wouldn't otherwise see or catch on to. And before we knew it, we realized we were a cottage industry waiting to happen. Yes, we know a lot of people (Eddie in particular has known a lot of people), but this book gives us the opportunity to share the parks' pinker side with so many more people than we'd otherwise get to know—although we're trying.

While in writing this book we were striving to share the love and enthusiasm we have for the parks (tempered, of course, by the resentment we feel for having spent enough money to send 47 kids to college), we also wanted to provide information to gay people who weren't just like us. Although

we are, at the time of writing, both single, gay men in our 30s (but look late 20s!), we realize many of you aren't. So, in an effort to broaden our perspectives a bit, we surveyed gays and lesbians from around the country and have included their input. Unless we thought it was stupid.

How to Use This Book

While we realize most of you are probably fairly bright (you did, after all, purchase this book) and can figure stuff out on your own, we want to take the opportunity to introduce you to a few of the features you'll find in this book. First of all, after each attraction description, we've included a Fairy Fact. Fairy Facts are little useless bits of ephemera that make you go, "Huh, I didn't know that." Mostly, we included them because as we were researching we found tons of information we thought was too cool to leave out. We also want you to be able to walk through the park with the quiet satisfaction that you know things about the attractions that most other guests won't. Still, we don't really recommend attempting to use any of these facts as pick-up lines. Eddie has. Crash. Burn. The thought makes us wince.

We've also taken the liberty (and why not, it's our book) of giving the entries completely biased and subjective ratings. It's a five-star system with a range of "sucky" to "fantabulous." These ratings should help you know at a glance whether an attraction or hotel is worth the time or money (things we try to spend with at least a little discretion).

There's a glossary in the back of the book, just in case you're confused by any of our "Disney-speak."

And while you're back there, take a look at our lists. They include shortcuts to what we like and don't like for when you're on the fly and don't have time to read full ride descriptions. There's also a list of places that are conducive to kissing (wait, don't go there yet!).

Change Is Good (Well, It Can Be)

"Disneyland will never be completed," said Walt of his original park. "It will continue to grow as long as there is imagination left in the world." In keeping with that vision, Disney resorts are constantly changing and evolving. This means there's always something cooking, whether it's new attractions, restaurants, hotels, and (of course) stores to buy lots of Disney stuff. It also means that things such as ticket prices, hotel rates, and even attractions can change with little notice, and sometimes even much-beloved rides will be shut down for good.

In recent years at Disneyland Park, the PeopleMover and the Circle-Vision theater were closed to make way for the thrill ride Rocket Rods. However, after just over a year of operation, Rocket Rods was closed down, and as of press time, nothing was scheduled to go in its place.

Of course, not all buildings remain empty: Mr. Toad's Wild Ride in Orlando made way for the Many Adventures of Winnie the Pooh; in both resorts Michael Jackson's campy *Captain EO* became *Honey, I Shrunk the Audience*; Take Flight in the Magic Kingdom became Buzz Lightyear's Space Ranger Spin; and at Disneyland Park, Walt Disney's Carousel of Progress became America Sings, which became Innoventions (which we find to be questionable progress at best).

For up-to-the-minute information, we suggest you visit the park's Web sites at www.waltdisneyworld.com or www.disneyland.com. While we pride ourselves on our intimate knowledge of the parks, things are bound to change. So don't be mad at us.

Part One
Stuff You Need to Plan

Chapter One
Gays 'n' Disney

Why do gay people love Disney so much?

People have actually written essays on this topic. But since you bought a guide, we'll spare you the academe in favor of a little dime-store psychology.

Fantasy: Let's face it, gay people love fantasy, artifice, and escapism: Hollywood, the theater, dance clubs—we like other worlds. And the Disney parks are all about transporting us to other worlds.

The Outsider Wins: Disney movies have always told stories of outcasts or underdogs who overcome and live happily ever after. From *Dumbo* to *The Little Mermaid,* Disney heroes are often thought of as "less than" by their contemporaries. Nowhere is that more clearly illustrated than in the lyrics of the late, gay Howard Ashman, who in *Beauty and the Beast* had the villagers crying, "We don't like what we don't understand. In fact, it scares us," as they hunted down the Beast. While anyone who has ever felt like a minority can relate to the lyric, the words especially resonate for gays and lesbians.

The "Family" Behind the Magic: It shouldn't surprise anyone that some of the biggest talents behind the scenes at Disney are gay. Steven B. Davison, creative director at the Disneyland Resort, who's responsible for such spectacles as Believe…There's Magic in the Stars and "it's a small world holiday," acknowledges that "some of the best designs that have come out of here have been from gay men. Knowing all the designers who I grew up here with, the most evocative parades and the most stunning things you saw came out of a gay sensibility." And while the 15-year Disneyland Resort veteran gives praise to Disney's heterosexual employees, "a lot of straight men who are brilliant designers have a stiffer quality about [their designs]."

It's Over-the-Top: We love a bit of fanfare. Hell, if we didn't, would our pride parades always be so fierce? Would Madonna have ever been a success? Would Carol Channing have even existed? "I'd come here and I was fascinated by how over-the-top everything was," recalls Davison of his youth visiting the park. "To me, that's what gay culture embraces a bit, being very over the top."

You Get to Be a Kid Again: For many gay and lesbian adults, childhood was a painful time. Many were taunted for being effeminate or a tomboy, while others found themselves feeling like the aforementioned outsider as they tried to figure out their place in the world. The parks speak to the child within us, who's getting a second chance—with a little less angst. Amen!

Gay Days at Disney

We're sure many of you have already heard of the unofficial Gay Days at both Walt Disney World Resort and Disneyland Resort. These take place without the endorsement of The Walt Disney Company. This is not because they hate us. It's just their policy not to endorse any groups that come into the park during normal operating hours. Disney has been very accommodating to the thousands of gay and lesbian guests who pour through their gates (it doesn't hurt that many of us have huge disposable incomes and tend to drop wads of cash while in the parks). Several area hotels and clubs get into the act with special parties and events to capitalize on the crowds. During those weekends, the parks are at their absolute gayest (and this book becomes almost irrelevant, as there's gay stuff at every turn).

Because Gay Days are unofficial, we blend in with all the straight folk in the parks. OK, so maybe "blend in" isn't the right turn of phrase. Gay Day attendees are encouraged to wear red shirts so that we can identify one another, stand out in the crowds, and show our strength in numbers.

Although we encourage you to visit the Disney parks at any time of the year, there's something unique about visiting during Gay Days. There's a relaxed yet giddy feeling in the air. You can hold hands with your boyfriend or girlfriend. You can cruise the hotties and be fairly certain they will cruise you back. For many people who find themselves somewhat repressed in their everyday lives (or in their everyday trips to Disney), it's a chance just to be yourself—and finally with family at America's number 1 family destination.

Gay Days at Walt Disney World Resort
When: The first weekend in June
Details: Visit www.gayday.com, www.gaydays.com
Back in 1991, Doug Swallow suggested he and some gay friends from his bulletin board group (remember life before AOL?) meet up at the Magic Kingdom one day in June, a tradition was born. Now, over a decade later, more than 100,000 gays and lesbians descend on Orlando every June. From its humble beginnings, the event has become a weeklong celebration that includes tea dances, circuit parties, and private parties at the parks. The main day is at the Magic Kingdom on Saturday, where at the afternoon parade the "red" converges, forming a blurry scarlet mass.

One of the highlights is the **Beach Ball** (www.beach ball.com), a nighttime party at Typhoon Lagoon presented by Watermark Entertainment Group. While it has become a little more "circuit party" in nature, with top DJs and a huge dance floor, it's hard to keep up that circuit-y attitude when you're screaming your head off going down a water slide.

Jeffrey Sanker (www.jeffreysanker.com) presents **One**

Mighty Party at Disney-MGM Studios, and while it's definitely a big circuit party, there's something really cool about going to one inside a Disney theme park. In the past, they've offered unlimited rides on the Twilight Zone™ Tower of Terror and the Rock 'n' Roller Coaster Starring Aerosmith. We do not advise the consumption of alcohol or drugs before riding (not that we'd ever advocate drug or alcohol use!). One time, right before the drop on the Tower of Terror, one tweaking guy cried out, "My X is kicking in!"

Mark Baker (www.markbakerpresents.com) always puts on a private party at Universal on the Sunday of the weekend, with live acts, dancers, and a light presentation that keep us entranced—even when we're sober!

There are also Gay Days at Epcot, Disney's Animal Kingdom, and Disney-MGM Studios (as well as Universal's Islands of Adventure and Sea World). Check out the Web sites for the details.

Gay Days at Disneyland Resort
When: The first weekend in October
Details: Visit www.gayday2.com

While a private company used to rent out Disneyland Park one night a year for gays and lesbians, the tradition stopped in 1997. In 1998 a new tradition was born: Gay Day 2 (the "2" indicates its younger-sibling status). After just a few years, more than 17,000 people flooded through the gates of Disneyland Resort on the first Saturday in October, and when Disney's California Adventure park opened in 2001, Sunday became the day to visit the new park.

Because it's only in its fifth year as of this writing, private events are starting but are not yet established traditions. The **Wonderland** party takes place on Friday night at the Disneyland Resort. Check out the Gay Day 2 Web site for more details.

And remember, wear a red shirt!

Commitment Ceremonies/Weddings

While Disney may be on the P.C. ball in many ways (e.g., it offers domestic-partner benefits to its employees), they are positively primeval in others. So if you want to have your fairy-tale wedding at either of the resorts, you may have to pretend it's a bar mitzvah. "Proof of a valid Florida marriage license is required prior to hosting your wedding ceremony at the Walt Disney World Resort," says a rep for the Orlando theme park. A Disneyland Resort publicist echoes the sentiment. "We require proof of a valid marriage license for a ceremony or vow renewal," he told us. "As you know, the State of California does not yet recognize same-sex couples in obtaining marriage licenses, so same-sex ceremonies just aren't held here."

Now, while we would never suggest boycotting our favorite vacation destinations (What? And risk losing book sales?), if you have a problem with this policy, we suggest you let your voice be heard. Hey, there was a time not too long ago when Disney didn't allow same-sex dancing!

Chapter Two
The Preliminaries
(a.k.a. All the Stuff You'd Better Think About Before You Go)

How Much Time You'll Need

If you want to see everything there is to see at the parks (and some of you may be perfectly happy not to—we don't understand you, but we know you exist), you pretty much have to allocate a day per park. In Florida, that means a minimum stay of four days; in California, two. If you have the time, we recommend spending a fifth day in Orlando, just so you can make it to one of the water parks, the golf course, or the outlet mall (a 10-minute drive to DKNY and Banana Republic at cut rates!). In California, unless you're heading out of Anaheim (Laguna Beach is half an hour away, Los Angeles is 45 minutes on a good day), there's not a whole lot to do in the area other than the parks, so two days is sufficient.

When to Go

Obviously, this question is best answered by your vacation schedule. That said, for most of the straight world, this question is answered by the kids' school calendar. Christmas, Thanksgiving week, and the summer months are always mob scenes at any of the parks. Ditto Easter. The quietest months are October, November, and December (excluding Thanksgiving week and Christmas week), January, and May. Weekdays are always best, but if you must go on a weekend, the Magic Kingdom and Disneyland

Park get particularly crowded on Saturdays (when the locals go). It's best to save those parks, if you can, for any other day of the week. And, of course, we always recommend going for Gay Days (first weekend in June in Florida, first weekend in October in California) because, even though the parks are crowded, lines are significantly less offensive when you can cruise and make new friends.

Now, before you start packing, there are some true downsides to going during the off-season. For starters, the parks open later (usually 10 A.M. instead of 8 A.M.) and close significantly earlier (as early as 6 P.M. in January). There are also many fewer shows and parades going on, and rides are frequently out of commission for refurbishment. Frankly, we think a "no line" park experience far outweighs another parade, but that's just us. The Disney Web sites provide daily schedules of both hours and entertainment so you can plan accordingly.

The weather in both Florida and California can vary significantly within a single day (a 20-degree split is not uncommon), so make sure that in fall and winter you have sweaters for the evenings. Summer months at both parks are hot. Florida takes the prize, however, with daily temperatures in the 90s. Factor in the humidity, and we recommend bringing only shorts, sandals, and a ton of hair product.

Additional Information

While we do profess to knowing everything, you may still have a couple of gnawing questions after reading the book (like our phone numbers). The Disney resorts can furnish you with additional help (although not our phone numbers—sorry). You'll also be able to use them as a starting point for making dining and room reservations.

Disneyland Resort
(714) 781-7290

Walt Disney World Resort
(407) 934-7639

Ticketing

While your airline reservations will probably be fairly straightforward, your ticketing options at the parks bear some thought. It's complicated, and what you choose wholly depends on what your agenda at the parks is. Options are as follows:

Length-of-Stay Passes: If you're staying on Walt Disney World Resort property, you can purchase an admission ticket good at all of the parks from the moment you check in until the end of the day you check out. This ticket offers convenience like you wouldn't believe. It means you can go back and forth from park to park as many times as you like within a day. Now, we know that from where you're sitting, that doesn't seem so important, but trust us, it is. On the day that you see Disney's Animal Kingdom, for example, you'll be done by 4 P.M. and will want to use those extra hours at the Magic Kingdom. Several times we've been with groups who start the day together and end up separated in different parks. The flexibility is terrific. Furthermore, a Length-of-Stay Pass at Walt Disney World Resort gets you into Pleasure Island (otherwise $19.95 each night), the water parks, Disney's Wide World of Sports, and DisneyQuest.

Hopper Passes: Hopper passes are different at Disneyland Resort and Walt Disney World Resort. At Walt Disney World Resort, Hopper passes come in two forms: Park Hopper and Park Hopper Plus. With either pass, you can float freely between the four parks. Hopper Plus passes include limited entry to the three water parks, DisneyQuest, and Pleasure Island. They come in five-, six-, or seven-day increments and allow you two, three, or four Plus choices, depending on which one you purchase (a five-day pass, for example, comes with two plus options, which would get you into Blizzard Beach and Pleasure Island once—additional visits would cost more). Standard Hopper passes come in only four- or five-day versions. The advantage of Hopper passes over Length-of-Stay passes is that Hoppers don't expire. If, for example, you only use five of your seven days, you can use the other two on a future visit (or give those two days to your Aunt Selma for her trip with her bridge club). And you don't have to stay at a Disney hotel to use them. The disadvantages are the limitations imposed on the Plus options and the fact that the minimum duration for a Hopper pass is four days. Length-of-Stay passes are good for as long or as short as your visit.

Disneyland Resort's Hopper passes are a bit less friendly. Available in either three- or four-day increments, they also allow free coming and going between parks. The bad news is that they expire 13 days after their first use.

Single-Park Passes: On both coasts, single day/single park tickets are available but, of course, you're restricted to one park only. That matters more at Walt Disney World Resort than Disneyland Resort, since Walt Disney World Resort has more parks.

Annual Passes: These are available at both Walt Disney World Resort and Disneyland, and while they're pricey, they do pay for themselves if you visit the parks more than once in a year. And the total flexibility they afford significantly ups their value.

Tickets are available in advance via the parks' Web sites, at Disney Stores nationwide, or at any Disney hotel. Otherwise, you can purchase tickets on your way in to the parks, but lines can be long and annoying.

Where to Stay

While we've broken the parks down by the two resorts, we have one fat, juicy section on the Disney property hotels. Of course, there are dozens of other hotels you could stay at, but really, do we seem like the kind of people who have the time to visit every hotel in Orlando and Anaheim? We have rides to go on, people. Plus we prefer to stay on property. When you get to that section, you'll understand why.

Should You Rent a Car?

At either Disneyland Resort or Walt Disney World Resort, having a car is completely unnecessary. That said, for our annual trip to Walt Disney World Resort, we always rent one (all of the national chains are available at the airport). Disney's transportation systems (which include bus, boat, and monorail) are all excellent and efficiently get you anywhere within park grounds. But let's say you want to go from one hotel to another (and we can envision one or two scenarios where that might be the case). You have to take a bus to the Marketplace at Downtown Disney or the Transportation Center and catch another bus to your destination. Ditto the return trip. That little jaunt can end up sucking an hour out of your day in transportation alone. You can do the round trip by car in 20 minutes or less. Furthermore, we like to occasionally escape to local bars, the outlet mall, and (gasp!) other theme parks. So while the bus system is extensive, we're spoiled. We like the car.

At Disneyland Resort, when we stay overnight, we don't set foot in our vehicles (except when someone gets lucky and the room is occupied). Unless you're planning excursions, a car at Disneyland Resort is completely superfluous.

Dining Overview:
The Skinny on Food

A girl's gotta eat, after all. And while we pride ourselves on frequent trips to the gym and relatively healthy diets, it all goes out the window when we enter a Disney resort. Besides, you're walking around all day, right? You'll burn it off. Um, sure.

While many people remember the Disney of years gone by, which offered little variety and even less quality in terms of dining, brush those thoughts aside. There are good eats to be found in every section of the resorts. While some guides lump all their restaurant reviews together, we've decided to break them down for you by location. After all, if you're in the Magic Kingdom, you're gonna want to know where to eat in the Magic Kingdom, not in Downtown Disney. So that's how to use the guide. You wanna know where to eat at the Disneyland Hotel? Flip to the Disneyland Hotel. Easy.

Furthermore, we've opted to review only Disney's sit-down restaurants. Let's face it, a Disney burger is a Disney burger, and if we reviewed every churro stand in the park, we wouldn't fit on most of the attractions—let alone have time to ride any of them. In our overviews, however, we do note some of the better eat-and-run and cafeteria options.

If you're interested in Character Dining (eating with Mickey and pals), check out page 27 for a full description.

Many of these sit-down restaurants offer what Disney calls priority seating—their form of reservations. Guests staying on Disney property can call ahead (up to 60 days in advance) to make priority seating reservations, while other guests can make them the moment they walk into the parks, subject to availability. A limited number of stand-by seats are always available. If you're traveling in a large group or are just dying to eat at Fulton's Crab House (and you should be), you will want to call ahead. It's worth it.

Gettin' There

Driving to the Disney Parks is very easy. Walt Disney World Resort is at the intersection of I-4 and U.S. 192, roughly 20 minutes south of downtown Orlando.

Disneyland Resort is on I-5, 45 minutes (average—with traffic that time can double) south of Los Angeles.

From the airport in either city, rental cars are, of course, readily available.

If you're not renting, taxis from either Orlando or Los Angeles International Airport (LAX) will cost you roughly $50 or more. There are hourly buses and shuttles at each, for significantly less. In Orlando, Mears Motor Transportation Service (407) 423-5566 is the most reliable. There are busses to Disneyland Resort that don't require reservations from LAX. Check with the airport ground transportation desk at baggage claim for details.

Guided Tours

Now, we know we've given you information. Lots of it. But, believe it or not, there are people who can give you still more.

Walt Disney World Resort Tours

At the Florida parks, there are several guided tours available for in-depth, backstage visits. These are particularly good if you've been to the parks several times and are ready for a new perspective (or if you need to hear someone other than your travel mate talk for a while). Unless otherwise indicated, all tours are for adults only (that's 16 or over, no matter how hard Jeffrey tries to tell you that a 14-year-old is fully grown). For reservations, schedules, and detailed information call (407) WDW-TOUR. Available tours include:

Keys to the Kingdom: Every day. A five-hour tour of the backstage workings of the Magic Kingdom. Included is a trip to the Utilidor, the infamous, nine-acre catacomb system built below the park.

Backstage Magic: M–F. A seven-hour tour covering a lot of the same territory as Keys to the Kingdom does but also including Epcot, Disney-MGM Studios (backstage at Fantasmic!), and lunch at Mama Melrose's Ristorante.

Hidden Treasures of the World Showcase: Tu, Th. This three-hour tour is an in-depth architectural tour of all 11 international replicas in the World Showcase Pavilions ("This pyramid isn't real, but if it were, here's why it would be significant…").

Gardens of the World: Tu, Th. A three-hour plant and horticultural look at Epcot. It's said to be far more interesting than it sounds.

DiveQuest: Every day. This three-hour tour of the Living Seas pavilion at Epcot is only for the scuba certified. It includes a 30-minute dive (equipment is provided).

Greenhouse Tour: Every day. This one-hour tour of the Living With the Land greenhouses can only be booked in the park on the day of your visit. Again, we hear it's better than it sounds.

Dolphins in Depth: M, W. Over 3½ hours you get up close and personal (we're talking feeling the heartbeat) of the dolphins of the Living Seas pavilion.

Undiscovered Future World (As opposed to the future that has already been discovered? How does that work?)**:** M, Tu, F, Sa. In 4½ hours, you'll get an inside look plus a visit to backstage at Illuminations and The Tapestry of Dreams.

Inside Animation: W, F. In 2½ hours, you'll get a detailed look at how the studio churns out animation at Disney-MGM Studios.

Disney's Magic Behind the Steam Train: M, Th, Sa (at 7:45 A.M.!). Takes guests to the train yards and, in two hours, details Walt's fascination with choo-choos.

Wild by Design: Tu, Th, F. A three-hour cultural tour of Disney's Animal Kingdom's lands. This one's notable for its usage of a new technology wherein guides speak into a mike that transmits to guest headsets, making crowding around your leader a thing of the past.

Backstage Safari: M, W, F. Hmm. What's missing here? Sure you get to see Disney's Animal Kingdom's animal warehouse and hospital in this three-hour tour but, um, there are no animals. They're all earning their keep out on the savanna. Kinda like going to your boyfriend's house while he's at work.

Disneyland Resort Tours

Tours are less behind-the-scenes than those at Walt Disney World Resort. On the two main excursions, available every day, guests must pay their own admission to the park, and tour charges are additional. Private tours of the park (if you want a more, um, intimate viewing) are also available. Call (714) 781-7290 for prices. Children are welcome but may be bored. Tours include:

Welcome to Disneyland: This four-hour tour (which includes three attractions, though you don't get to cut in line) is full of little-known park trivia.

A Walk in Walt's Footsteps: Disneyland Resort created this tour in celebration of Walt's 100th birthday. Highlights include a visit to the Club 33 lobby, a private lunch in the

Disney Gallery, and a behind the scenes look at the Enchanted Tiki Room.

Disabled in the Parks

Parking

Parking for the disabled is available at all the parks. Make sure to tell the attendant as you pull in, and he or she will direct you to the ground level area.

Wheelchairs

If you need a wheelchair, they are available for rent at the parks (and for resort guests, at the hotels) and come with maps showing the best ways to travel by chair. There are also electric wheelchairs available that look significantly more fun than several of the actual rides (after all, they go at about twice the speed of the Speedway cars). Most attractions and shows have wheelchair seating available. For those that don't, if the guest can transfer from their chair to the ride vehicle, Disney makes this as easy as possible for the guest and their party. It should be noted, however, that cast members cannot assist with this transfer.

Since most rides can't accommodate a wheelchair in their queue, nonambulatory guests should ask for the disabled entry as they arrive at a ride. Usually it's at the exit, and wait time is minimal. Should you have a lesser disability, as Jeffrey did when he wrenched his ankle in Disney's Animal Kingdom, crutches are also available at first-aid stations.

We should note that while we really appreciate the service Disney provides, we've seen it abused by people who don't need it but use it to avoid lines. A perfectly healthy (if somewhat overweight) female couple we know delight in telling the story of how they skipped every line in the parks by pretending to be wheelchair-bound. We hate them and know in our hearts that Disney karma will eventually hurt them.

Guests With HIV

We know of an HIV-positive guest who didn't need a wheelchair but was unable to stand in long lines. Main Street's City Hall issued him a special pass allowing him to skip the lines. Again, kudos to Disney.

Visual Disabilities

Braille guidebooks, cassette tapes, and portable tape players are available to guests during their visit to the Disney parks. Service animals are also welcome in most locations around the resort but must remain on a leash at all times. (Some attractions, however, will not allow animals, in which case someone from your party must remain outside the attraction with the animal.)

Hearing Disabilities

Disney provides numerous services to their hearing-impaired guests including Assistive Listening Systems (a wireless device that amplifies sound), Reflective Captioning (for shows that involve projections), and sign language interpretation (with seven days' notice at Walt Disney World Resort, three at Disneyland Resort). Guests can request interpretation at Walt Disney World Resort by calling (407) 824-4321 (voice) or (407) 827-5141 (TTY) and at Disneyland Resort by calling (714) 781-4555 (voice).

A Final Note

We have particular admiration for guests with limitations who choose to go to the parks. Getting around in a wheelchair or on crutches in a massive crowd strikes us as a little slice of torture. Our hats are off to anyone who will take on that inconvenience. If it were us, we'd be too busy moping and feeling sorry for ourselves. You won't catch sentiment like this again, so don't think we're going soft or anything.

Chapter Three
The Disney Resorts With Kids

Ewwwwww. Just kidding. While we realize there's an ever-growing legion of gay parents, this book is not ultimately designed as a guide for families—more of a guide for "family." That's not to say that parents won't find good bits of guidance throughout the book—we often note rides that are more appropriate for children (or adults for that matter).

If you're planning a trip with your kiddies to either of the Disney parks, here are a few good things for you to know:

Baby-sitting: Now that you're at the park, here's how to ditch the little ones! If you're staying on Disney property, all Disney hotels offer baby-sitting services so you can get a little private time. At many of the resort properties, there are kid clubs where your younguns can frolic with others in a supervised environment while you dine. It's like day care at night. Contact the front desk for details and rates.

Strollers: While we often wonder why parents would take a child in a stroller to an expensive theme park, when most teeny-tiny tots we have encountered would be equally entranced by the local mall, it's a question that shall never be answered. In any case, strollers are available to rent at the entrances to all the parks.

Changing Stations: They have them in all the bathrooms, people, so please don't swap diapers while on Pirates of the Caribbean.

Height Requirements: Be aware that many of Disney's thrill rides have height requirements. This is not to piss you off but rather to ensure that your child does not slip out of their seat and plummet into a Space Mausoleum. Luckily, if there are two of you with a kid, you can do a "Baby Swap" (as they are called): Adult A goes on the ride while Adult B waits with the child. When A returns, B goes on the attraction without having to wait in line. You should alert the first cast member you see working that attraction so that you can do the swap. Note that the procedure is different for each ride. Of course this means you have to go on the ride alone, but hey, you can use the peace and quiet on Space Mountain, right?

Lost Children (or "Lost Adults," as Disney likes to say): Because Disney parks are crowded and bustling and there's tons of stuff to look at, it's easy to lose a child (especially if you're a bad parent). Cast members are notorious for keeping a diligent eye out and making sure kids stay calm and safe. At Disneyland Park or the Magic Kingdom, go to City Hall. At Epcot, go to Baby Services near the Odyssey Center, which bridges Future World and World Showcase. At Disney-MGM Studios, go to Guest Relations at the entrance to Hollywood Boulevard. And at Disney's Animal Kingdom, go to the Baby Center on Discovery Island. Lost Children at California Adventure is on Fisherman's Wharf past the Boudin Bakery where the baby care center is.

Chapter Four
Characters

Anyone who's ever been in the same state as a television has seen a Disneyland Resort or Walt Disney World Resort commercial in which guests happily frolic with Mickey or Dopey or whomever and it's all a little bit of fairy-tale magic. It is therefore reasonable to expect that when you enter the parks, you will encounter said characters. In fact, for many people (particularly crazy ones), both with and without kids, character encounters are a highlight. Up until the mid 1990s, characters were liberally peppered throughout the parks. You never knew who you'd see, but there were always characters to pet, hug, and share a Kodak moment with. Then things began to get a bit more scientific. At Epcot's World Showcase, characters indigenous to a given region would hang out at those pavilions. Belle, the Beast, and Quasimodo stayed close to France, while Pooh and Mary Poppins trolled the streets of England. Now, while some characters roam freely, the majority are in designated character meeting areas at specific times, which can be found in your guide maps. The days of serendipitously happening upon Pinocchio are pretty much gone. Instead, people wait for ages to snap a picture with Ariel. It's like going to see Santa at Macy's. There is an advantage for those people determined to see as many characters as possible: Now they know where and when to find them. But we prefer our street encounters to be just a bit more organic.

If you're really a character diehard, you can get a little more personal time with the lil critters during character dining meals.

All of the parks and many of the hotels feature restaurants with character dining, which means that at some point during your meal, Mickey or Pluto will drop by your table for some quality time. It's always sort of cute but not worth prioritizing at the expense of park time.

If you have no need to actually get close to—or touch!—a character but wouldn't mind seeing them from afar, you need not engage in any of the above. Most Disney parades feature characters, as do many of the shows. If you're content to watch Donald go by on a float, rest assured that you'll have your chance without having to wait in line for 45 minutes.

Chapter Five
Negotiating the Parks

Now, we hate to sound patronizing, we really do, but we want to emphasize that before setting foot in any of the Disney parks, it's important to understand how they work. Not doing your homework on this is like not reading the manual before hooking up your wide-screen TV and adding seven hours to doing it. We know you can get along just fine without this info, but you'll be happier having it. Comprehending basic flow and traffic patterns of the parks will only help make your day smoother and easier. So trust us and read this part.

The amount of time it takes to get into, onto, or around every attraction at the Disney parks depends on a combination of simple criteria, some variable, some not. Here are the factors:

The Variables

The Weather: Rainy days in Florida significantly diminish attendance at the Magic Kingdom and Disney-MGM Studios. And that's why Eddie loves to go in the rain and walk right onto every ride. Jeffrey prefers to stay in the hotel and complain. Now, Eddie knows that the rainy method of touring pretty much destroys your hair and makeup, but think of all of the time you'll save—with which you can recoif. Rain actually increases attendance at Epcot because so many of its attractions are contained within indoor pavilions. Disney's Animal Kingdom, is, of course, a particular bummer in the rain, since the animals seem to care as much about keeping their fur dry as you do about preserving the pleats on your linen shorts.

At the California parks it seldom rains. It does get cold at night during the winter months, however, and that temperature dip does help make the park just a bit quieter. It also makes several rides significantly less fun. Splash Mountain comes to mind.

Time of Day: The early morning hours are as close as you can come to seeing the parks without crowds. Unfortunately, that's a small window, and once it's closed, it's closed for good. For that reason (and we know you'll hate us for this) we recommend that you always (as in *always*) get to the parks at opening. You'll be amazed at how much more you can get done, and you'll be able to head back to the hotel for an afternoon siesta or tanning instead of spending the entire day in lines in withering heat.

If you insist on going against counsel on this one or if you're the type for whom noon is early no matter what we say, there are a few other tips that can help make up for some of the time you lost.

The Disney parades and spectacles (Illuminations, fireworks, Fantasmic!) are extremely popular. Wait times diminish significantly during them, so if you're willing to skip a parade (and many of them are skipable), you can save yourself some serious line time.

Meal times also help alleviate lines, so if you can manage to eat unusually early or unusually late, you'll benefit from shorter lines.

How Much of the Ride Is Running: This is something over which you have no control, but many of the rides at the parks have varying capacity levels. Space Mountain at Walt Disney World Resort, for example, has two identical tracks.

When the park is crowded, both are open, making lines move much faster. Other rides, like "it's a small world," can add extra boats to help increase capacity. While it's not always easy to tell from the outside, on some rides (Disneyland Park's Matterhorn Bobsleds, for example) you can see if the ride is utilizing full capacity before you decide to get in line.

The Fixed Factors

Slow/Fast Loaders: The way a ride loads on or dispatches guests helps determine how long your wait will be. Fast loaders include rides that take in large numbers at once (Pirates of the Caribbean or The Great Movie Ride come to mind). Even though these rides are popular, they load quickly because they can take a large number of guests in each of their vehicles, so lines are always relatively short. Other fast loaders include Epcot's Spaceship Earth or Disney's California Adventure's Grizzly Peak, which feature vehicles on a continuously moving conveyer belt so that people are always getting on and off without the ride ever having to stop. Thus, many of these rides can be ridden at any time of day without too much waiting.

Slower loaders are usually rides that can handle only a few people per vehicle (Snow White's Scary Adventures, Peter Pan's Flight) or, worst of all, rides that come to a complete standstill during loading and unloading (Dumbo the Flying Elephant or Disney California Adventure's Maliboomer, for example). While most rides have guests inside while loading is going on outside (boats continue to cruise through "it's a small world" while loading happens elsewhere), on the attractions where that's not the case, lines can be treacherous. On those rides, even when there are many fewer guests in line, the wait can be longer than that of a fast-loading ride. We tell you all of this so that when we refer to a slow or fast loader, you know what the hell we're talking about.

Location: Sometimes a ride's location has a direct effect on the length of its lines. Spaceship Earth is the first attraction every guest entering Epcot's front gate hits and therefore has its heaviest crowds in the morning. Similarly, Star Tours and MuppetVision 3-D are somewhat tucked away at Disney-MGM Studios, so in the mornings most people haven't found their way there yet.

Seatings: Several attractions are presented in theater-type spaces. Wait times will depend on how much time is left in the previous show. So you should always ask before getting in line. Epcot's American Adventure runs almost half an hour. If a showing has just started as you arrive, it's better to return just before a later show than to wait the half hour.

FASTPASS: And finally, the life preserver, FASTPASS. For the most popular rides that have crowds no matter what, Disney created this free service in 1999 to great success. Here's how this godsend works: At several rides in each park, FASTPASS kiosks can be found near the entrance. When you insert your park ticket into a FASTPASS kiosk, you'll get a slip of paper that will give you a specific one-hour time window during which you should return to the ride. When you do, you'll be directed to a special FAST-PASS line, which is infinitely shorter than the standard, standby line. You will breeze by hordes of others who will scowl as you walk right up to the front. It feels like being on the VIP list at Studio 54. The drawback to FASTPASS is that you can only hold one at a time. So, until you've used a pass, you can't get another (which, we've found, puts a real kink in our scalping scheme). Still, it's a great system. And strangely, it's one that many guests don't bother to avail themselves of, choosing instead to wait in the longer lines. But then, we're confused by what they choose to wear too, so who are we to judge?

Chapter Six
Where to Sleep...Or at Least Check In: The Disney Resort Hotels

Disneyland Resort Hotels

There's something special about staying at one of the three Disneyland Resort properties. Maybe it's the proximity to the two parks. Maybe it's the disturbingly friendly people at the front desk. Maybe it's the early admission to the parks that they sometimes offer. But a vacation at the Disneyland Resort starts from the moment you enter the lobby. Ostensibly, the hotel is just a place for you to crash after spending every waking moment inside the park gates. Well, maybe. But if you are there for a few days or aren't as maniacal about the parks as we are, you may actually want to spend some time just relaxing. All hotels feature heated pools, hot tubs, arcades, and numerous gift shops (often with merchandise specific to the hotel). They can be more expensive than neighboring hotels, so if you're making a reservation, you should always ask if there are any specials being offered— they usually accept an AAA discount, for example. Hey, it never hurts to ask, right? And if you have a few extra bucks to burn (or just want to impress your new boyfriend/girlfriend), ask about Concierge Rooms; they are the sweetest suites money can buy.

Disney's Grand Californian Hotel

Atmosphere: ✪✪✪✪✪
Quality: ✪✪✪
Price: Expensive
Number of Rooms: 751
Etc.: 🍴 🍽 🍹 🎵

Even if you're not staying at this hotel, you must, must,

must go look at the cavernous lobby. Designed by Peter Dominick of the Urban Design Group of Denver (the same folks who created Disney's Wilderness Lodge and Disney's Animal Kingdom Lodge at Walt Disney World Resort), this Craftsman-style resort is jaw-droppingly stunning. The lobby features an always-burning, immense fireplace, and the entire hotel gives nods to architect Frank Lloyd Wright. And if you're looking for a cocktail, the hidden Hearthstone Lounge, tucked into the back corner of the lobby, is perfect for a nightcap. The rooms that overlook Disney's California Adventure are the best: It feels like you're sleeping in the park. The rooms overlooking Downtown Disney offer a nice view, but the noise could keep you up if you're early to bed. The hotel features two large pools (one with a water slide for the kids), two hot tubs, and a nearby snack bar. Jeffrey enjoyed the hot tub until a family of 17 joined him. Eureka Springs is a small health club offering a variety of spa treatments. As for the rooms themselves, they're fairly standard with slightly nicer accents. And the bathroom looks like it was copied from the Holiday Inn handbook—not that there's anything wrong with Holiday Inn, but when you're paying Ritz-Carlton prices, you want something a little more luxurious.

Resort Dining

Storytellers Cafe
Price: Moderate
Meals: B, L, D, ☺

This lovely restaurant is adorned with seven large murals on the walls depicting moments from famous California stories (alas, they left out the William Higgins classic *Sailor in the Wild*). Breakfast offers a reasonably priced, eclectic buffet in a sophisticated atmosphere—with some characters wandering throughout the restaurant (although not as many as at the animalfest at Goofy's Kitchen in the Disneyland Hotel). Lunch and dinner offer a broad American menu, with hearty portions and quality cooking. And they start you off with a basket of bread that's so yummy (love the corn bread!) that Jeffrey always asks for an additional one to go. Cheap bastard.

Napa Rose
Price: Expensive
Meals: L, D

The hotel's most upscale restaurant offers a wide range of wines to accompany the delicious California cuisine. It's totally romantic (rosebuds are incorporated throughout the room's design) and features an efficient and knowledgeable staff. Eddie was still savoring his salmon the next day. This grossed Jeffrey out.

Disneyland Hotel
Atmosphere: ✪✪
Quality: ✪✪✪✪
Price: Expensive
Number of Rooms: 990
Etc.: 🍴 🏊 🎵

The Disneyland Hotel has been around since the beginning of time. And that's a good thing. Because unlike some of Disney's newer properties, the Disneyland Hotel features spacious, accommodating rooms and large, diverse common areas. What the hotel lacks, however, is character. Built before Disney started theming its hotels, the Disneyland Hotel, like Disney's Contemporary in Florida, is a nice, fairly basic, upscale property with ample amenities but few distinguishing traits. The hotel features three restaurants, but since the opening of Downtown Disney in 2001, the food and shopping options within an easy walk of the hotel have increased considerably. The recently renovated Never Land pool area, which features charming Peter Pan settings, is fun but a little too central to provide any peace or quiet time. It's just a hop, skip, and a jump to the Lost Bar, where you won't find Tinker Bell—but you may find a lost boy.

Resort Dining

Granville's Steak House
Price: Expensive
Meals: D

Expensive but excellent. Or so we're told. Since neither of us actually eats red meat, Granville's hasn't been a priority for us. But reports are consistently wonderful, citing Granville's as one of the park's best eateries. "One of the best steaks I've ever had," beams James from Anaheim, Calif. And who are we to disagree?

Hook's Pointe & Wine Cellar
Price: Moderate
Meals: B, L, D

Overlooking the Never Land pool and the Lost Bar, Hook's Pointe is a good choice for mesquite-grilled fare. It's the resort's best kept secret for breakfast, offering a wide selection of eats in a kid-lite environment. A bit pricey but not disappointing.

Goofy's Kitchen
Price: Moderate
Meals: B, L, D, ☻

For Jeffrey, there is no other buffet at the resort. Yes, the characters can become annoying (especially when they encourage you to dance). And there are so many kids, you could easily fill three "it's a small world" attractions. But the food is good (try the peanut butter and jelly pizza or the bagels and lox or the sugary pastries or the...), and the service is especially attentive.

Disney's Paradise Pier Hotel
Atmosphere: ✪✪
Quality: ✪✪✪

Price: Expensive
Number of Rooms: 502
Etc.:

After existing as the Disneyland Pacific Hotel, Disney's Paradise Pier was rechristened when Disney's California Adventure park opened its doors in 2001. There's a gate to the park exclusive for hotel guests. The hotel, like the Disneyland Hotel next door, is nice but uninspired: Rooms are pretty and bright.

Resort Dining

PCH Grill

Price: Moderate
Meals: B, L, D, ☻

The atmosphere in the PCH, which looks like a mosaic explosion, is a bit utilitarian, which is a shame because the food is quite good. It specializes in wood-fired food and California cuisine. Breakfast is with "Minnie and Friends," a moniker that disturbs us in its ambiguity. After all, how do we know we'll like Minnie's friends?

Yamabuki

Price: Expensive
Meals: L, D

Disneyland Resort's only Japanese restaurant is pricey but excellent. The sushi is particularly fresh and particularly expensive.

Walt Disney World Resort Hotels

While staying at a Disneyland Resort Hotel is a good thing, staying at a Walt Disney World Resort hotel is a great thing. Every hotel is themed with loads of attention to detail. From the Mayan pyramids of Disney's Coronado Springs to the 33-acre savannah at Disney's Animal Kingdom Lodge, Walt Disney World Resort hotels are unlike any other. Additional advantages to staying at the Disney resorts include unlimited use of their transportation systems (buses, watercraft, and the monorail system, which links select hotels with the Magic Kingdom, Epcot, and the Transportation and Ticket Center), free parking at the theme parks, preferred tee times (for those of you who like boring sports such as golf), and a variety of children's activities (not to mention baby-sitting and child-care options when you want to leave the lil' ones). You can make advance dining reservations ("priority seating") up to 60 days before your arrival. All hotels feature pools, arcades, restaurants, and, of course, gift shops (with some merchandise exclusive to the resorts). As with the Disneyland Resort, rooms can be pricey, so make sure you ask your reservation specialist if there are any discounts (like AAA or AARP) are available. And many of the hotels offer suites and Concierge rooms, for all you masters who like to be waited on hand and foot. Disney categorizes the hotels by their proximity to the parks.

MAGIC KINGDOM RESORTS

Disney's Contemporary Resort

Atmosphere: ✪✪✪✪
Quality: ✪✪✪✪
Price: Expensive
Number of Rooms: 1,041
Transportation: 🚌 ⛴ 🚡 🚈
Etc.: 🍽 💻 🎮 🍸

Somehow after all these years (it opened in 1971), Disney's Contemporary still feels…contemporary and is Jeffrey's favorite Disney resort. It's also one of the oldest resorts, so the standard

Disney's Contemporary Resort with Magic Kingdom Park in the background

© Disney Enterprises, Inc.

rooms are larger than any others at Walt Disney World Resort (save for Disney's Grand Floridian's pricier standards). Rooms in the A-frame tower overlook either the parking lot and Magic Kingdom or Bay Lake (where you can watch the water show at night), and the monorail, which speeds through the center of the building, sends Jeffrey's heart racing. The three-story "garden" buildings mostly overlook the lake. As for the decor, well, they recently renovated, and it looks like a postmodern explosion. Everything is so intentionally mismatched, you'd think the future was about clashing. The Fantasia gift shop is decent, but BVG, the shop across the concourse, offers more high-end merchandise. There are a large pool and numerous water activities to keep you busy (including fun little boats you can take out) as well as a fitness center. There's also a cafeteria restaurant (adjacent to a large arcade and movie screening room) that offers mediocre food but can be good for a meal on the run.

Resort Dining

Concourse Steakhouse

Price: Inexpensive/Moderate

Meals: B, L, D

Located on the concourse level (surprise!) of the hotel, this unassuming restaurant—which boasts the monorail whizzing overhead (vaguely unnerving, actually)—offers a lot more than just steaks (which we non–beef-eaters hear are pretty good). There's a little something for everyone, including seafood, pasta, chicken, and burgers. It's a relative bargain at breakfast, however, and a welcome reprieve from the screaming children found next door at Chef Mickey's. And don't forget to try the Mickey Sticky Buns. (Stop—no, we mean it—stop!) A piece of heaven with cinnamon.

Chef Mickey's

Price: Inexpensive/Moderate

Meals: B, D, ☻

If it's carb-loading you want, this is the place. Despite the annoying dances the characters encourage you to do (if we hear the "Disney Macarena" one more time, we may go postal), there's a great array of food at this bang-for-your-buck buffet, especially at breakfast. You want breakfast pizzas? How about Mickey-shaped waffles? A make-your-own omelet? You won't need to eat again for the rest of the day. But of course, you will.

California Grill

Price: Expensive

Meals: D

Without a doubt our favorite restaurant in the entire resort. Trust us, it's worth the price. In fact, Jeffrey loves it so much he threw his 30th, um, we mean *21st*, birthday party here. The restaurant offers a wide range of California cuisine in a warm atmosphere. Those of you who like Wolfgang Puck's Spago will feel right at home with the sumptuous flat-breads, designer pizzas, and creative fare.

Disney's Grand Floridian Resort & Spa

Atmosphere: ✪✪✪✪✪
Quality: ✪✪✪✪
Price: Expensive
Number of Rooms: 900
Transportation: 🚌 ⛴ 🚤 🚝
Etc.: 🍴 🍽 ☕

Yep, it's beautiful. This resort (considered by many to be the Kingdom's finest) is reminiscent of the Hotel del Coronado in San Diego, with its Victorian design. From a distance the place looks like a postcard from the 19th century. The opulent five-story lobby is the gateway to a complex of spread-out buildings, which can make getting to your room a bit of a schlep (but they'll take you to your room in a little cart if you ask). Rooms are fairly spacious, but for the exorbitant prices you may expect more. The service, however, can't be beat. You can take a dip in the spectacular, recently renovated pool area or lie by the white sand beach along the Seven Seas Lagoon. On the shore are cozy cabanas you can cuddle in. Not that we would know anything about that. Unfortunately, the spa gets mixed reviews. While Sue, a frequent spa-goer from Boston, says she loved her massage, she felt the place itself "lacked the panache of most day spas."

Resort Dining

Victoria & Albert's

Price: Expensive
Meals: D

The finest of the fine-dining restaurants at Walt Disney World Resort, Victoria & Albert's has won more awards than Tom Hanks. The almost disturbingly attentive service, ever-changing menu of fresh foods, and elegant design make this a dining experience you won't forget (particularly because you'll be paying for it for years to come). Please note, it's one of the few restaurants in the entire resort that actually requests that men wear a jacket and that ladies don evening attire (which we're pretty sure doesn't mean a nightgown). Perfect for getting all cozy with the one you love.

Cítricos

Price: Moderate/Expensive
Meals: D

This sunny and colorful European restaurant offers an open-air kitchen (for those of you suspicious of chefs). It specializes in beef and lamb but offers other foods. While we like it just fine, it's not a must-dine.

Gasparilla Grill & Games

Price: Inexpensive
Meals: B, L, D

There's a little bit of everything here, from standard breakfast fare to pizza, nachos, and the specialty, top-your-own burgers. Great for kids. Not great for people who don't like kids.

Grand Floridian Cafe

Price: Moderate
Meals: B, L, D

With soups and salads, steaks and seafood, this is an eclectic eatery. There's a bit of a Southern (read: deep-fried) feel to the place, but there are many healthy offerings as well. But please, you're at Walt Disney World Resort. Don't be healthy. A good spot if you're spending the day by the pool, but don't come running back here for a meal.

1900 Park Fare

Price: Moderate

Meals: B, D,

1900 offers a more sophisticated buffet (especially at dinner, when the prime rib is a specialty) than some of the other resorts. It's a good place for dining if you're staying at the hotel. Otherwise, for a better buffet hit Chef Mickey's or Boma at Disney's Animal Kingdom Lodge.

Narcoosee's

Price: Expensive

Meals: D

OK, so the Seven Seas Lagoon isn't salt water. It's not even a natural formation. But there's something wonderful about eating seafood on the edge of the water in this strange, octagonal building. The mainly seafood fare gets rave reviews—especially from Eddie, who won't shut up about the tuna. And you get a fabulous view of the fireworks over the Magic Kingdom.

Disney's Polynesian Resort

Atmosphere: ✪✪✪✪

Quality: ✪✪✪

Price: Expensive

Number of Rooms: 853

Transportation: 🚌 🚤 🚶 🚝

Etc.: 🍴 🍽 ☕

Like Adventureland's Enchanted Tiki Room attraction? Enough to live there? 'Cause you can. Disney's Polynesian (or the Polly, as we like to call it) is designed to be a tropical paradise, featuring waterfalls and exotic foliage. We think it's closer to a kitsch paradise, featuring loads of bamboo and bad floral prints. The whole feel is meant to be very native and tribal (which, in Disney terms, means wood beams and rocks, not loincloths). The rooms are comfortable but feature one too many batik prints for our eyes to handle. In fact, they're downright ugly. But that's actually part of the charm. Several of the rooms have balconies, a feature that is lovely unless you're on the ground floor, making access a little too easy for our comfort. For some, however, that's a selling point. It's situated on the Seven Seas Lagoon, and you can't beat the convenience. And the lushly landscaped pools (there are two) are superior.

Resort Dining

Ohana
Price: Moderate
Meals: B, D

Anyone who saw Lilo and Stitch knows that Ohana means "family." Since to us, that means "other homos," we love it here. And the food's pretty good. Everything is grilled on skewers and brought to your table for a reasonable fixed price. Since we love an all-you-can-eat meal where we don't have to get up and go to the buffet, we've been known to graze here all night. Jeffrey claims the bread is a particular treat, but since he inhales it, he's the only one who knows. The atmosphere, like that of the hotel, is South Seas kitsch. With a fire pit. For naughty children.

Kona Cafe
Price: Inexpensive
Meals: B, L, D

Coffee shop with bamboo seats. Fine for breakfast if you're staying at the Polly but otherwise not worth the trip.

Disney's Wilderness Lodge
Atmosphere: ✪✪✪✪✪
Quality: ✪✪✪
Price: Expensive

Number of Rooms: 728

Etc.:

Like Disneyland Resort's Grand Californian, Disney's Wilderness Lodge, well situated off the Seven Seas Lagoon, is an expensive, gorgeous, intricately detailed space with surprisingly small rooms. The rustic, Pacific Northwest theme includes a massive stone fireplace, lush pine landscapes, totem poles, redwood and timber accents, and waterfall courtyards. Offsetting the grandeur of the common areas is the quaintness of the rooms (they say cozy, we say tiny), which include details such as patchwork quilts and etched armoires. This place is perfect for bears and lesbian logger types with money. We're neither. And frankly, the place is a little too quiet for our Walt Disney World Resort pace. But if you're a Yosemite–Muir Woods kind of person, this is your hotel. Now try wearing the requisite flannel in the Florida heat.

Resort Dining

Artist Point

Price: Expensive

Meals: B, D

Surprisingly casual (because it's hard to dress up in the middle of the forest), this restaurant features a variety of seafood, poultry, and game (meaning, you can eat Bambi) and is quite good for the price. We particularly like the maple-glazed salmon. The atmosphere is very pretty, although we prefer seating by the large windows as opposed to next to the massive, two-story artwork.

Whispering Canyon Café

Price: Moderate

Meals: B, L, D

OK, here's where this hotel stops feeling like a serene, classy national park and degenerates to basic Western. Not that that's a bad thing. Yummy barbecue and grille are loaded onto a lazy Susan atop your barrel-motif table, and you get to chow down like a country bear.

Disney's Fort Wilderness Resort and Campground

Atmosphere: ✪✪
Quality: ✪
Price: Inexpensive
Number of Rooms: 418 cabins, 784 campsites
Etc.: ▣

It takes a certain brand of person to choose to stay in a mobile home at Walt Disney World Resort. And while we enjoy Frito pie just as much as the next guy, we're not that kind of person. Don't misunderstand—we're all for the joys of camping, but for us, that usually involves nature as opposed to a plot of landscaped Disney property. To us, Walt Disney World Resort and a camping trip are not particularly compatible. But hey, that's us. Our lesbian galpals Lindsay and Claire, who are far more butch than we, adore spending the night in the great outdoors. So don't let our bias sway you. But don't expect to pee outside of your tent either.

Resort Dining

Trail's End Buffeteria

Price: Inexpensive/Moderate
Meals: B, L, D

Basic American food buffet for three meals. Yep, that pretty much sums it up. C'mon, it's called a buffeteria!

Shades of Green

Atmosphere: Unknown
Quality: Classified
Price: Four years' service

Number of Rooms: 288
Etc.:

Just so you know, we don't expect any of you to be staying at Shades of Green. And it's not because we don't think you like golf (ladies, we *know* you like golf). But rather, because Shades of Green, though on Disney property and maintained by the mouse, is actually owned by the U.S. armed forces and available only to members of the U.S. military. So unless you're really looking to put "don't ask, don't tell" to the test, our code of conduct dictates "don't stay." Needless to say, we've never been inside. We don't think they'd like us. We've never even trolled the grounds looking for drunken sailors. But it should be noted that while the hotel is off-limits to us (pending the outcome of our lawsuit), the three golf courses are available to all resort guests.

Resort Dining

Who knows? But reports say both full-service and buffet dining are available in the canteen.

EPCOT RESORTS

Disney's Caribbean Beach Resort
Atmosphere: ✪✪
Quality: ✪✪
Price: Moderate
Number of Rooms: 2,112
Transportation: 🚌
Etc.: 🍴 ☕ 🍸

This festive resort is built on 200 acres that surround a 42-acre tropical lagoon. There are five "villages" made up of small buildings, themed in traditional styles of Caribbean islands: Trinidad, Martinique, Barbados, Aruba, and Jamaica. Each village has its own pool. There are six counter-service restaurants to choose from, including the Cinnamon Bay Bakery and Montego's Deli, which all border a 500-seat eating area. Because it was the first moderately priced resort, we find it to be more in need of a face-lift than Bea Arthur. If you're making a reservation, check to see if you can get a renovated room. If you can't, we suggest Port Orleans or Coronado Springs as better alternatives in the same price range. Because it's large, walking to the bus stops can be a bit of a hassle (as is the case at many of the moderate and inexpensive resorts).

Resort Dining

Captain's Tavern
Price: Moderate
Meals: D

The nautical theme is so authentic, we find ourselves getting seasick. While the food is adequate, you'll find better almost anywhere else.

Disney's Beach Club Resort
Disney's Yacht Club Resort

Atmosphere: ✪✪✪✪
Quality: ✪✪✪✪
Price: Expensive
Number of Rooms: 572
Transportation: 🚌 ⛴ ➊
Etc.: 🍴 🏊

We have taken it in upon ourselves to lump these two resorts together. They're remarkably similar, save for different paint jobs on the buildings and outfits for the cast members. Reminiscent of traditional New England archi-

tecture, these classy, deluxe hotels, with open, airy rooms, are even nicer and more user-friendly than Disney's Grand Floridian. For quick eating, Beaches and Cream, a counter-service restaurant, offers fast goodies all day long. These hotels share a large swimming area called Stormalong Bay (complete with a life-size shipwreck) for a cross-pollination of hotties.

Resort Dining

Cape May Cafe
Price: Moderate
Meals: D

Located in Disney's Beach Club, this restaurant has the dubious distinction of being the only place we've dined at that serves both mussels and barbecue ribs. Actually, the buffet is quite nice, featuring traditional breakfast fare in the morning and a New England–style clambake at night (where Jeffrey gorged himself at the shrimp bar).

Yacht Club Galley
Price: Moderate
Meals: B, L, D

After you're done staring at the kinda cool seascape mural with moving sailboats, you can enjoy the tasty food at this eatery, which, naturally, offers a variety of seafoods. The breakfast buffet is quite good too.

Yachtsman Steakhouse
Price: Expensive
Meals: D

For those of you who like to eat meat (don't go there), this is the place. But while it does offer other eating options (we like the lobster), if you don't have a hankering for beef, you may want to look elsewhere.

Disney's BoardWalk

Atmosphere: ✪✪✪✪
Quality: ✪✪✪✪
Price: Expensive
Number of Rooms: 372 (plus 520 villas, part of the Disney Vacation Club, Disney's time-shares)
Transportation: 🚌 🚢 🚶
Etc.: 🍴 🍸

Imagine Atlantic City at the beginning of the 20th century. You know, before all the crime, casinos, hookers, and Pia Zadora ruined it for everyone. While there may not be a real Ferris wheel or a roller coaster to ride, both are incorporated into the colorful architecture that makes this place one of the most festive. The rooms are decently sized (Jeffrey loves all the closet space) and the detail (like the cherry furnishings) is lovely. The carnival-themed pool, with its coaster-style slide, is a blast. The real draw of the hotel is the entertainment complex that lines the hotel's boardwalk. Inside Atlantic Dance, which recalls a 1930s dance hall with sparkling design, it still don't mean a thing if you ain't got that swing. Admission is extra, but if you gotta dance, you gotta dance. Jellyrolls is a lively bar featuring dueling pianos. Enjoy a yummy treat at Seaside Sweets and browse the other numerous stores.

Resort Dining

Big River Grille & Brewing Works

Price: Moderate
Meals: L, D

The food is just fine here. And when every other place has a 16-hour wait, the food is great. We're not big beer drinkers, but they brew their own ales here (beware, there are no commercial beers available).

ESPN Club

Price: Moderate

Meals: L, D

Just to prove that we'll go to the ends of the Earth for you folks, we descended into the testosterone-drenched world of ESPN. Sports? We majored in underwater basket weaving. And we think they had a few basket-weaving competitions on the more than 80 monitors showing every game on earth (or pretty close to it). They even have televisions in the bathrooms. There's The Yard, with an arcade, sports, and virtual reality games. Sports Central is the main dining room, which makes a delicious fresh fin tuna sandwich. You can also eat in Sidelines, where you get a table with your own sound box to switch back and forth between all the games being shown around you. There are gobs of memorabilia on the walls, which means nothing to either of us. But maybe it will all mean something to you.

Flying Fish Cafe

Price: Expensive

Meals: D

The food here is delish. The whole place looks like a roller-coaster ride. The seafood rocks. And you can't forget the warm chocolate lava cake with its gooey, delicious center. We sure haven't.

Spoodles

Price: Moderate

Meals: B, L, D

Ah, there's nothing that says "boardwalk" like Mediterranean food. While the decor (which includes an open kitchen and neat light fixtures) is really cool, the place is super noisy. The food is good but not great—although we love the pizzas.

Walt Disney World Swan and Walt Disney World Dolphin

Atmosphere: ✪✪
Quality: ✪✪✪
Price: Moderate/Expensive
Number of Rooms: 2,268
Etc.: R, C, B, ✪

Looming on Epcot's horizon are these two turquoise monstrosities. Can you tell we're not fans? It's not that we have a problem with swans or fish (although Jeffrey does), and it's not the peculiar interiors, which feature still more turquoise and coral motifs. It's the fact that these are Disney property hotels that feel nothing like Disney property hotels. The Swan and Dolphin are actually operated by Westin and Sheraton respectively. So while you get the good service these chains are known for, you pay the prices Disney's known for without the Disney experience. And while you can't beat the location (walking distance to both Epcot and Disney-MGM Studios), if you want to stay at a nice chain hotel, you can do it elsewhere for a lot less money.

Resort Dining

Because they're not really Disney properties, we won't go into detail about the more than a dozen restaurants these hotels offer. **Gulliver's Grove** is too expensive for its average American dishes, but the moderately priced **Palio,** which offers fresh Italian, is not too bad. There's good, decently priced sushi at **Kimonos,** even if the name hinges on offensive. The jungle-themed **Harry's Safari Bar and Grill** is too pricey for its steak-and-seafood menu (seafood in a jungle theme— uh, OK, we get that). Your best restaurant bet here is **Juan & Onlys,** which serves up spicy Mexican cuisine that rivals the food at Epcot's Mexican pavilion. Our recommendation is, unless you're staying at these hotels, skip their restaurants with the possible exception of Juan & Onlys.

DOWNTOWN DISNEY RESORT AREA

The Villas at Disney Institute

Atmosphere: ✪
Quality: ✪✪✪
Price: Expensive
Number of Rooms: 584
Etc.: 🍴 🛎 ☾

How vanilla are you? If the answer is "like a Nilla Wafer," you might like the Institute. No theme, no motif, not even any real color to speak of. You'd hardly know you're at Walt Disney World Resort. Now before you skip to the next hotel, there are some true assets here. First of all, the all-suite hotel's complete lack of atmospheric fun makes it less popular with kids, making Disney Institute the property's most quiet locale. It also offers a rich variety of accommodations, from the utilitarian bungalows (which we don't like) to the atrium ceilinged town houses with full kitchens (which we very much do). And with Downtown Disney (for shoppers) and Pleasure Island (for partiers) a short walk, this hotel is easily Disney's most grown-up. A full spa is available as well. Not that we've ever taken the time, but it's always good to know where to go for a mani/pedi.

Resort Dining

The Gathering Place

Price: Moderate
Meals: B, L, D

Like your average convention Hyatt. We ate there once. And only once.

Disney's Old Key West Resort

Atmosphere: ✪✪✪
Quality: ✪✪✪
Price: Expensive
Number of Rooms: 761 Villas
Etc.: 🍴 🎶

They call it Disney Vacation Club. We call it time-share. The setting is lovely, the rooms are spacious, and the service is reportedly excellent. But it's still a time-share (although occasionally, when units are unoccupied, they are available to nonowners). And there's something less exotic about a Florida theme when one is actually in Florida. For the record, Old Key West means O-o-old Key West, not 1980s gay Key West.

Resort Dining

Olivia's Café

Price: Moderate
Meals: B, L, D

Moderately priced family restaurant with charming atmosphere of pastels and palms. Kinda makes you want to wear your sweater over your shoulders. There's a whole lotta fried food. Eddie likes the fritters, Jeffrey the chicken.

Disney's Port Orleans Resort

Atmosphere: ✪✪✪
Quality: ✪✪
Price: Moderate
Number of Rooms: 3,056 (1,008 at French Quarter; 2,048 at Riverside)
Etc.: 🍴 🅿️

Think Louisiana. Think New Orleans and bayou country. Think antebellum mansions. Think Mardi Gras. Now think about all of those things sanitized with Lysol and you've got Port Orleans, a moderately priced property with sections divided between the wrought-iron ambience of the French Quarter (sans naked people throwing beads from balconies—sans balconies, actually) and the watering hole and plantation atmosphere of Riverside (sans, well, you know). It sounds more gracious than it actually is, but this property is just fine. Since Port Orleans used to be two separate hotels, there are pool areas on either end, but the rooms are comparable: basic and standard but perfectly adequate. Of course, you're more than welcome to spice things up with your own voodoo dolls.

Resort Dining

Boatwright's Dining Hall
Price: Moderate
Meals: B, D
Very average Cajun food in a setting designed to look like a riverboat construction site (we don't really get it either).

DISNEY'S ANIMAL KINGDOM RESORT AREA

Disney's Animal Kingdom Lodge
Atmosphere: ✪✪✪✪✪
Quality: ✪✪✪✪✪
Price: Expensive
Number of Rooms: 1,293
Etc.: 🍴 🍸 ☕

Lions and tigers and bears, oh my! Well, no bears actually. Unless that's you. But there are also zebras, giraffes, and gazelles at this place, which was built adjacent to a 33-acre African "savanna" and offers prime viewing of the animals from almost every room and sweeping vistas from the lobby. The hotel itself is stunningly crafted with amazing African inspired design and architecture. Everything is in wood tones with splashes of color, making this property a feast for the eyes.

Authentic tribal art fills the common spaces, including a 16-foot mask in the lobby. It's expensive, but along with Disney's Grand Floridian it's arguably the nicest of the World's hotels. The rooms are equally beautiful, if on the small side, with hand-crafted furniture from Zimbabwe. If watching rhinos frolic gets you excited (and who doesn't thrill to the sight of a cavorting rhino?), there's also a spa where you too can indulge in mud.

Resort Dining

Jiko: The Cooking Place
Price: Expensive
Meals: B, D
Surprisingly, Jiko isn't an African restaurant. Rather, it features cuisine influenced by much of the globe (yes, more fusion food: baked chicken with grapefruit and olives, for example). It is truly exceptional and, unlike many of Disney's eateries, worth the price.

Boma: Flavors of Africa
Price: Moderate
Meals: B, L, D
Boma includes a wood-burning grill and rotisserie, though we're partial to its breakfast buffet . We've made no secret about how much we like a buffet at which we can stuff our faces until we're immobile, but of all the Walt Disney World Resort breakfasts we've enjoyed, Boma comes out on top, hands down. The food is outstanding, the setting beautiful, and the service excellent. Well worth a special trip to the hotel. Or to Florida, for that matter. You think we're kidding, but you haven't sampled its pastries.

Disney's Coronado Springs Resort
Atmosphere: ✪✪✪✪
Quality: ✪✪
Price: Moderate

Number of Rooms: 1,967

Etc.: 🍴 🛏 🍸

For our money, Disney's Coronado is the best of the moderately priced resorts. Though a bit out of the way, the hotel boasts its very own 15-acre lagoon around which its Mexican themed buildings, grouped into "villages," are situated. Of course, walking around those 15 acres to get to the main building gets *muy* tiresome, particularly when it's *muy caliente* and we're in a *muy grande* rush, but it is pretty. The lagoon's center features the main pool and the five-story Mayan pyramid–water slide, but there are three other "quiet pools" on property. We vote for those because we favor the simple equation: fewer kids = less urine. The hotel's common areas feature lots of tile mosaic and stucco and all of that Santa Fe chic stuff that makes Martha Stewart wet. The rooms themselves are average but comfortable. Eddie particularly likes this hotel for the Pepper Market, a huge food court from which you buy individual items instead of full meals. So if all you want is three eggs, you can get them without sides you'll never eat. And it reminds him of Tijuana, where he buys all of his drugs, um, hair product. Not that it's ever mattered to us, but this hotel does have the country's largest ballroom (ooh, aah) and convention facilities. It is, in fact, the only mid-priced convention hotel on property. But we figure, if we're gonna crash a convention, we'll head over to Disney's Grand Floridian, where we might actually meet a doctor.

Resort Dining

The Maya Grill

Price: Expensive

Meals: B, D

OK, so you can watch them cook it, and OK, we're told there's some "fusion" going on with this cuisine. But we gotta say it's awfully pricey for Mexican food and slightly out of place in this otherwise moderate resort. The food's fine, but there are more interesting choices at better values to be had elsewhere.

All Star Resorts

Atmosphere: ✪✪
Quality: ✪
Price: Inexpensive
Number of Rooms: Each resort (there are three) has 1,920
Etc.: ☕

We're not snobs…OK, we're snobs. Bursting with small children, thanks to their affordable prices, these three hotels are our worst nightmare come to life, chasing us down, and eating us. Each hotel has its own theme: music, movies, or sports. And there are some fun design elements: The Music Resort boasts a pool shaped like a guitar and one like a grand piano; the Movie Resort has gigantic characters from movies like *101 Dalmatians* and *Toy Story* overlooking the place; the Sports Resort's pool has figures of Disney characters shooting water pistols. There are no sit-down restaurants, only food courts, which makes nice dining a chore (it's a long bus ride anywhere). And the rooms are small. To be fair, it is clean and pretty well kept up (and they are the cheapest hotels on property). But we would rather sleep on Tom Sawyer Island.

DISNEY'S WIDE WORLD OF SPORTS RESORTS

Disney's Pop Century Resort

Atmosphere: N/A
Quality: N/A
Price: Inexpensive
Number of Rooms: 5,760!

Transportation: 🚌
Etc.: 🖥️

At press time, this enormous complex, a paean to the popular culture of the 20th century, had yet to open. Flanked with gargantuan models of pop icons like Play-Doh, Rubik's Cube, and a laptop computer, this hotel breaks down into two sections, the "Legendary Years" (showcasing 1900–1950) and the "Classic Years" (highlighting 1950–1999). Each section will have its own lobby, food court, arcade, and three pools in unusual shapes (a bowling pin, a flower, etc.). We imagine the inexpensive rooms will be similar to those at the All Star resorts (only newer). But we can already hear the pitter-patter of thousands of children.

DOWNTOWN DISNEY RESORTS

In the Downtown Disney area of the Walt Disney World Resort, there are a good number of chain, non–Disney-owned hotels. These places provide the amenities commensurate with their sister hotels throughout the country. They tend to be a bit more affordable than the Disney resorts, but they offer none of the Disney property privileges (early admission, package delivery, etc.). Those of you sensitive to sensory overload might prefer these hotels because they offer no theme. Unlike the properties off site, however, they are served by Disney's transportation system, making park access significantly easier. We never stay at these hotels because we prefer to give ourselves over to the entire Disney experience. If you want soap without Mickey on it, however, the Downtown hotels include:

Wyndham Palace Resort & Spa
Number of rooms: 1,013
Amenities: three pools, spa facilities, beauty salon, nine restaurants
Activities: tennis, boat rentals, children's playground

Grosvenor Resort Hotel

Number of rooms: 626

Amenities: two pools, two restaurants

Activities: tennis, racquetball, shuffleboard, basketball, playground

Doubletree Guests Suites Resort

Number of rooms: 229

Amenities: all suites (separate bedroom and living room, three televisions, refrigerator), pool, whirlpool, restaurant

Activities: tennis

Courtyard by Marriott

Number of rooms: 323

Amenities: two pools, restaurant

The Hilton

Number of rooms: 814

Amenities: two pools, whirlpool, seven restaurants

Hotel Royal Plaza

Number of rooms: 394

Amenities: pool, restaurant

Activities: tennis

Best Western Lake Buena Vista

Number of rooms: 325

Amenities: pool, restaurants, a nightclub

Part Two
Disneyland Resort

A Little History

One Saturday in 1940, Walt Disney was sitting on a bench eating peanuts and watching his daughters go around on a carousel. "I felt," said Walt, "that there should be something built where the parents and children could have fun together. So that's how Disneyland started. I started with many ideas, threw them away, started all over again. And eventually it evolved into what you see today at Disneyland. But it all started from a daddy with two daughters wondering where he could take them where he could have a little fun with them too." Who knew that kingdoms could have such humble origins? But after kicking the idea around for a good 15 years, Walt built Disneyland. He originally saw it as a park on a parcel directly across the street from his studio in Burbank Calif., but when that space proved too small for his vision, the Anaheim site was chosen. "Herbie," he told designer Herbert Ryman, "I just want it to look like nothing else in the world. And it should be surrounded by a train." Once financing for the park came through, construction happened very quickly. The entire park was built in 257 working days, and on July 17, 1955, Disneyland opened its doors. With it, one man irrevocably changed the face of entertainment, travel, and ultimately, America.

Disneyland was built in a city and, as such, was bound by the borders of major thoroughfares (a fact that Walt came to loathe, later saying, "The one thing I learned from Disneyland was to control the environment"). Expansion was extremely limited. While new attractions opened with regularity, they were almost always replacing older ones. Toontown, which opened in 1993, was the park's first major extension, albeit a relatively small one. In 2001, after buying neighboring hotels and razing them to build a massive parking structure, Disney's California Adventure park opened on what had once been the Disneyland parking lot. The addition of the new park meant that the Disneyland could now be a multiday vacation destination, much like Walt Disney World Resort in Florida. So while Walt's immortal quote about his empire ("It all started with a mouse") may be immortalized in bronze, this particular dream all started with a merry-go-round.

Chapter Seven
Disneyland Park

<u>Main Street, U.S.A.</u>

Walking through the Disneyland Park entrance turnstiles and onto Main Street, U.S.A. is a transformative experience that can inspire giddiness akin to hearing the opening bars of the overture from *Gypsy*. So spectacular is the detailing of this turn-of-the-century, pristine, gaslit, barbershop quartet, knickerbocker, Hayley Mills atmosphere that you instantly feel like a character in *The Music Man* (it helps, of course, that they pipe in music from that score). It's lined with horse-drawn carriages and old-time buses that will transport you from one end of the street to the other if you're too pathetic to walk your lazy ass down the block. The buildings (all of which contain either food or the usual selection of Disney-branded everything) run the gamut from a firehouse to an old bank. There's a cinema with continuous showings of old black-and-white Mickey Mouse cartoons playing on six screens. ("To some, it's boring," says Michelle from Pontiac, Mich. "To me, it's an oasis.") And there's the always-popular Candy Kitchen where caramel apples and fudge are whipped up right in front of you, sending children into a frenzy the likes of which only a busload of queens en route to a Cher concert can match. The shopping includes stores with one-of-a-kind Disney character watches, hand-blown crystal, massively expensive collectible figurines, and a music shop that has kiosks where you can create your own CD of Disney park music (OK, yes, fine, Eddie admits to listening to the music at home—you'd be amazed at

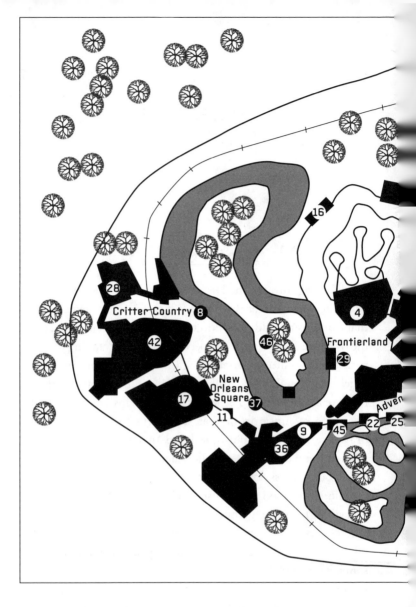

1. Alice in Wonderland
2. Autopia
3. Astro Orbitor
4. Big Thunder Mountain Railroad
5. Casey Jr. Circus Train
6. Chip 'n' Dale's Treehouse
7. Columbia Sailing Ship
8. Davy Crockett's Explorer Canoes
9. Disney Gallery
10. Disneyland Monorail
11. Disneyland Railroad
12. Donald's Boat
13. Dumbo the Flying Elephant
14. Enchanted Tiki Room
15. Fantasyland Theatre
16. Festival Arena
17. Gadget's Go-Coaster
18. Goofy's Bounce House
19. Great Moments with Mr. Lincoln
20. Haunted Mansion
21. Honey, I Shrunk the Audience
22. Indiana Jones Adventure

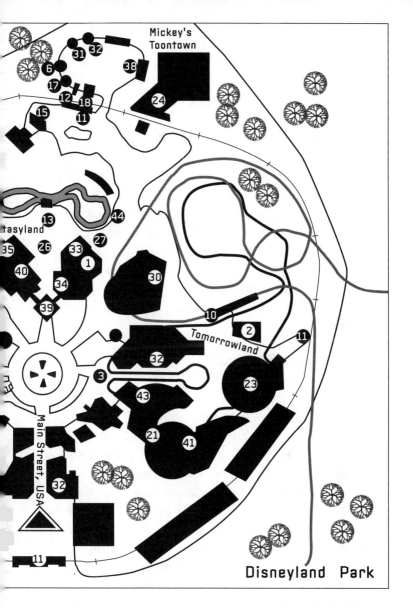

Mickey's Toontown

tasyland

Tomorrowland

Main Street, USA

Disneyland Park

. Innoventions
. it's a small world
. Jungle Cruise
. King Arthur Carrousel
. Mad Tea Party
. Many Adventures of Winnie
  the Pooh
. Mark Twain Riverboat
. Matterhorn Bobsleds
. Mickey's House
. Minnie's House
. Mr. Toad's Wild Ride
. Peter Pan's Flight

35. Pinocchio's Daring Journey
36. Pirates of the Caribbean
37. Rafts to Tom Sawyer Island
38. Roger Rabbit's Car Toon Spin
39. Sleeping Beauty Castle
40. Snow White's Scary
    Adventures
41. Space Mountain
42. Splash Mountain
43. Star Tours
44. Storybook Land Canal Boats
45. Tarzan's Treehouse
46. Tom Sawyer Island

how helpful "Yo Ho, A Pirate's Life for Me" can be after a really lousy date.)

Main Street also serves as the park's information central, where essentials such as guest relations, lockers, stroller and wheelchair rentals, and lost and found can be, well, found.

Look out for the eucalyptus tree behind City Hall. It was planted at the beginning of the 20th century, giving it the distinction of being the only truly authentic antique on Main Street (other than Eddie when he visits).

Crowning Main Street is the central hub around which are entrances to Tomorrowland, Adventureland, Frontierland and, through the iconic and majestic Sleeping Beauty Castle, Fantasyland.

Disneyland Railroad
Overall Rating: ✪✪✪✪
Attraction Debut: 1955

After walking your ass off all day long, this pleasant, low-key, smooth ride is Jeffrey's first choice for kicking back and cooling off (even if the guided voice-over pointing out landmarks along your way can get a bit grating). The train travels around the perimeter of the park, making stops at Main Street U.S.A., New Orleans Square (where you can hear Walt Disney's speech from the park's opening day—if you know Morse code), Mickey's Toontown, and Tomorrowland. In between stations the train chugs through an underwhelming Grand Canyon diorama and a "Primeval World" complete with Audio-Animatronics dinos. It's best to board the train at Main Street, as other stations can be more crowded. For those looking to cruise the park for cuties, be forewarned, you see very few from the train. However, if you come with (or have met) that certain someone, the train can sometimes offer a nice place to nuzzle up. "As quaint and dusty as my grandmother's furniture," says Chris from West Hollywood, Calif. "But the park would not be the same without it."

Fairy Fact: All those cute animals you see on your ride through the Grand Canyon? Yeah, they're taxidermied. Yep. Walt had a bunch of cute, dead animals stuffed for your enjoyment. Adds a new dimension, don't it?

Great Moments With Mr. Lincoln
Overall Rating: ❸❸❸
Attraction Debut: 1965, replaced by The Walt Disney Story in 1973, returned in 1975

Completely retooled and revamped in 2001, the new Mr. Lincoln is a warm, patriotic, and moving multimedia attraction—quite an achievement considering the snoozefest it replaced. Now guests are given headsets that, with crystal-clear sound technology, transport viewers into several Civil War settings, including Lincoln's Oval Office, the battlefield, and an army hospital where a nurse informs you that you've, gulp, lost a leg. No soft-sell, war-is-glamorous stuff here. The conclusion is still the same, with an Audio-Animatronics Lincoln trotting out one of his orations. But now the opening act makes him more compelling. "No gay Republican should miss this attraction," notes James from Lancaster, Calif. This used to be Eddie's favorite spot for a make-out session (after all, it's a 15-minute show in a dark, air-conditioned, unpopulated theater), but now he has to admit that Abe gets his attention, even if Lincoln was the original Log Cabin Republican.

Fairy Fact: Like several Disneyland Resort attractions, Great Moments With Mr. Lincoln premiered at the 1964 New York World's Fair. The plan was to move the attraction to Disneyland Resort after the closing of the fair, but Abe was so popular that Walt rushed the opening of the California version, making it the first Disney attraction to show in two locations concurrently.

☕ Blue Ribbon Bakery and Gibson Girl Ice Cream Parlor

Price: Inexpensive
Meals: Open all day

We've singled out these two counter restaurants because they're so darn mouthwatering. For those who count every calorie and gram of fat, we remind you that you're probably out all day walking. You'll burn it off. Really. Now get yourself a cinnamon roll, oozing with sugary frosting, or a scrumptious Rice Krispie brick. They also have some sandwiches, which we don't really recommend, as well as fresh fruit. Let's pause to say that we don't want to be with *anyone* who goes to Disneyland Resort to eat an apple. If that's you, stay at home and run on your treadmill some more. We'd write more, but we have to go eat.

🍴 Carnation Cafe

Price: Moderate
Meals: B, L

One of two full-service restaurants in the park, Carnation offers a splendid array of foods, from pancakes and eggs at breakfast to pasta and sandwiches at lunch. None of it is outstanding, but it's all just fine—and the friendly wait staff is a welcome break from the often pushy crowds. The outdoor seating is great for people-watching (our lesbian galpals Claire and Lindsay always make a point of spending an hour cruising park arrivals), but it's very limited, so there may be a wait.

Adventureland

While there are no hunky, shirtless tribesmen or Amazonian women to greet you as you enter this land, where else can you go from Asia to Africa to South America just by walking a few feet? Adventureland's counter restaurant, the Bengal Barbecue, offers

delightful food on a skewer, which is relatively healthy, if not altogether filling. And the shopping is great—if you're dying for a pith helmet. Because Adventureland jams several attractions into a small amount of space, its walkways are often so clogged you may find yourself compelled to throw the slow-moving children and meandering gawkers out of your way. Since we're all about efficiency, we say do what you must.

The Enchanted Tiki Room

Overall Rating: ✪✪
Attraction Debut: 1963

OK, we know this one's ancient and kind of boring. After you get through the infectious opening number (you remember: "In the tiki tiki tiki tiki tiki room, in the tiki tiki tiki tiki tiki room"), the Audio-Animatronics Polynesian bird and flower show with Don Ho luau music can be irritating. But what can we say? We like it. It's kitschy and tacky and weird. Kinda like a Trader Vic's cocktail come to life. Some are less enthusiastic about the attraction. "I would rather be enclosed in a room with Britney Spears," shudders David from Boston. Others offer advice that doesn't require seeing the show. "Check out the pineapple stand out front," enthuses James from Anaheim. "They have some of the best pineapple frozen yogurt anywhere."

Fairy Fact: The Enchanted Tiki Room, which featured the debut of Audio-Animatronics, was originally designed to be a dinner-theater attraction. But when test audiences saw the show, they were so entranced by the birds (go figure) that they stopped eating, making table turnover too slow for restaurant operations to be feasible (or profitable).

The Jungle Cruise

Overall Rating: ✪✪✪✪
Attraction Debut: 1955 (expanded several times until Indiana Jones Adventure was built, at which time it was reduced)

Another Disney classic, this one takes guests on a boat ride through an Audio-Animatronics jungle. The quality of this attraction depends on the personality of your live tour guide/captain. (We can only imagine what the ride was like when its skippers were Robin Williams and Kevin Costner before they woke up Vietnam and danced with wolves.) The bad news is that the guides deliver a spiel of ancient puns and jokes not heard since your grandmother's trip to the Catskills in '53. (Regarding the alligators: "They're always looking for a hand out." Ba-dum-bum.) The good news is that the guides are up close and personal, available for flirting, heckling, or some combination thereof. And in our experience, even the straight ones love the opportunity to have the monotony broken. So we like to help. That's just the kind of people we are.

 Fairy Fact: Each of the boats on the cruise has its own name, including the *Nile Princess* and the *Congo Queen*. Who designed this ride?

Indiana Jones Adventure
Overall Rating: ✪✪✪✪✪
Attraction Debut: 1995

If you watched *Raiders of the Lost Ark* and wished you could be a part of the action, you're about to get your wish. Without a doubt, Indy is one of the best rides in any Disney park. An action adventure ride in an oversize jeep through the Temple of the Forbidden Eye, it takes you through snakes, fire, and everything that makes Harrison Ford our hero. They warn you to not look into the eyes of Mara (the goddess who protects the temple's treasures of wealth, eternal youth, and seeing the future) or you're doomed. Well, let's be real, folks, whether or not you look into her stony eyes, you're on a track and you're not getting off, so stare all ya want! The hydraulic car lurches, spins, and tosses you all over the place, and there are a few good

scares that promote hand-squeezing. While you drive, see if you can spot the skeleton sporting a set of Mickey ears with "Bones" embroidered on it. And those sound effects you hear? They're actually recordings of Big Thunder Mountain Railroad in action. The only bummer is that since they instituted FASTPASS on this always-crowded ride, guests miss much of the elaborate waiting area, which was designed to keep patrons amused while in line.

Fairy Fact: On the waiting line, there's a pole in the chamber that has spikes and skeletons. If you pull on the pole—bang!—the ceiling collapses! OK, it only comes down a couple of inches, but it's still cool!

Tarzan's Treehouse

Overall Rating: ✪✪

Attraction Debut: 1999 (opened in 1962 as the Swiss Family Treehouse, which was remodeled to become Tarzan's home)

What can we say about Tarzan other than "Woo-hoo!" Rarely are Disney characters drawn so damn studly. We think Jane's a bit prissy, but after a little time with this loin-cloth-wearing bohunk, even *she's* got to let her hair down. If you missed your daily workout on the StairMaster, the numerous steps up into this walk-through attraction in an immense, man-made tree are all the calf-toner you need. "Too much walking," groans Billy from Maynard, Mass. "Are you insane?" Books made of brass tell you Tarzan's story (CliffsNotes version) as you walk by numerous moments from the hit Disney film. The interactive activities at the bottom (complete with drums kids love to bang—loudly) can be skipped, but the top of the treehouse offers a lovely view of the park.

Fairy Fact: That treehouse may look imposing, but there are actually only 72 steps up and 67 coming down, proving the point that getting up is harder than going down.

New Orleans Square

While it's true that strands of sparkly beads abound in New Orleans Square, we're sorry to report that the custom of showing your, um, goods in order to obtain them isn't much practiced. But before you walk away dejected, know that there's jazz, beautiful wrought-iron balconies, gumbo (served in sourdough bread bowls), and a riverboat. It's New Orleans lite. But it is very pretty and features more shopping and food than any other land. The stores are particularly notable for their concentration of non-Disney stuff. The jewelry store sells the real McCoy. Ditto the crystal shop. It's ridiculously priced but fun to browse through. Unlike Disneyland's other sections, this one doesn't exist in the Florida park, making it unique.

Pirates of the Caribbean
Overall Rating: ✪✪✪✪✪
Attraction Debut: 1967
⚡

"Dead men tell no tales." Ooh, we just love saying that! It's a boat ride through the land of swarthy sailors at a fraction of the price of an Atlantis cruise. Walt was deeply involved in the creation of Pirates, but he died just before the completed version opened. In 1997 Disney reworked the ride, adding new Audio-Animatronics that make these randy pirates all the more lifelike. Far superior to its Walt Disney World Resort counterpart, this immense attraction takes you from the bayous of Louisiana (complete with fireflies) down a waterfall into a haunted cavern and out into a town overrun by looters. "I love that some of the animatronic pirates seem to have spent a lot of time in Key West, if ya know what I mean," cracks Bob from Buffalo, N.Y. As you finish the ride and ascend the ramp back to civilization, take note of the mural to the left boasting a cozy pair of female pirates, Anne Bonny and Mary Read, who clearly have no need for any Long John

Silvers in their lives. (In real life these ladies, though straight, had a penchant for wearing men's clothes.) And keep an eye out for the pirate straddling the cannon in a not-too-subtle fashion. Avast ye mateys, thar be squalls ahead! Indeed.

 Fairy Fact: During the 1997 revamp, Disney sanitized the men chasing the women because they were considered too politically incorrect. Looting and pillaging of villages is, however, apparently OK.

The Disney Gallery

Situated above Pirates of the Caribbean is The Disney Gallery, featuring a modest exhibit of art showing the development of the parks. There's also a shop selling high-end lithographs and posters. Tucked behind the gallery is a small outdoor patio that's always empty. On a first date and looking for a spot to chill away from the masses? This is it. Adds Dustin from Chicago: "This is the best place to find 'family.' Who else would forgo yet another ride on Indiana Jones to look at overpriced Disney art?"

Fairy Fact: The space was originally supposed to be a larger apartment for Walt, replacing the one he had on Main Street, but he died before it was completed. It became office space and later the gallery.

The Haunted Mansion
Overall Rating: ✪✪✪✪✪
Attraction Debut: 1969

❼

Housed in a gothic, Southern plantation–style house (which was actually built six years before the attraction was even designed), this ride has a reputation as the one in which fooling around is easiest. And it is. But seizing the opportunity to get all steamy with your date in a dark, enclosed, private "doom buggy" does a disservice to one of Disney's absolute best. The Mansion, though it opened in 1969, features some of the park's most captivating effects (including the crystal ball–encased Madame Leota, who raises the dead using a variety of instruments found in a 1970s discotheque: a tambourine, a bell). So we recommend riding this fast loader twice, thereby covering everyone's agenda. Oh, and did we mention that Disney has infrared cameras tracking your every move? "I find the women in goth outfits in the Haunted Mansion really sexy," admits Michelle from Pontiac. "I mean, if I saw a girl in a bar wearing one of them I wouldn't approach her. But it works for the ride."

In 2001 the mansion began getting a seasonal overhaul to become "Haunted Mansion Holiday" from October to December. Using the plot and characters from Tim Burton's *The Nightmare Before Christmas* to do the haunting, the mansion looks entirely different. The holiday version is as fabulous as the original, but be warned, as with "small world holiday," lines are very long. Make sure you get there early or FASTPASS.

Fairy Fact: The broken head singing in the final graveyard sequence is that of Thurl Ravenscroft, the original voice of the Disney trains—and of Tony the Tiger. The face of Madame Leota is actually a former Disney employee named Leota Toombs (the voice is that of Eleanor Audley, who lent her vocal chops to *Sleeping Beauty*'s Maleficent and *Cinderella*'s stepmother). You actually get to see and *hear* Leota at the exit: She's the china doll who hopes you're coming back.

⑪ Blue Bayou

Price: Expensive
Meals: L, D

Blue Bayou is one of only two full-service restaurants at Disneyland Resort. It puts you right on the bayou, inside Pirates of the Caribbean. The food is fine but definitely not worth the exorbitant prices you're going to pay. Lunch is cheaper than dinner. Reservations are hard to get, so if you're

determined to eat there, book right when you get to the park. Some disagree with us and think it's a requirement. "If you think that this restaurant is too expensive for you, you're wrong," states James from Anaheim. "Go for lunch and enjoy the best Monte Cristo sandwich I've ever tasted." But for God's sake, people, when those freaks on the Pirates boats sail by encouraging you to "throw them a roll" from your table, don't do it!

Critter Country

Critter Country is much like Frontierland in feel, but there's less Davy Crockett and more flannel. It's almost like a Frontierland annex where all of the cute furries were forced to live. So instead of cowboys and Indians, you get Pooh and friends. Instead of a mine train, you get singing animals. But the overall feeling is lumberjack, lesbian-friendly rustic.

Davy Crockett's Explorer Canoes
Overall Rating: ✪✪✪
Attraction Debut: 1956 (as Indian War Canoes, renamed in 1971)

For those of you dying to get in a workout while you're at the park—or those just wanting to show off your rowing skills—here's your chance. This is the one ride at Disneyland Resort you propel yourself. And don't think you can just sit back and let everyone else do the paddling for you: This is an everyone-participates kind of ride, as you row, row, row your boat around the Rivers of America. "It's the butchest I've ever felt," recalls Skypp from Southern California. "Worth going just to see the manly men rowing," gushes James from Anaheim. The guides will interact with you, especially if your cell phone rings mid ride. Just be careful what you say to them; when Jeffrey got a call from Eddie mid journey, the guide asked what Eddie was saying. "Something about stroking,"

Jeffrey quipped. From the back, a lady exclaimed, "This is a children's ride!"

Fairy Fact: There was a brief time when the canoes were propelled by motors, but the batteries kept dying, leaving the guests stranded.

Splash Mountain

Overall Rating: ✪✪✪✪✪
Attraction Debut: 1989

Splash Mountain is all about Brer Bear's butt. That butt is relentless. It's at every turn of this outstanding flume ride based on the animated–live action feature *Song of the South* (you know, the film Disney won't release on video because plantation musicals with racial stereotypes just don't entertain the way they did back in 1946). Brer Rabbit is trying to escape from his boring life—and from Brer Bear and Brer Fox who'd like to turn him into rabbit stew. The Audio-Animatronics on this always-packed attraction are not as sophisticated as they are on the newer Splash Mountain at Walt Disney World Resort, but they're working on sprucing up the attraction here. As you go down the Slippin' Falls or the five-story plunge into the briar patch, however, Brer Bear's butt will be indelibly marked in your brain. This is the most bear-friendly attraction in the park.

Fairy Fact: Many of the Audio-Animatronics characters used on the ride were taken from an attraction called America Sings, which closed in 1988. (Grouses Deb from Los Angeles, "Did they really need to recycle *all* that crap?") Legendary animator Marc Davis (creator of Tinker Bell, Cruella De Vil, and Maleficent) designed the characters for America Sings using his own model sheets from *Song of the South*. Ironically, those characters ended up in the *Song of the South* ride.

The Many Adventures of Winnie the Pooh

Overall Rating: N/A

Attraction Debut: 2003

While still under construction at press time, this dark ride (standing on the site where the park's original cubs—the Country Bears—once ruled the roost), promises to be nearly identical to its Magic Kingdom sibling, a description of which can be found on page 154.

Fairy Fact: The Winnie the Pooh stories represented here were actually told by Disney in three separate short films made in the '60s. It wasn't until 1977 that they were united and released as the feature, *The Many Adventures of Winnie the Pooh* (although we think it's a stretch to call three stories "many").

Frontierland

Cowboys your thing? How about leather jackets with fringe and cowgirls in suede skirts? If so, then Frontierland's your town. Though it's less popular now than when Disneyland opened and every show on TV was a Western, Frontierland still has its fans. Shockingly, though, Disney still gets away with selling toy rifles and guns across the way from the shootin' arcade. We half-expect Charlton Heston to make personal appearances.

New to Frontierland is the Rancho del Zocalo Restaurante, which roughly translates to "Overpriced Burritos and Tacos Next to a Roller Coaster Restaurant." But you get a lot of bang for your peso—portions are *grande*.

Big Thunder Mountain Railroad

Overall Rating: ✪✪✪✪

Attraction Debut: 1978

⚡

There's really not much that's gay about a runaway train, now is there? Except that it's set in a mining town, where typically women were scarce. Anyway... This rollicking ride through caves, hills, and an earthquake (it is California, after all) is a hell of a lot of fun. It's definitely not the most thrilling roller coaster in the world, but Disney's impressive attention to detail (including the Gold Rush–era town and a menagerie of western animals like rattlesnakes and, uh, goats) are a feast for the eyes. For the most fun, sit in the back—you get more thrill for your ride. And for an extra head rush, keep your eyes and head locked on the bleating goat as you sail by it. Don't say we didn't warn you!

Fairy Fact: The landscape of the ride is inspired by Bryce Canyon in Utah. While you're waiting in the queue take time to note a true park rarity: something real. The waiting area is peppered with authentic mining equipment from the 1800s, and the train on display is from the 1978 Disney film *Hot Lead and Cold Feet* (starring the talents of Karen Valentine and Don Knotts).

Tom Sawyer Island
Overall Rating: ❂❂❂
Attraction Debut: 1956

Though the Disney guide map says this place is part of Frontierland, it's actually accessed via a raft in New Orleans Square. In any event, Tom Sawyer Island is an oversize jungle gym for kids. There are rope bridges, forest paths, a fort, and a treehouse to explore. Grown-ups enjoy the respite from pavement and FASTPASS kiosks. There are also several winding caves. Now, we'd never be so trashy as to advocate something as crass as copping a feel or grabbing a prolonged kiss with your sweetie on Disney property. If we were to, however, the caves on Tom Sawyer Island would be on our list of the top five spots.

Fairy Fact: The fort, called Fort Wilderness, was actually built in Disneyland Resort's backstage area, disassembled, trucked over to Frontierland, floated across the river log by log, and reassembled on the island.

Mark Twain Riverboat and Sailing Ship Columbia

Overall Rating: ✪✪

Attraction Debut: Riverboat, 1955; Columbia, 1958

Need a break from yelping kids and pushy adults? These boat rides on the man-made Rivers of America are a welcome escape from the mayhem. The *Mark Twain* looks like it was ripped from the movie version of *Show Boat,* and the *Columbia* is a replica of an 18th-century merchant ship. During busy times, both boats are operational, with minimal wait times. The detail work on the ships is impressive, but mostly you'll just appreciate the cool breeze off the stagnant water to take you away from the hustle and bustle for a few minutes. Bring your own mint julep.

Fairy Fact: Before Disney became concerned about reinforcing negative, stereotypical notions of history, the cabin that you sail by on your voyage featured a dead settler lying out front with an Native American's arrow in his heart.

Fantasmic!

Overall Rating: ✪✪✪✪✪

Attraction Debut: 1992

Fantasmic! is an attraction that defies description. But it is one of the park's absolute highlights. Make it a priority. Shown seasonally on the Rivers of America, the body of water around which Frontierland, New Orleans Square, and Critter Country are situated, the 25-minute multimedia attraction is like nothing else at Disney. The spectacle consists of live performers (doing some particularly queer choreography with ribbons), sequences from the animated classics projected on mist shot up from the river, puppetry, a fabulous score, and finally lasers and fireworks in a magnificent pyrotechnic display. The story, about Mickey's dream being invaded by Disney's villains, makes absolutely no sense. But who cares? It's a big, expensive crowd-pleaser, and we can't get enough of it.

The Mark Twain Riverboat follows one of Davy Crockett's Explorer Canoes

Seeing Fantasmic!, however, isn't always all that easy. While the view is very good from almost anywhere around the "Rivers," we really think it's worth the effort to grab an unobstructed view from front and center. But since people camp out along the riverbank for several hours prior to the evening's first show, we typically wait until the second showing, when they have one. Our strategy is to stand by Tarzan's Treehouse for the

finale of the first show, and as the crowd disperses we dash in and stake out the just-vacated territory along the water. Then we send out emissaries for coffee and pastries (the chocolate Mardi Gras cake from the French Market is a particular favorite of Eddie's). During Fantasmic! the lines for the Haunted Mansion and Splash Mountain are at their shortest because people don't try to get through New Orleans Square during the show. If you're sitting in that vicinity, you can dash from the show to either of those rides and find shorter-than-usual lines. But if your sugar mama's paying, you can get reserved seating with all-you-can-eat dessert and coffee for a mere $41. The only catch: Seats are limited and go on sale 30 days in advance—so ya better reserve early if you're hankering for unlimited fudge pie. Call (714) 781-4400 for reservations.

Fairy Fact: Cast members in the show use the fort on Tom Sawyer Island as a dressing room to get ready for Fantasmic!—something that would have really confused Davy Crockett.

Fantasyland

Since so many of us live in Fantasyland on a daily basis (he'll call, I know he'll call), it's fairly safe to say it's the gayest of the Disney settings. After all, it's the land of Once Upon a Time and Happily Ever After. Walking through it (if you can imagine it without all of those other people cluttering up your fantasy), the sense of magic, fairies, witches, and everything else we hold dear is palpable. Of course, children think so too, and they value those things just as much as we do (thank you, Dr. Freud). Therefore, if you want a slightly quieter Fantasyland experience, we advise visiting very early, before the kiddies are up, or very late, after they've been tucked in or are too catatonic to engage in the whining that is pervasive throughout the middle of the day. Fantasyland also contains the majority of the rides based on the animated classics. Most of these are "dark rides." While, for many, the dark rides' gentility classifies them as "kiddie rides," we disagree. They're well worth a visit with or without small fry in tow. If you're the type who's bored by a poisoned princess or a flying lost boy, you're not really gay.

Fantasyland is also the place you're most likely to meet the storybook characters. And since posing with a princess (or as one) has appeal to, oh, one or two of you, we recommend checking out the courtyard just inside the castle.

Sleeping Beauty Castle

Overall Rating: **✪**

Attraction Debut: 1957 (for the walk-through attraction)

Serving as the portal from Main Street to Fantasyland is "the castle." It is, of course, known the world over as a landmark right up there with the Empire State Building, the Eiffel Tower, or Siegfried and Roy (oh, come on—they *define* Vegas). Walt thought that the original conception, based on Bavaria's Neuschwanstein Castle, looked too literal. Thus he rotated the top of the model 180 degrees, creating the design of what currently stands. The castle's massive drawbridge has been raised and lowered only twice: once at the park's opening in 1955 and again for the opening of the refurbished Fantasyland in 1983. What most people don't know is that the castle actually houses an attraction: a walk-through diorama telling the *Sleeping Beauty* story. OK, the animatronics look like they're circa 1911, but hey, this is the story with four, count 'em, four fairies (three good, one evil). On that score alone, it's worth a peek. Most people like to enter Fantasyland by going through the castle, but we recommend taking the path off to the right and coming in the side way. That route will take you past Snow White's Wishing Well, and, well, if you're anything like us, you'll want to grab the opportunity to make some wishes.

Fairy Fact: Sleeping Beauty Castle was meant to serve as a preview for the animated film, which opened a mere four years after the Castle first lowered its drawbridge.

Snow White's Scary Adventures

Overall Rating: ❸❸❸

Attraction Debut: 1955 (as Snow White's Adventures, remodeled into the "Scary" version in 1983)

Jeffrey is loath to admit that when he first went on this attraction as a small child (three weeks ago), he was so terrified by one of the opening special effects that he shut his eyes for the rest of the ride. Well, he never said he was butch. While the ride is a bit short (and sort of cuts off before the end of the story—like you don't know what happens), this abbreviated version of *Snow White and the Seven Dwarfs* is definitely charming, with a few good scares (so be wary if you have small children) and a very cool magic mirror.

Fairy Fact: Running your hand over the brass apple on your way into the building can create thunder and witchy cackles.

Pinocchio's Daring Journey

Overall Rating: ❸❸

Attraction Debut: 1983

Old men who create little boys to play with. Do we even want to go down this road? But any attraction that features a Blue Fairy is just fine with us. This dark ride rapidly tells the story of Pinocchio. You follow his adventures as he goes from his quaint village to a tortuous puppet show to Pleasure Island and into the mouth of a big fat whale. All the while his conscience, Jiminy Cricket (who looks awfully fey with his top hat and umbrella), tries to give him good advice. Our advice? Take a whirl. It may be simple, but it's quick and there's never a line. We'd like to go back to Pleasure Island, please.

Fairy Fact: While the Audio-Animatronics characters on the attraction are safely out of harm's way, be kind to the living ones you see strolling around the park. Once an unsuspecting Honest John (the fox) from *Pinocchio* was caught by some eager girls who snapped a photo—while copping a feel.

We suggest you ask characters politely before engaging in groping.

Peter Pan's Flight
Overall Rating: ✪✪✪✪
Attraction Debut: 1955

One of the most beloved rides in Disneyland Resort, even though lines are long and slow. "When I was a child," remembers Deb from Los Angeles, "I actually believed that if I rode it enough times I wouldn't grow up." Peter Pan's Flight takes guests soaring above a moonlit London and into Never Land for an encounter with Disney's biggest queen, Captain Hook, and most famous fairy, Tinker Bell. "The most romantic ride in the park," coos Chris from West Hollywood. "My partner and I always kiss as we fly in our little ship over Big Ben and the twinkling lights of London." Plus, which of us hasn't discussed that Peter guy in therapy?

Fairy Fact: Some of the cannons and such on Captain Hook's pirate ship were taken from the long ago dismantled Chicken of the Sea boat that once stood nearby.

King Arthur Carrousel
Overall Rating: ✪
Attraction Debut: 1955 (completely refurbished in 2003)

Yep, it's a carousel. It's beautiful, particularly at night, but it's still a carousel. Walt insisted that every horse on this carousel be mobile, no small feat considering they're all over a hundred years old. And no two of them are the same. The attraction features pictures of *Sleeping Beauty,* which is weird since its name comes from *The Sword in the Stone.* But who are we to quibble? We never ride it anyway.

Fairy Fact: When the park originally opened, the carousel was much closer to the castle itself (the teacups were where the carousel now stands). Too close, in fact. And on opening day, the crowds created such a bottleneck, with people jumping the guard fence to get aboard the horses, that they closed it down.

Mr. Toad's Wild Ride
Overall Rating: ✪✪✪
Attraction Debut: 1955

This ride is unique because unlike any other in the park, its plot, concocted by Walt Disney Imagineer Ken Anderson, has nothing to do with the source material or Disney's film, and considering that very few people remember Disney's version of *Wind in the Willows,* it's odd that Mr. Toad is as popular as it is. It is beloved, however, even if it ain't all that wild. But for some kids, it can be a bit intense, thanks to a bizarre ending in which guests are hit by an oncoming train and sent to hell. "I went on this ride with my friends' 4-year-old son," recalls Bob from Buffalo. "He loved it until the part where the devil came up. Boom! He instantly started crying. We agreed with him that 'it was scary!'" Whatever. We feel at home in hell.

Fairy Fact: Above the entrance to Toad Hall, in Disneyfied Latin the shield reads "Toadi Acceleratio Semper Absurda," which roughly translates to "Speeding With Toad Is Always Absurd."

Dumbo the Flying Elephant
Overall Rating: ✪✪
Attraction Debut: 1955 (remodeled in 1983)

The last time Jeffrey saw elephants fly was after a particularly hedonistic night at the Roxy in New York. In fact, upon recently visiting this attraction, where riders board an elephant and fly in circles high above Fantasyland, he was suddenly jonesing for a cosmopolitan. While it's essentially a kids' ride and one of the slowest loaders in the park, there's something delightfully giddy about soaring over Fantasyland in a big elephant.

Fairy Fact: The ride's original concept was to have the film's pink elephants flying overhead, since there is only one Dumbo. But when it occurred to someone that those pink elephants were actually the result of Dumbo's alcohol-induced hallucination, it was decided that 10 Dumbos were preferable to promoting booze to minors. Let the record note, Jeffrey has no problem promoting booze to anyone.

Casey Jr. Circus Train and Storybook Land Canal Boats

Overall Rating: ✪

Attraction Debut: Both in 1955

Sure, we've all wanted to be a prince or princess at one point or another. (Eddie, in fact, has perfected being a prince-*hunting* princess.) But on this attraction, it all comes down to property values. Both of these kids' rides offer "See the Homes of the Stars!" from many of Disney's classic features. From Snow White's cottage to Aladdin and Jasmine's palace, the miniature replicas of these properties (complete with adorable bonsai trees dotting the landscape) are precious. The boat ride (which enters through the mouth of Monstro—the whale from *Pinocchio*) comes complete with a tour guide, whom Eddie perpetually flustered with comments about the moral consequences of a woman living with seven adult men. The train, while cute, is a little less comfortable, as it was clearly designed for people smaller than us to enjoy.

Fairy Fact: When the ride first opened as Canal Boats of the World, guests were taken on a boat tour of…dirt. We're not kidding. Disney had run out of money and had nothing to put there. So, while a host would describe what was actually going to be there one day, you got to look at dirt.

Fantasyland staple: it's a small world

it's a small world

Overall Rating: ✪✪✪✪
Attraction Debut: 1966

⚡ (during the winter holidays)

Yes, the song is incessant and annoying, and yes, it's kind of weird to see Audio-Animatronics children of many nations dressed in adult clothing doing things like belly dancing. Still, this is required viewing, and we don't just mean for NAMBLA members. This ride is simply a Disney classic. Although some of you disagree: "It's an *annoying* world," quips Michelle from Pontiac. We still say you can't make a trip to Disneyland without it. If you visit during the holidays, you can see the holiday version, which is beautiful, if a bit odd; the tykes all sing "Jingle Bells." When was the last time you saw a sleigh in Egypt?

☀ **Fairy Fact:** Originally, when the ride was designed for the 1964 New York World's Fair, the concept was for all of the children to sing their own national anthems. Cacophony ensued, breeding the song we love to hate.

The Mad Tea Party

Overall Rating: ✪✪
Attraction Debut: 1955

Anyone who's ever been to a carnival has ridden a ride where guests control the spinning action of their rotating vehicle. The only difference here is that the cars are shaped like teacups. "I've thrown up on it," says David from Boston. "So I think it was fun." Our recommendation is to skip this slow loader in favor of parking it on a bench with a tall frozen lemonade and watching other fools spin themselves into oblivion. Unless, of course, sitting in china is your thing.

☀ **Fairy Fact:** While the teacups are a pretty intrinsic part of the Fantasyland topography, they haven't always been where they are. Originally where the carrousel now stands, the entire party was relocated to its current site, appropriately in front of Alice in Wonderland.

Alice in Wonderland
Overall Rating: ✪✪✪✪
Attraction Debut: 1958

For our money the best of the dark rides, Alice takes guests through a Technicolor, kaleidoscopic Wonderland. But can we just point out that that girl Alice is a circuit queen–fag hag? Look at the company she keeps: Tweedle Dee and Tweedle Dum? The Mad Hatter and the March Hare? A fastidious rabbit and a massive queen? Come on. And let's not forget about the "magic cookies" and pieces of mushroom she ingests. Give that girl a glow stick and send her twirling.

Fairy Fact: Alice's voice belongs to Kathryn Beaumont, who recorded the role first for the film in 1951, then for the ride in 1958, and again for the ride's renovation in 1984. P.S. She's also Wendy in Peter Pan.

Matterhorn Bobsleds
Overall Rating: ✪✪✪✪
Attraction Debut: 1959

The best thing about this turbulent roller coaster—the first ever tubular steel coaster—is how you're seated: between the legs of your companion. And because you're being tossed to and fro, it makes for the perfect opportunity to get a hold of your main squeeze and squeeze away. Cast members in outrageously fey, little Swiss Miss costumes board you on your "bobsled" and send you up the alpine Matterhorn Mountain (which has a 10-story elevator inside) where you encounter the Abominable Snowman (or woman—who really knows?) as you go flying down the man-made peak. It's not exactly the scariest roller coaster in the world (although we're told the A track, closer to Tomorrowland, has sharper curves, bigger drops, and goes two miles an hour faster), but the distinctive seating and somewhat rickety feel (don't worry, it's a metal coaster, it just *feels* rickety) provide that extra thrill. As you whiz by the Snowman, look for the Wells Expedition Camp,

a tribute to Frank Wells, The Walt Disney Company's president from 1984 until 1994, when he was killed in a helicopter accident.

 Fairy Fact: The Matterhorn was designed to mask the late, lamented Disneyland Skyway's ugly support tower. The mountain was built over the steel frame and the Skyway cars went right through the alps.

Mickey's Toontown

You know some gay Walt Disney Imagineer had a field day creating the park's newest land. The area, which opened in 1993, is based on Toontown from the Disney film *Who Framed Roger Rabbit* and there's not a straight line in this place (which will be comforting to those of you who are sick of all things straight). Splashy, curved buildings make up this Technicolor paradise, which is impressive for its attention to clever detail. The manhole cover below talks back to you while the safe above you comes crashing down. Fireworks explode in the munitions factory while a mailbox vociferously refuses your letters. Even the water at the drinking fountains comes out in color. The could-induce-nausea Jolly Trolly bobs and dips, weaving its way from one end of town to the other. On the far side of the tracks reside Mickey, Minnie, and Disney's toon all-stars. Who knew they all lived on the same cul-de-sac? And there's a mediocre food court with fare like pizza and ice cream. Our favorite landmark is a rubber-barred prison cell, perfect to re-create that night when you got busted in the park.

Roger Rabbit's Car Toon Spin
Overall Rating: ✪✪✪✪
Attraction Debut: 1994

⚡

It's a dark ride with a twist. Literally. While the format is the same as that of other dark rides, the vehicles are cars, which, like the teacups at the Mad Tea Party, spin at the whim of the rider. But be warned, advises Deb from West Hollywood: "While I was trying to spin my little car, I broke a nail. Not good." People have complained that if you spin, you miss many of the ride's details, all of which are fabulous. We say, if you miss something, ride it again. (That's actually our philosophy on everything.) "The FASTPASS killed this ride," says Bruce from West Hollywood. "The real fun of the ride was the waiting areas. Now you just race through the queue with the FASTPASS or stand outside in the sun for an hour without one." This ride is also notable for its inclusion of that drag queen role model Jessica Rabbit. In fact, if it weren't for that cleavage of Grand Canyon proportions, you'd have a tough time convincing us she's not a man.

Fairy Fact: The idea for a passenger-controlled, spinning dark ride was actually conceived in the '70s for an intended Ichabod Crane ride. Guests would spin around in pumpkins, looking for the Headless Horseman.

Chip 'n' Dale Treehouse
Overall Rating: ✪
Attraction Debut: 1993

We are very suspicious about those two wacky chipmunks. "There's nothing gayer in Disneyland than the neat, creatively yet tastefully decorated treehouse where these two young chipmunks share their lives together," states Chris from West Hollywood. "All they need now is a hot tub!" The treehouse is designed for younguns to climb through. It really offers nothing for adults—except a place to temporarily deposit the kids.

Fairy Fact: Wanna know how to tell the difference between Chip and Dale? The goofy Dale has a bright red nose, a tuft of hair on his head, and a Lauren Hutton space between his front teeth. The more responsible Chip has a brown nose.

Goofy's Bounce House

Overall Rating: ✪
Attraction Debut: 1993

Unless you're shorter that 52 inches, there's no way you're getting into this attraction. We don't care if you're on the list, sweetie. Built for kids, this up-close look at the Goofster's home is actually a cute variation on the "moonwalk" attractions of Jeffrey's youth (Eddie's midlife), with inflated walls, floor, and furniture too. It's all very cute, but you're not getting in. No, we checked twice. Try crashing someone else's bounce house.

Fairy Fact: You are required to wear shoes at all times inside Disneyland Resort. Except here. No shoes allowed inside Goofy's abode. You wanna pop the furniture?

Gadget's Go Coaster

Overall Rating: ✪
Attraction Debut: 1993

A gentle coaster for younger kids, this may be the only roller coaster in the park some queasy queens can handle. The concept is that you have been miniaturized and are traveling in an acorn. Now, we can think of lots of things we'd like to do if we were miniaturized, and traveling around in an acorn isn't one of them. And in this day and age of super coasters, even children think Space Mountain is tame. Plus the ride is barely a minute long.

Fairy Fact: We'll go out on a limb here and assume that most of you don't watch the animated series *Chip 'n' Dale Rescue Rangers*. Kids do, though. And they know that Gadget is that show's girl genius-inventor. And this coaster is done up to look like one of her creations with pencils and paper clips for bridges and oversize toy blocks as support beams.

Minnie's House

Overall Rating: ✪✪
Attraction Debut: 1993

Girlfriend, it doesn't get any gayer than this pink palace

for Mickey's longtime love. It's decidedly more feminine than Mickey's home, which is right next door, but let's face it, Minnie's a lipstick kind of gal. Her sitting room boasts seats that look comfy but are really not, her fridge is stocked with enough cheese to choke a horse (let alone a mouse), and her *très* gay vanity mirror is heart-shaped. Interactive kitchen displays let you turn on appliances, perfect for your inner June Cleaver. You can usually meet the mouse herself right out front. "A little too Midwestern for my taste," observes Dustin from Chicago (who, we guess, would know). "But the kitchen is to die for!" Fun for photo ops, but not a must-see. At the wishing well out back, you can toss in a coin and Minnie speaks to you from inside. Times are tough when Minnie's at the bottom of a well collecting change.

Fairy Fact: While Mickey's birthday is widely recognized and celebrated, Minnie is exactly the same age, having debuted in *Steamboat Willie* in 1928 right alongside Mickey. While we applaud her reserve on this subject, we think it's time that attention be paid.

Mickey's House
Overall Rating: ❂❂
Attraction Debut: 1993

Is it an attraction or just a long, themed line pretending to be one? We'd never be so cynical as to suggest the latter. But if we were that cynical, we might also point out that the end of the line, er, attraction, at which you get to personally visit with Mickey in his dressing room, has several offshoots, suggesting that there are multiple dressing rooms—and multiple Mickeys—operating at any given moment. Good thing we're sweet innocents who'd never notice or point out that kind of thing.

Fairy Fact: Mickey's digs are located in Toon Hills (notice the hills and the city's version of the Hollywood sign behind Chez Mouse). The central area of town is Toon Square and

Roger Rabbit is located in Downtown Toontown. In case you were mapping it out.

Tomorrowland

Sorry, folks, this is not the future land where lesbians and gays can get married and the Boy Scouts don't discriminate. But rather, it's Disney's vision of tomorrow. Or rather it was until it reopened in 1998 after an overhaul as *yesterday's* vision of tomorrow. But somehow it all works as a fun, retro look at the future. We were thrilled when the reasonably priced counter-service restaurant Redd Rockets Pizza Port, which features tasty pasta, salads, and (oh, right) pizza, opened along with the rest of "new" Tomorrowland. That renovation introduced a new entryway to the land, complete with the suspiciously phallic, otherworldly rock formations. Barbarella, eat your heart out.

Astro Orbitor
Overall Rating: ✪
Attraction Debut: 1998
While the ride itself looks really sleek, it's essentially just Tomorrowland's version of Dumbo the Flying Elephant—although we're told it goes a little higher and a little faster. (With the opening of the flying dinosaurs at Disney's Animal Kingdom and The Magic Carpet of Aladdin in the Magic Kingdom, it seems like Disney's solution to attraction additions is different versions of the Dumbo ride.) It's definitely fun for kids, but when you stop to consider that this ride was once in the center of Tomorrowland, elevated high above the old PeopleMover, the displacement to ground level is a bit depressing. Like Dumbo, it loads slowly, so be prepared to wait a while.
Fairy Fact: The redesigned ride, now based on the

Orbitron in Disneyland Paris Park, has had more names than Elizabeth Taylor: Astro-Jets, Rocket Jets, Tomorrowland Jets, and now the Orbitor.

Star Tours
Overall Rating: ✪✪✪✪
Attraction Debut: 1987

⚡

At Star Tours, based on the *Star Wars* films, the line (as with many of the rides at the Disney parks) is half the fun. You walk through the Star Tours shuttle terminal and into a Droidnostics Center, as you prepare to board flight ST-45 for a light speed trip to the Moon of Endor—with the help of a sophisticated flight simulator that rockets you into space. RX-24 (Rex for short) is your robot pilot, who is kinda new to his job, and his blunders send you crashing through a comet field, into the tractor beam of an Imperial Star Destroyer, and onto the Death Star for the ride of your life. Unfortunately, while rumors persisted that Disney was going to update or refurbish the ride when the new *Star Wars* movies opened, it remains the same. C-3PO and R2-D2, who greet you as you enter, have apparently, post-*Jedi*, been relegated to working for an elaborate travel agency. And don't try to convince us that the mincing couple aren't a little more than just "good friends."

Fairy Fact: Listen, if you can, to the banter between C-3PO and R2-D2; they refer back to events in the *Star Wars* films. And that's Paul Reubens (yep, Pee-wee) as the voice of Rex.

Disneyland Monorail
Overall Rating: ✪✪✪
Attraction Debut: 1959 (new trains added over the years)

OK, no one can tell us that this transportation system, which runs between Tomorrowland and Downtown Disney, isn't shaped like a giant, er, hot dog. (*This is a children's ride!*)

For an enchanting view of both parks, or to escape for a meal at Downtown Disney or the resorts, we recommend taking the Monorail. While not as sophisticated as its newer sister vehicles at Walt Disney World Resort, the ride is low-key. "The best way to escape the park and hit the hotel bar for a midday drink," says Bruce from West Hollywood. It's also an easy way to enter the park via Downtown Disney, but if you decide to leave with plans to return, make sure you get your hand stamped as you disembark.

 Fairy Fact: Walt discovered the monorail while driving through Cologne, Germany. The original was set up on a one-mile test track that cut through a wheat field. The German engineers were shocked when they visited Disneyland. They had spent seven years testing theirs without passengers. Walt had his up and crammed full of people in just one year.

Autopia

Overall Rating: ✪✪
Attraction Debut: 1955 (most recent revision in 2000)
⚡

For Jeffrey, who is pretty much the living personification of road rage, Autopia is almost as unnerving as driving down the 5 freeway on his way to the park. *The cars don't go fast enough! Damn those 7-year-olds!* But for some people, the adorable new cars and delightfully designed scenery are a pleasant break from the stress of everyday driving. Sponsored by Chevron, this slow-loading attraction is designed like a raceway's observation bleachers, and the waiting line has an entertaining large-screen television that displays friendly-looking cars telling (mostly) bad jokes. While it's true the cars don't go very quickly (a whopping seven miles per hour), just think of it as a pleasant Sunday drive—before you race to the next ride.

Fairy Fact: When the park opened in 1955, aluminum was the metal of the future, so the cars' original bumpers were made out of the flimsy metal. By then end of their first week in operation, thanks to the crumpling bumpers (and a myriad of other problems), just one car was left standing. Each car cost $5,500 to replace, at that time more than the cost of a new, real car. Until 1970 drivers got a souvenir driver's license as they left the ride.

Innoventions

Overall Rating: ✪
Attraction Debut: 1998

Jeffrey calls this attraction "Infomercials." It seems mainly to exist as a source of revenue for the park by providing kiosks for a plethora of companies to promote their wares. To be fair, some of the computer programs will be entertaining to kids and teens, and not every display feels like it's shoving a corporate logo down your throat (well, at least not to those of us with no gag reflex). "Save your time and go to the Sharper Image at your local mall," says David from Boston.

 Fairy Fact: We feel taunted by the fact that Tom Morrow, your robotic host, sings "There's a Great Big Beautiful Tomorrow," the theme to the late, lamented Walt Disney's Carousel of Progress, which used to occupy the Innoventions building. But Tom is voiced by Nathan Lane and looks almost exactly like the bionic Timekeeper over at Walt Disney World Resort's Tomorrowland, a robot voiced by Robin Williams, Lane's *Birdcage* lover. Go figure.

Space Mountain

Overall Rating: ✪✪✪✪✪
Attraction Debut: 1977
⚡

Space Mountain had the distinction of being the Disneyland Resort's best coaster until California Screamin' debuted in 2001. Still, this one holds its own. It's in the pitch black and a rock score pumps into speakers directly behind

riders' heads. Throw in a beer and it could be any bar in West Hollywood. "Any place that promises thrills in the dark is my kinda place," states Billy from Maynard, Mass.

Fairy Fact: Despite its impressive exterior, the ride was actually built 17- feet into the ground so as not to tower over the Matterhorn or the Sleeping Beauty Castle.

Honey, I Shrunk the Audience
Overall Rating: ✪✪✪
Attraction Debut: 1998

Inspired by the hit Disney films *Honey, I Shrunk the Kids* and *Honey, I Blew Up the Kid,* this fantastic 3-D movie makes guests part of the show—at times literally. Dr. Nigel Channing (Eric Idle) of the Imagination Institute is about to present Dr. Wayne Szalinski (Rick Moranis, reprising his role from the films—as do others from the movies, such as Marcia Strassman) with the Inventor of the Year award for creating a replicator. Mayhem ensues, including mice scurrying through the theater, a dog sneezing on guests (blech!), and the entire audience being miniaturized. While almost nothing could be gayer than the Michael Jackson 3-D movie, *Captain EO,* which was the last inhabitant of this theater, it's still a blast.

Fairy Fact: The film was directed by openly queer director Randal Kleiser (*Grease*).

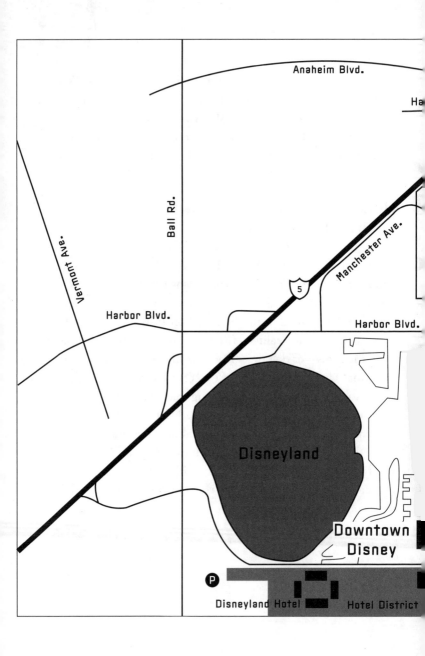

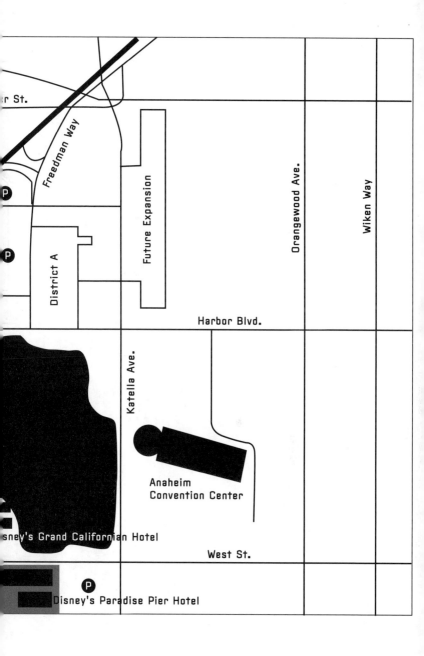

r St.

Freedman Way

P

District A

P

Future Expansion

Harbor Blvd.

Orangewood Ave.

Wiken Way

Katella Ave.

Anaheim
Convention Center

sney's Grand Californian Hotel

West St.

P

Disney's Paradise Pier Hotel

Chapter Eight
Disney's California Adventure Park

California, here I come! I left my heart in San Francisco. I wish they all could be California Gir... Well, you get the point. Celebrating the fun and excitement of the Golden State, Disney created this $1.4 billion park expansion, which opened in 2001, directly facing Disneyland, on what was once the parking lot. Let's face it—overall, there ain't no gayer state than California. San Francisco? West Hollywood? Palm Springs? Each city gayer than the next. But don't expect a "Trolley Down the Castro" ride or a "Seedy Back Rooms of Los Angeles" walk-through attraction. Here at Disney's California Adventure (or DCA, as we like to call it—especially because it takes less time to type) it's all good, clean fun.

The park is divided into three lands: Golden State, which looks at the beauty of California; Paradise Pier, which explores the joys of an old-time oceanside amusement park; Hollywood Pictures Backlot, which puts you center stage in the glamour of Tinseltown. And, of course, there are more restaurants and shops than you'll ever have time to spend money in—which won't keep Disney from trying to help you on that quest.

Alas, while the new park opened with gobs of fanfare, initially the people didn't come. Some blamed the lack of rides for kids (something Disney is working rapidly to fix). Others note that for a park that relies heavily on local visitors (Walt Disney World Resort relies on out-of-town tourists), the idea of Californians exploring California seems, well, redundant. That has not stopped us from going over and over and over again.

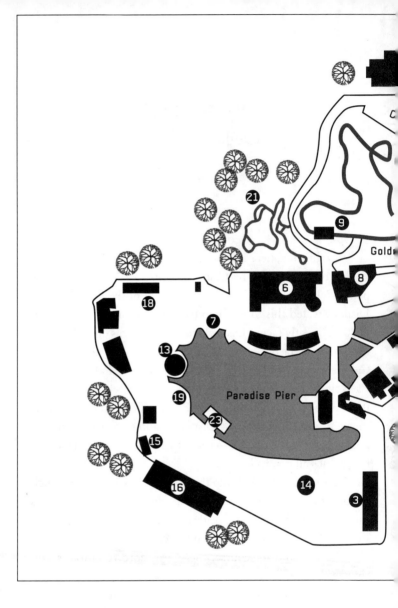

1. Backlot Stage
2. Boudin Bakery
3. California Screamin'
4. Disney Animation
5. Flik's Fun Fair
6. Golden Dreams
7. Golden Zephyr
8. Golden Vine Valley

9. Grizzly River Run
10. Hyperion Theater
11. It's Tough to Be A Bug
12. Jim Henson's Muppetvision 3-D
13. Jumpin' Jellyfish
14. King Triton's Carousel
15. Maliboomer

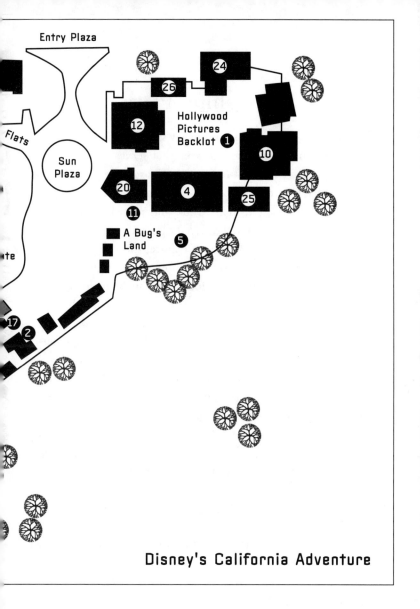

Disney's California Adventure

. Midway
. Mission Tortilla Factory
. Mulholland Madness
. Orange Stinger
. Playhouse Disney
. Redwood Creek Challenge
  Trail
. Soarin' Over California

23. Sun Wheel
24. Superstar Limo
25. The Twilight Zone Tower of
    Terror (2004)
26. Who Wants to Be A Millionaire
    Play It!

Sunshine Plaza

When you walk into Disney's California Adventure you're in Sunshine Plaza, an area that serves as an entrance foyer as well as a hub connecting sections of the park. As you pass under the monorail track–Golden Gate bridge replica (the SlimFast version, thank you), and past the wave mural mosaics constructed of over 11,000 tiles, you can't help but be struck by the plaza's dominant feature, the massive, 50-foot Sun Fountain. Made of gold titanium, the sculpture is inlaid with smashed glass particles for maximum sparkle. To keep the sun always, um, sunny, it is actually illuminated by computerized heliostats that follow the actual sun, reflecting its light onto the fountain all day. At night, Disney resorts to electricity. The plaza's other landmark is the full-size replica of the Golden Zephyr steam train, symbolic of the industry that brought millions to settle in the state. Now the Zephyr serves as the facade of several stores and eateries (our favorite being Bu-r-r Bank Ice Cream). The train's nose is the real McCoy, discovered in a railway yard in Moline, Ill. What the Imagineers were doing in Moline is anybody's guess.

Golden State

Unlike those of Paradise Pier and Hollywood Pictures Backlot, the borders of the Golden State section of the Park are somewhat blurry. And while the other two retain singular themes, Golden State incorporates several smaller themed areas. The Condor Flats section (home of Soarin' Over California) acknowledges California's reliance on the aviation industry, while A Bug's Land (formerly Bountiful Valley Farm) gives a nod to the state's agriculture. Unfortunately, neither comes equipped with pilots or farm hands. The Bay Area gives a whiff of San Francisco, including a **Fisherman's Wharf** food court but sans the Castro. There's also the Grizzly

Peak Recreation Area (home of the children's playground and the whitewater ride), evoking the redwood–Russian River territory. The Winery is right out of Napa or Sonoma, although the Napa outlet stores are nowhere to be found.

Soarin' Over California
Overall Rating: ✪✪✪✪✪
Attraction Debut: 2001
⚡

Sweetheart, you can see all the sights of California without ever leaving Anaheim. Perfect for the girl on a budget. Guests board what is best described as a flight simulator that sends them swooping over an 80-foot bowl-shaped screen as film from all over the state is projected around them. It gives you the sensation of, well, soarin' over California—complete with smell-o-rama! (Yep, as you go over orange groves, you're misted with the scent of that citrusy fruit.) It's the best ride in the park. "Fight, kick, scream—do whatever you can do to get in the front row," advises Mark from Northridge, Calif. Patrick Warburton (best known as Puddy on *Seinfeld*) plays your flight attendant (Or is he a pilot? Eh, who cares) who guides you in your safety instructions.

Fairy Fact: Our friends Bruce and Chris are standing next to the Dumbo ride in the film's final shot. We don't care that you don't know them. They're very nice.

Grizzly River Run
Overall Rating: ✪✪
Attraction Debut: 2001
⚡

If you like artificial mountains gushing with gorgeous waterfalls and boasting peaks that look like grizzly bear heads, this is a fabulous attraction. As a river-raft ride, it's just OK. Hampered by size (you are smooshed into tiny rafts) and length ("It's already over?"), the River Run is, unfortunately,

Riders splash down the Grizzly River Run

anticlimactic (as is everything hampered by size and length). On the bright side, you definitely get wet—thanks to the numerous "leaky pipes" around you. A few of the spills are thrilling, and we've been doused by a good slide down the slope. But while Jeffrey enjoys a brief thrill (years of therapy required, kids), it's worth it only if you have FASTPASS or if lines are short. And do you really want to mess up your hair? **Fairy Fact:** Think those slopes are steep? Eh. The longest drop is only 22 feet high.

Redwood Creek Challenge Trail

Overall Rating: ✪
Attraction Debut: 2001

OK, so it's essentially Tom Sawyer Island without the island. But Jeffrey had fun running over the rope bridges and climbing the tower. Clearly he had too much sugar. The Trail is definitely geared toward educating kids. (There are guides for tracking animals by their footprints and the like.) Eddie thought the authentically costumed Disney park rangers in their wide-brimmed hats, hiking boots, and hunter-green uniforms were dreamy. They thought he was a lunatic. **Fairy Fact:** The three ranger stations are called Mount Lassen Lookout, Mount Shasta Lookout, and Mount Whitney Lookout—all after mountains in Northern California.

Golden Dreams

Overall Rating: ✪✪✪✪✪
Attraction Debut: 2001

One could argue that Disney's California Adventure is too heavily reliant on attractions that are on film, as opposed to actual rides. And while Golden Dreams is yet another film, it is extraordinary. Hosted by Whoopi Goldberg (as Caliphia, Queen of California—OK, sure), the film is a multicultural history of California, telling the state's story through scenes ranging from the Gold Rush to the summer of love.

Excellently cast, the movie, which is a bit sophisticated for kids, is among Disney's best. It ends, like Epcot's American Adventure, with a touching and inspiring montage of significant Californians, including Harvey Milk, Elizabeth Glaser, Elizabeth Taylor, and Sonny Bono, who wasn't gay but may as well have been.

 Fairy Fact: Tony-winner Heather Headley (Disney's *Aida*) sings the movie's theme song, "Just One Dream."

Boudin Bakery

Overall Rating: ✪
Attraction Debut: 2001

The Boudin Bakery isn't so much an attraction as an advertisement for the sourdough loaves sold at the end of a walk-through exhibit where you can watch bread being baked through huge windows. Narrated by Rosie O'Donnell and Colin Mochrie (*Whose Line Is It Anyway?*) on overhead monitors, the tour is pleasant enough but not worth making a special trip for. Unless, of course, the thought of Rosie and vats of dough gets you going.

Fairy Fact: The "mother dough," used to bake the bread here, comes directly from the original Boudin Bakery in San Francisco.

Mission Tortilla Factory

Overall Rating: ✪
Attraction Debut: 2001

The Mission Tortilla Factory, like the Boudin Bakery, is a walk-through demonstration. Without Rosie to enliven this one, however, the tortillas are pretty flat. Oh, God. You see what this attraction makes us stoop to?

Fairy Fact: The tortilla machine used here is deliberately slowed down, churning out just 25 tortillas a minute. A typical machine makes 2,000 every 60 seconds.

Flik's Fun Fair

Overall Rating: ✪
Attraction Debut: 2001

In an effort to make Disney's California Adventure more kid-friendly, Disney took the section of Golden State known as Bountiful Valley Farm and turned it into A Bug's Land, adding this kiddie-ride area based on the Disney-Pixar film *A Bug's Life*. Included are **Flik's Flyers** (a small hot air balloon simulator), **Tuck & Roll's Drive 'Em Buggies** (an oh-so-slow bumper car ride under P.T. Flea's circus tent), **Heimlich's Chew Chew Train** (an oh-so-short railroad), **Francis's Ladybug Boogie** (a unique spinning ladybug ride, à la the tea cups), and **Princess Dot's Puddle Park** (a place for kids to get soaking wet much to their parents' chagrin). The attention to detail is staggering: Look for the one four-leaf clover overhead or at the tissue-box bathrooms. But unlike the fare across the way, these are not attractions that can be enjoyed by adults and kids alike. Nice to visit, but ya don't wanna stay.

Fairy Fact: You enter the Fair walking through a box of Cowboy Crunchies—featured in another Disney-Pixar creation, *Toy Story 2*.

It's Tough to Be a Bug

Overall Rating: ✪✪✪✪
Attraction Debut: 2001

Going down a long and winding path that leads you into an ant hill, you arrive inside a waiting area surrounded by—no, not ants—Broadway show posters, of course. Placards from hit bug shows like *Beauty and the Bees, My Fair Ladybug,* and *A Stinkbug Named Desire* adorn the walls as you're serenaded by an insect chorus buzzing out hits like "I Could Have Danced All Night" and the like (tell us a straight person concocted that). Eddie would have been content to spend the day in the pre-show area, but Jeffrey voted for the actual attraction: a 3-D "be kind to your neighborhood bug" film, using characters from the hit *A Bug's Life*. Once you put on your "bug eyes" (3-D glasses), Flik the ant (voiced by Dave Foley) proudly parades a host of his creepy-crawly friends for your enjoyment. The fun comes off the screen (you may want to hold your breath when the stinkbug, Claire de Room, shows up), and things go awry when grasshopper Hopper arrives to teach us humans a lesson. The showstopping finale will leave you high kicking (or buzzing, your choice) out of the theater. "If you don't laugh and scream," says Keith from Orlando, "then you're dead."

Fairy Fact: Other voices in the attraction include those of Jason Alexander (as the dung beetle), Cheech Marin (as tarantula Chili), and French Stewart (as the Termite-ator).

Golden Vine Winery

Overall Rating: ✪✪
Attraction Debut: 2001

Remember when we talked about the park's reliance upon filmed attractions? Well, the Golden Vine Winery "tour" is one of those. And this one isn't particularly exceptional. The film is a minidocumentary on winemaking, tracing a grape's journey from the vine to DUI. Well, not quite that far. It's a perfectly harmless film, if a little sterile. If only they'd hand out samples…

Fairy Fact: The Winery tour is narrated by Jeremy Irons, making him a record holder as the only celebrity on four attractions (this one, Spaceship Earth at Epcot, The Timekeeper at the Magic Kingdom, the recently closed Legend of the Lion King).

⓫ The Vineyard Room

Price: Expensive
Meals: L, D

Disney took over the food preparation at this upscale eatery, originally operated by Robert Mondavi, with a little

help from its Napa Rose chef, Andrew Sutton. The eclectic menu, ranging from salads and pastas to more hearty fare, is sumptuous. Service, however, is less than stellar. And of course, there's lots of wine.

Hollywood Pictures Backlot

Hooray for Hollywood! La, la, la, la, la, la, la—Hollywood! (Does anyone really know all those lyrics?) Disney has taken its Disney-MGM Studios theme park in Orlando and essentially condensed it with varying degrees of success. Surrounded by glamorous old Hollywood architecture, Eddie was certain that his close up was going to come at any minute. And he was ready. The detail work on Hollywood Boulevard, which is occasionally used for filming, is quite impressive, including facades of the Max Factor building and the (Disney-owned) El Capitan Theatre. If you're starving, you can get a bite at Award Wieners (those Oscar-caliber hot dogs) or the Hollywood and Dine food court, which offers a diverse selection of decent food. This is also your best place for catching Disney characters from the latest animated feature release (usually hovering by the fantastic Animation Pavilion). The only things missing from this Hollywood Boulevard are the drunks and the hookers. Oops, Jeffrey's here. Now they're just missing the hookers.

Animation
Overall Rating: ✪✪✪✪
Attraction Debut: 2001

The most striking part of the Animation building is undoubtedly its lobby. Guests walk past a sparkling "Once Upon a Time" into a huge atrium lined with massive screens showing musical animated scenes in varying stages of completion. Hercules will be singing on one screen, for example, while another will show still paintings from that film's background art. The effect is absolutely beautiful. "Disney's executives should be required to visit this attraction once a month," says Chris from West Hollywood, "to be reminded about what the public really wants, loves, and expects from Disney."

From that lobby, guests can choose a number of rooms to explore. The Sorcerer's Workshop features interactive displays where you can draw your own animation, lay your own vocal tracks over an animated Disney scene, or take a personality test to find out which Disney character you're most like. (For the record: Jeffrey: Hades; Eddie: Tinker Bell. No comments until your own results are in, please.) The Screening Room shows the Walt Disney biopic *One Man's Dream*, also presented at Disney-MGM Studios. And the charming presentation *Drawn to Animation* features a live, faux animator who interacts (via video screen) with *Mulan*'s Mushu to reveal the genesis and development of an animated character. Like any Disney attraction with a live host, this one can be delightful or deadly depending on the human. Mushu remains pretty much the same.

Fairy Fact: Several of the voice talents from Disney Classics were brought back to dub dialogue for their characters in this pavilion. Present are Pat Carroll (Ursula), Jerry Orbach (Lumiere), and David Ogden Stiers (Cogsworth).

Jim Henson's Muppetvision 3-D
Overall Rating: ✪✪✪✪✪
Attraction Debut: 2001
⚡

When Disney was in negotiations to purchase the Muppets just before Jim Henson's death, there was the fear that the sensibilities of Disney and Henson wouldn't quite blend. Well, the opening of Muppetvision 3-D ended those fears. While the attraction is at Disney, the mood is definitely Muppet, with all of their typical irreverence and wit intact

(including a poke at the Mouse). The bulk of the attraction is a 3-D film (and an excellent one at that, including Miss Piggy croaking out "Dream a Little Dream") with some terrific effects, but the atmosphere is heightened by Audio-Animatronics Muppets (Waldorf and Statler, two men eternally sharing a theater box—you do the math—heckling; the Swedish Chef tangling the film from the projection booth as he did in *The Muppet Movie*). The waiting area features some priceless video footage and is also chock-full o' gags, including a large cargo net hanging from the ceiling holding orange and green cubes of gelatin—that would be a "a net full of Jell-O" (get it?).

 Fairy Fact: Muppet creator Jim Henson died shortly after making this film. It stands as the last big-screen performance of Henson as Kermit the Frog.

Who Wants to Be a Millionaire—Play It!
Overall Rating: ✪✪✪✪
Attraction Debut: 2001

⚡

All you type A, competitive queens get ready. If you ever sat back in your chair watching Regis and thought, *I could do that,* now's your chance, smarty-pants. Walking into a sound-stage that looks identical to the set used on the hit TV game show, audience members are directed to seats equipped with boxes on which you play along. As you answer the multiple-choice questions, your speed and accuracy help determine who will be the next player to join your Philbinesque host in the infamous "hot seat." You'd better hope your "fastest finger" is fast; you're playing against 600 people simultaneously for a chance. While you can't win cash, Disney does present winners with pins, hats, and other prizes.

Fairy Fact: This is a working soundstage from which the producers could actually shoot an episode.

Superstar Limo

Overall Rating: ✪

Attraction Debut: 2001

More like Supersucky Lame-o. Sorry, we had to say it. You board this dark ride to discover that you're Hollywood's newest superstar (please, we already knew that). Then it's a quick tour of the county before you arrive at your big premiere at Grauman's Chinese Theater. Throughout your journey, you encounter other megastars like yourself. Antonio Banderas and Melanie Griffith (looking more like Matt Lauer and Katie Couric) greet you in Beverly Hills, Cindy Crawford douses you with (thankfully unscented) perfume, and yes, even Cher turns up, in sequined flippers, when you hit Malibu (which for some reason has a Muscle Beach—a Venice attraction, many miles south of Malibu). "If you're into watching car crashes," warns Dustin from Chicago, "the Superstar Limo is for you: a chain-reaction pileup of bad, bad, executive decisions." While it's amusing just to see how distorted some of the actors look, it's more amusing to do something else. Anything else.

 **Fairy Fact:** Yes, that really is Joan Rivers lending her voice to a puppet that looks shockingly less plastic than she does.

The Twilight Zone™ Tower of Terror

Overall Rating: N/A

Attraction Debut: 2004

While coming up with exciting rides is always fun, copying existing rides from your other theme parks is infinitely easier and cheaper. So they are wisely setting up this jaw- (and stomach-) dropping Disney-MGM Studios staple here at DCA, set to open in 2004. Flip to page 197 to see what the fuss is all about.

Playhouse Disney—Live on Stage!

Overall Rating: N/A

Attraction Debut: 2003

While Rolie Polie Olie, Stanley, and Bear (of the Big Blue

House) may not sound like any Disney characters you've ever heard of, these fine folks are regulars on the Disney Channel. And this 20-minute show transports them from the small screen to the stage. Unless you have small children, stay far, far away. **Fairy Fact:** The building recently housed another daytime TV attraction—the ABC Soap Opera Bistro, visited frequently by the network's sudsy stars. Wonder if Susan Lucci will come back and cut a rug with Bear.

Paradise Pier

If you dumped vats of Clorox on the Santa Cruz boardwalk, you'd get Paradise Pier, a beach community carnival without the seediness usually found at similar haunts. The look of Paradise Pier—meant to evoke the kinder, gentler 1920s—is absolutely beautiful, but the rides are primarily versions of carnival attractions, making the Pier not quite up to Disney's usual standard. It is fun, though. And these days it's hard to find an atmosphere that will justify massive corn dog consumption. **Strips, Chips and Dips** and the **MaliBurrito** stands feature scrumptious chicken strips and burritos respectively, but **Pizza Oom Mow Mow** (boasting pies in the shape of surfboards) is a must-miss.

California Screamin'
Overall Rating: ✪✪✪✪✪
Attraction Debut: *2001*
⚡

California Screamin' is a roller coaster, pure and simple. No gimmicks, no theme, just a great coaster. There are, however, some design elements that make it exceptional. As with Disneyland's Space Mountain, a score is piped in through a speaker directly behind the rider's head, adding a truly fabulous auditory element. The ride also glides without any sharp, uncomfortable jerks. And the views of the park and Paradise Pier are beautiful, particularly at night.

Fairy Fact: Though the coaster is a tribute to the old wooden rides of yore, this one's made of 5.8 million pounds of steel. Stacked 16 feet high, that steel would cover three football fields.

King Triton's Carousel
Overall Rating: ✪
Attraction Debut: 2001

This carousel is so dull, they took out the additional *r* that exists in King Arthur's Carrousel at the park next door. When he was a kid Jeffrey had a merry-go-round in his backyard that was more exciting—he would spin in a circle until he fell down. Thank you, we'll be here all week.

Fairy Fact: Though the calliope playing is a gay '90s band organ (the other gay '90s, not the Ricky Martin '90s) the music is decidedly '60s, including "Surfin' Safari" and "Sea Cruise."

Sunwheel
Overall Rating: ✪✪✪
Attraction Debut: 2001

While the Sunwheel appears at first glance to be no more than a huge Ferris wheel, what differentiates this particular disc is the fact that two thirds of its compartments slide on an inner track as the wheel rotates. Views are also fabulous, but the Sunwheel is most notable for the fact that it offers one of the park's few opportunities to be completely secluded. The ride's not really long enough for anything more than a cuddle, but at those altitudes, that usually suffices for us.

Fairy Fact: The wheel is inspired by the Wonder Wheel on Coney Island.

Maliboomer
Overall Rating: ✪✪✪
Attraction Debut: 2001

⚡

Ever wonder what it was like to be inside one of those

The Sunwheel shines in front of California Screamin'

"test your strength" games where some guy using a mallet sends a disk soaring up to (hopefully) ring a bell and win a prize? If you said yes, get help. The Maliboomer, sort of a reverse "free fall" ride, sends you shooting up ultrafast, and we guarantee you'll ring the bell every time. And when you shriek like the girl that you are (real or not) don't worry about the residents of Anaheim. Those plastic windows in front of you are actually scream shields used to comply with the city's sound codes.

We advise a FASTPASS, or go into the "single riders" lane—do you really want to see the look on your lover's face when he or she is about to hurl? Again? We thought not.

Fairy Fact: The ride shoots you up 200 feet using a high-powered compressed-air launch system. A sensation you may also experience after one too many MaliBurritos.

Orange Stinger

Overall Rating: ✪✪
Attraction Debut: 2001

Remember that carnival ride where you got on a swing that lifted off the ground and went around in circles? Well, if you want to ride it again, now's your chance. Only this time you're inside an orange and the sound of bees swirls around you. "It's a fun old carny ride," states Chris from West Hollywood. "But as you're flying around, you can't help wonder, *Why am I inside this giant orange? And what is with the sound of all those bees?*"

Fairy Fact: Like the Pier's giant dinosaur that doubles as a sunglass shack, the huge orange is based on roadside convenience stands that used to dot Route 66.

Jumpin' Jellyfish

Overall Rating: ✪
Attraction Debut: 2001

Strictly for kids (or very small, frightened adults), this is sort of like a miniature Maliboomer (see page 120). You're lifted up in a brightly colored "jellyfish" and then gently dropped to the ground, thanks to the fish's parachute.

Fairy Fact: While it's a kiddie ride and moves pretty slowly, the tower is a surprisingly high 50 feet.

Mulholland Madness
Overall Rating: ✪✪✪
Attraction Debut: 2001

And Eddie thought driving with Jeffrey was dangerous. We adore this wild minicoaster. No, it doesn't boast huge drops or loops, but the hairpin turns and sudden dips are a blast. Yes, we know it's a "preexisting coaster" (meaning Disney just bought it from a coaster company that sells the exact same ride all over the country), and we realize that the actual Mulholland is a tight, winding road, not a freeway (which Disney people seemed to forget when redressing the ride). But we still love it. Love it. Love it.

Fairy Fact: This is the only continuously loading roller coaster either of us has ever been on. The cars never stop (unless there's an emergency, of course)—they just slow down and you get in. But don't assume this makes it a fast loader. It's not.

Golden Zephyr
Overall Rating: ✪
Attraction Debut: 2001

Board one of six silver rockets and spin around and around and around. It's neither a thrill ride nor relaxing. It's not even golden. It could, however, make you dizzy. The bright and shiny rockets provide a lovely view of Paradise Pier but are more fun to watch spinning from the ground than to actually be on. When the ride first opened, it was shut down frequently because of wind (it has since been reweighted to fly during heavier gusts). In the summer heat, you could fry an egg on the silver surface.

Fairy Fact: Thanks to the wonders of computer technology, your rocket ship will drop you off in the exact spot you launched from.

⓫ Ariel's Grotto

Price: Moderate

Meals: L, D, CD

Wolfgang Puck started up this eatery as Avalon Cove when DCA first opened, but by the time the year was out, so was Wolfie. We tend to find character dining sometimes annoying, and the mediocre selection on a prix-fixe menu is uninspiring. However, upstairs at the bar (where you can knock one back), the lobster nachos are a must-have. Plus the bar offers a great view of parades and water shows (when they're happening). The name change from Avalon Cove to Ariel's Grotto created an interesting situation; it's the first time an attraction and a restaurant have shared the same moniker. (Ariel's Grotto is a character meet-and-greet in both Disneyland and the Magic Kingdom.)

Chapter Nine
Downtown Disney, Anaheim, Other Area Parks, and More

Nighttime at Disneyland Resort

While we realize that for many of you, the setting of the sun means the putting on of leather pants and breaking out the martini shaker, Disneyland Resort does offer some great options for nighttime entertainment.

Inside the gates of Disneyland Park and Disney's California Adventure, there's always something happening at night. But because schedules and shows can change seasonally, we didn't include them in the reviews. So please check online ahead of time or in the foldout brochures Disney gives out when you get to the park. At Disneyland Park, **Fantasmic!** (which we do review) is always worth the one- to two-hour wait you'll have to put in for a good seat. You won't need to carve out space to look up to the heavens and watch **Believe…There's Magic in the Stars,** one of the most outstanding fireworks displays we've ever seen. Usually there will be one parade at night as well.

Across the way at Disney's California Adventure, the company brought back the **Main Street Electrical Parade** (now called **Disney's Electrical Parade** since its move to the new park) at night. And at press time, it had developed **Disney's LuminAria,** a holiday show on the lagoon at Paradise Pier incorporating light, fireworks, and projections, which was rumored to be coming back on a regular basis.

The Disneyland Hotel also offers the **Fantasy Waters Show** (at the cleverly titled Fantasy Waters Amphitheater) where water leaps and jumps to the music of Disney. Or you could just hang out with us and watch Eddie leap and jump to the music of Disney. Your choice. Shows are nightly (but check a schedule).

Downtown Disney also has numerous nightspots that are open until well after park closing, and **House of Blues** usually has an interesting roster of talent coming in to perform. The bars at all of the hotels are open late as well.

The Anaheim area also has a somewhat limited gay nightlife of its own. Please refer to our **Anaheim Gay Life** section on the following page for details.

Downtown Disney, Disneyland Resort

With the opening of Downtown Disney, Disneyland Resort has become a place with things to do almost around the clock. Situated right next to Disney's California Adventure and Disneyland, Downtown stretches in a long, narrow strip from the ticket windows to the Disneyland Hotel, incorporating the restaurants and bars there. Downtown combines shopping, restaurants, and after–park hours bars and clubs to keep the adults as happy as the kids. Moreover, Downtown has provided Anaheim's locals with an extremely popular evening entertainment "mall," tapping into a whole new market for Disney.

While Downtown's stores are nothing extraordinary, they're fun for a browse. Included are **Sephora** (makeup)**, Illuminations** (candles), **Department 56** (re-e-eally ugly Christmas ornaments), and, of course, a massive **World of Disney** store. The bigger restaurants include the chains **House of Blues** (where there's live music nightly), **ESPN Zone** (where there are straight men watching games nightly), and the **Rainforest Cafe** (where there's rain every 20 minutes or so). Of these, Skypp from Southern California recommends the Zone: "Cute guys walk in here *all* the time."

There's also **Ralph Brennan's Jazz Kitchen**, which serves up excellent N'awlins cooking amid live jazz (try the fried green tomatoes or the coconut shrimp). **AMC** has a massive multiplex for those who just want to veg with a tub of popcorn. Jeffrey adores the delicious Italian fusion at the pricey **Catal**, which is operated by the high-end Patina Group, as is the more Italian-y Italian restaurant, **Naples**, which serves up great pastas and pizzas. Unfortunately, unlike its Florida counterpart, Downtown has no specific location favored by gay and lesbian guests, making cruising a bit harder. Park staff still favors the **Lost Bar** at the Disneyland Hotel, but Eddie's had luck at Catal's outdoor coffee bar, **The Uva**.

Anaheim Gay Life

Sadly, unlike Orlando, Anaheim is not exactly a gay mecca. This is kinda shocking to us given the large number of gay people Disneyland Resort employs. Many attribute the lack of a gay scene to the fact that Anaheim is located in conservative Orange County. Of course there's an abundance of homo havens in Los Angeles and San Diego, and there are even queer pockets in nearby Long Beach and Laguna Beach. But for those who don't want to travel, your options are somewhat limited (save for hanging out at the cast member entrance). You can also plug into the Web sites for **Gay Orange County** (www.gayoc.com) or the **Orange County/Long Beach Blade** (www.metrog.com/headline/blade/blade.html) for listings and information. Here are the places to hit (and since things can change, please call ahead) that are just a quick cab ride away:

OZZ (6231 Manchester Blvd., Buena Park, [714] 522-1542) features a dance club, restaurant, and cabaret. It's your best bet for a good time locally. We hear **Frat House** (8112 Garden Grove Boulevard, Garden Grove, [714] 373-3728) can be a bit dicey given the neighborhood, but hey, things change, right? The *caliente* club **El Calor** (2916 W. Lincoln Blvd., Anaheim, [714] 527-9973) features a mostly Latino crowd and is gay *only* on Wednesday nights.

Surrounding Theme Parks— California

Knott's Berry Farm

Given its proximity to Disneyland Resort, guests with an extra day may choose to visit Knott's, once a berry farm—now a theme park. While there's a good degree of theming (most of the place has the feel of an old Western town), the Ghost Town at Knott's pales in comparison to Disneyland Park's Frontierland. Knott's, however, does offer more thrill rides than Disneyland, including the **Supreme Scream**, a free-fall ride that makes the Maliboomer look like a kiddie ride (Jeffrey cowered by a cotton candy stand as Eddie shot up into the stratosphere). The **Ghostrider,** designed to look like an old-fashioned coaster, is great, and the brand-new '50s-themed **Xcelerator** coaster has cars designed like '57 Chevys and gets you rockin' at speeds up to 82 mph. But their **Camp Snoopy,** a kiddie area featuring the Peanuts characters, feels like it's trying too hard to slap some characters onto attractions. We go for the food: You don't even have to pay park admission to dine at **Mrs. Knott's Chicken Dinner Restaurant,** a prix-fixe (at a nominal $11.95 per person), old-style, sit-down restaurant that features some of the best down-home cooking in Southern California. But beware— people line up at the door for *hours* to eat there.

How to get there: From Disneyland Resort, the place is just a hop, skip, and a jump (or several skips, if you're Eddie) away. Get on the I-5 north. Get on the 91 Freeway west, and exit at Beach Boulevard. Turn left at the end of the ramp. Proceed south one mile to the auto entrance lanes on your right past La Palma Avenue.

SeaWorld

A theme park to satisfy your inner marine biologist. SeaWorld is great if you (a) love creatures of the sea; (b) enjoy sitting through lots of shows and walking through attractions; and (c) don't care at all about rides. Sure, it has the wet and wild **Shipwreck Rapids!** which really is a great rafting ride, but that's pretty much it (unless you count the Skytower, with its aerial view, and the ski lift–like **Skyride,** both of which cost extra). But the shows, which include the signature exhibition with Shamu the killer whale, and some of the exhibits (like the **California Tide Pool,** which always gets Jeffrey excited for some reason), are all solid. Unless you feel a desperate need to go under the sea, it's probably not worth the trip.

How to get there: SeaWorld is in San Diego, 90 miles (about two hours) south of Disneyland Resort. From Disneyland Resort, take the I-5 south. Exit at Sea World Drive and turn west toward SeaWorld's park entrance. For details visit www.seaworld.com or call (619) 226-3901.

Legoland

C'mon, you remember Legos, those plastic bricks you could stick together to build tiny little dungeons where little Lego people would torture one another. OK, maybe that was just Jeffrey. Don't laugh. Eddie used his to build mini-sets from his favorite musicals. Here the Legos are larger than life. While we loved walking through parts like Miniland, where you can see miniature versions of sites from California, a New England harbor, New Orleans, Washington, D.C, and New York City (because it's Miniland, the Chelsea gym bunnies are too small to see), it's mostly just fun for kids.

How to get there: Legoland is about 60 miles south of the Disneyland Resort. Take the I-5 south and exit at Cannon Road in Carlsbad. Go east, following signs to Lego Drive. For details visit www.legoland.com or call (760) 918-5346.

San Diego Zoo

Founded in 1916 (the same year Eddie was born), the San Diego Zoo has one of the most elaborate collections of animals in the world. (There are more than 4,000 animals, which is vaguely the number of people Eddie has, uh, met in his lifetime.) It's also immense (making a day at Disneyland Resort look like a cakewalk), so bring comfy shoes. The pandas are the must-see attraction at the park, and there are a variety of tours worth checking out. Plus the **Old Globe** theater is steps away, so you can do the zoo during the day and see a show at night.

How to get there: The zoo ain't close to the Disneyland Resort (about two hours south), but for many, it's worth the trip (if only to reenact the opening credits from *Three's Company*). From the Disneyland Resort, take I-5 South to the State Route 163 north exit, then the Zoo/Museums (Richmond Street) exit. For details visit www.sandiegozoo.com or call (619) 234-3153.

San Diego Wild Animal Park

The Wild Animal Park makes the San Diego Zoo look puny (it's 20 times larger). Founded in 1972 (a few years before Jeffrey was born), this 1,800-acre wildlife preserve has more wild animals than a night in West Hollywood. You view the extensive wildlife (lions and tigers and bears, Dorothy) several ways, including walking the extensive trails and taking the Wgasa Bush Line Railway, a five-mile, 55-minute guided train tour where you get a great look at all the animals.

How to get there: The wild animal park is a bit closer to Disneyland Resort (about 90 minutes) than the zoo. From Disneyland Resort, take I-5 south, exit at State Route 78 east at Oceanside. Proceed east to I-15 south. Exit at Via Rancho Parkway and follow the signs to the park. For details visit www.sandiegozoo.com or call 760-747-8702.

Universal Studios Hollywood

When Universal Studios opened as a tourist attraction in 1964 it was a unique entity. It wasn't an amusement park but a working movie studio that had thrown open its doors for the public to see the "behind-the-scenes magic" of Hollywood. Almost the entire experience was a tram tour, encompassing Universal's vast backlot and featuring such movie landmarks as the *Psycho* house and *Spartacus* Square. Things like an automated Jaws and King Kong were added for excitement, but the place was first and foremost a studio with a bit of window dressing thrown in. Well, those days are gone. While Universal remains a working studio, most of the production facilities are kept very separate from what the public sees. Instead, the bulk of the amusement park is made up of rides and attractions that while movie-themed could just as easily exist anywhere. That's not to say they're all bad, but the park has lost the authentic feel it had when it was simply a studio.

Of the attractions, the **Back to the Future** flight simulator ride (the best of the genre), **Terminator 2: 3-D** (so lifelike you can you almost smell Schwarzenegger's sweat), and the **Jurassic Park** ride (where massive animatronic dinos prey on you before the final splashdown) are the headliners and are all excellent. Less impressive (read: downright lame) are a **Waterworld** stunt show (millions spent on that before anyone realized the movie was a stinker), the **Backdraft** experience (not quite a classic), and the sickly sweet **E.T.** ride, which pretty much destroys the film's integrity by presenting a plastic, nonsensical story about saving E.T.'s planet. The backlot tour is still there, but it's decidedly less historical in perspective and significantly more focused on Universal's current slate of movies. But you can be sure to find family at **Lucy: A Tribute**, a walk-through exhibit tracing Lucille Ball's career with video narration from Lucie Arnaz. (That's pretty much the park's gayest feature now that live, buff, Hercules and Xena are no longer roaming the grounds for Kodak moments.) The bonus of being at a studio is never knowing when you might catch a glimpse of real Hollywood; last time we took the tram, Steven Spielberg went speeding by on a golf cart. Granted, a Spielberg sighting may not be worth the admission, but it's something.

How to get there: From the Disneyland Resort, take the I-5 north. When it merges with the 101, get on the 101 Hollywood Freeway north to Universal Center Drive and follow the signs to Universal Studios Hollywood.

Part Three
Walt Disney World Resort

A Little History

Eager to avoid the spatial limitations of the California park, when Walt began planning Walt Disney World, he went looking for vast, undeveloped spaces. He chose 27,500 acres (48 square miles) of central Florida swamp and farmland filled with citrus groves, wild boar, alligators, and every imaginable bird and bug. But Walt was determined to build in a space where he could insulate his guests from the strip malls and cheap hotels that had sprung up in Anaheim right after Disneyland opened. To buy all of that land without being gouged, Walt kept his name out of all of the transactions and used layers of dummy companies to make the purchases. And though Walt never lived to see Walt Disney World completed, he was intimately involved with its creation, in the end working through planning details with his brother, Roy, from a hospital bed. The Magic Kingdom opened on October 1, 1971, and was an immediate success. On the same date, 11 years later, Epcot opened its doors, to be followed by Disney-MGM Studios in 1989 and Disney's Animal Kingdom in 1998. With these four parks plus the development of three water parks and the nightlife center Downtown Disney, the Disney company has managed to monopolize not only the Florida theme park consumer but the entire entertainment dollar. Yearly park profits exceed $1 billion, and, as of this writing, the resort has seen more than 500 million guests. Walt Disney World Resort has its own taxing authority, makes its own zoning decisions, and sets its own building codes. It generates its own power and has its own environmental protection department. With the development of Celebration, a model community of 20,000 close to the resort, Disney's is an all-encompassing empire. But it's more than likely that Walt's words on Disneyland's 10th anniversary are as true now as they ever were: "It's all just been sort of a dress rehearsal, and we're just getting started. So if any of you are resting on your laurels, I mean just forget it, because…we are just getting started."

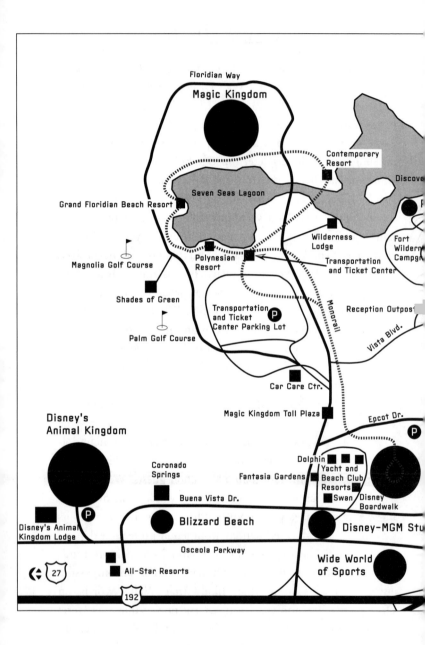

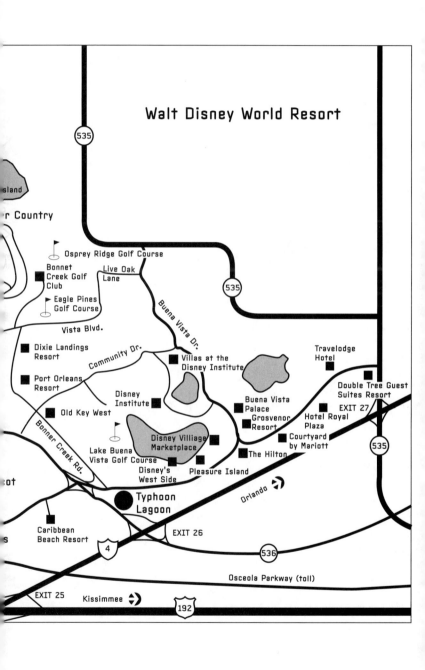

Chapter Ten
Magic Kingdom Park

With no developed property for miles and miles, Walt Disney World Resort could stretch out in a territory twice the size of Manhattan. The result, which started with the Magic Kingdom, is a park that, while like Disneyland in feel, is much more spacious. Attractions are farther apart, making for a smoother and more pleasant crowd flow. The park never feels empty, however, owing in part to the fact that everything is simply bigger. From Main Street's edifices to the castle itself (this one is Cinderella's) everything is taller and bigger (size queens take note). And when the weather hovers around 85 degrees for much of the year, the extra breathing room is a necessity. The Magic Kingdom also differs from its older sister in that it features a new land, Liberty Square, in lieu of California's New Orleans Square. The rest is thematically similar, with the park's five lands all connecting at Main Street, U.S.A.

How to get there: From the Transportation and Ticket Center you can hop on a monorail or ferry to get to the park. From the resorts, you can take a bus directly to the Magic Kingdom, and if you're staying at Disney's Contemporary, you can walk around the lake.

Main Street U.S.A.

Sure, the sweet scent in the air is pumped in, and it's hard to tell if the twittering birds are real or recorded. But ya know something? We don't care. We can't help smiling as we walk

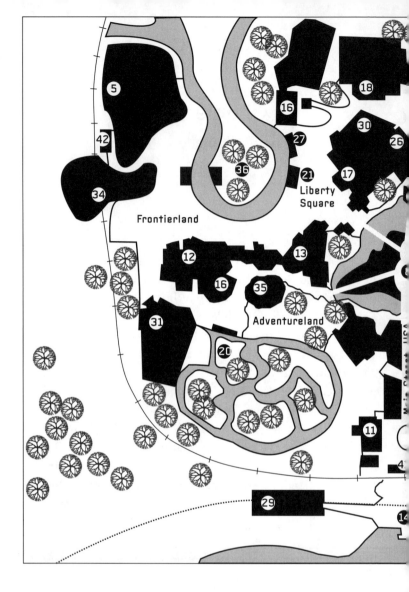

1. Alien Encounter
2. Ariel's Grotto
3. AstroOrbiter
4. Barnstormer
5. Big Thunder Mountain Railroad
6. Buzz Lightyear's
   Space Ranger Spin
7. Carousel of Progress
8. Central Hub
9. Cinderella Castle
10. Cinderella's Golden Carrousel
11. City Hall

12. Country Bear Jamboree
13. The Diamond Horseshoe
    Saloon Revue
14. Donald's Boat
15. Dumbo the Flying Elephant
16. Enchanted Tiki Room,
    Under New Management
17. The Hall of Presidents
18. The Haunted Mansion
19. it's a small world
20. Jungle Cruise
21. Liberty Belle Riverboat

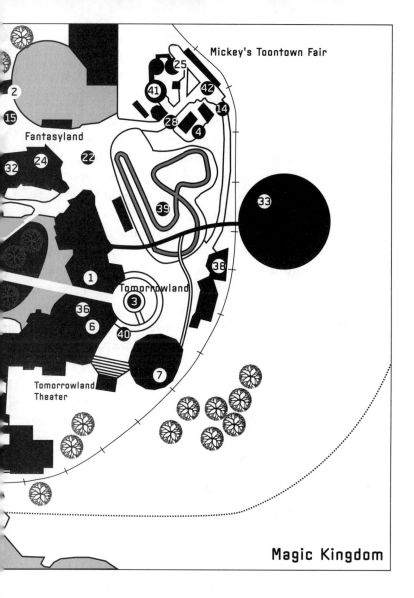

Magic Kingdom

22. Mad Tea Party
23. The Magic Carpets of Aladdin
24. The Many Adventures of
    Winnie the Pooh
25. Mickey's House
26. Mickey's PhilharMagic
27. Mike Fink Keelboats
28. Minnie's House
29. Monorail Station
30. Peter Pan's Flight
31. Pirates of the Caribbean
32. Snow White's Scary
    Adventures
33. Space Mountain
34. Splash Mountain
35. Swiss Family Treehouse
36. The Timekeeper
37. Tom Sawyer Island
38. Tomorrowland Arcade
39. Tomorrowland Speedway
40. Tomorrowland Transit
    Authority
41. Toontown Hall of Fame
42. WDW Railroad Station

down Main Street, the hub of the Magic Kingdom where all the lands converge. Fire engines and trolleys shuttle lazy guests from one end of the street to the other. The two-story buildings are much bigger than those in the West Coast counterpart, and that means lots more shopping and eating. A close inspection of the windows on the second floors reveals names of Main Street's proprietors. Not so coincidentally they're the people involved with the creation of the park like Walt's brother Roy O. Disney. (Walt's window is one of the few that faces the castle.) Main Street stores are designed with an artificial perspective to make the buildings seem bigger and the street longer. The upper stories are smaller so that the buildings look taller. Ground floors are 90% life-size, second floors 80%, third, where they exist, are 60%. The Emporium, the Main Street Gallery, and Disney Clothiers (which make up the "Magic Kingdom Mall") are open late so you can save the bulk of your buying until you exit the park. In addition to the full-service restaurants, there's Casey's Corner, where you can pick up hot dogs and fries. Also found on this stretch of old-time Americana are candy, cookies, ice cream, and…oh, stop us. Please.

Walt Disney World Railroad
Overall Rating: ✪✪✪
Attraction Debut: 1971

OK, so you just got into the park and you're rarin' to go. Then your companion, if he or she is anything like Eddie, makes you ride every ride, buy every tchotchke, and eat every churro. And oh yeah, you're staying another five hours until park closing. Jeffrey suggests you sit. Take five (or 15 or however long it takes to make a full loop) on this relaxing ride around the park. Sure, you can hop off in Frontierland or at the Toontown Fair, or you can just keep going around and around and around…

Fairy Fact: The steam-powered trains are the real McCoy and were found in the Yucatan.

🍴 The Crystal Palace

Price: Moderate
Meals: B, L, D, CD

We love a buffet, and the food here is decent. (Although we're partial to the buffets at Disney's Animal Kingdom Lodge and Disney's Contemporary Resort.) Characters make it a treat for the kids. Priority seating is available.

🍴 Tony's Town Square Restaurant

Price: Moderate
Meals: B, L, D

Mama mia! One of the better restaurants in the Magic Kingdom, this Italian eatery, inspired by the joint in *Lady and the Tramp,* serves up pastas and pizzas and lots of high-carb eats. In keeping with the theme, Eddie likes to push a meatball toward Jeffrey with his nose. It's enough to make you a vegetarian. Priority seating is available.

Adventureland

Adventureland at Walt Disney World Resort is just slightly more tame than the Disneyland Resort version. This jungle trek feels colonized. The natives aren't particularly restless; in fact, they're expatriates from the Orlando rest home. There's still some African influence here, but it's all rather mellow. Of course, when looking for adventure, there's always the opportunity to create your own…

Swiss Family Treehouse

Overall Rating: ✪
Attraction Debut: 1971

For more than three decades guests have been visiting this attraction, and that damn Swiss family is never home! How rude. They might at least leave out a cheese plate. While it offers a nice view (and good cardio as you climb), looking at how people live in trees is not the most fun way we can think of to kill time.

☀ **Fairy Fact:** The tree (which boasts real Spanish moss intertwined in its 330,000 fake leaves) is unofficially christened Disneyodendron eximus: out of the ordinary Disney tree. There are four such trees in the world: the Swiss family trees here and at Disneyland Paris Park, Tarzan's Treehouse at Disneyland Park, and The Tree of Life at Disney's Animal Kingdom.

The Enchanted Tiki Room, Under New Management

Overall Rating: ✪✪✪

Attraction Debut: 1971 (as the Tropical Serenade, revamped in 1998)

OK, yes, it's still Audio-Animatronics singing birds in a Hawaiian luau, but after 30 years of squawking, the Tikis have been revised and rejuvenated. The new version features *Aladdin*'s Iago and *The Lion King*'s effete Zazu as the attraction's new owners. More important, the music has been updated and replaced. Although we know you'll all be disappointed to learn that there's no more sing-along to "Let's All Sing Like the Birdies Sing." Instead it's "Hot! Hot! Hot!" (Which reminds us, when *is* Buster Poindexter getting his A&E *Biography*?)

☀ **Fairy Fact:** The preshow birds, power agents William and Morris, are voiced by Don Rickles and the late Phil Hartman.

Jungle Cruise

Overall Rating: ✪✪✪✪

Attraction Debut: 1971

⚡

Walt Disney World Resort offers better cruising than Disneyland Resort on this ride (for one thing, it's longer here—and size matters, no matter what your last date said), but refer to the description on page 70 for the basics.

☀ **Fairy Fact:** While the cruise's animals were crafted at

44

Disney, the sounds they make are authentic. They were recorded in Africa and South America. And speaking of sound, while you're in line for the ride, listen for Cole Porter's "You're the Top" in the background (no, not because it's a Merman song but because it includes the lyric "You're Mickey Mouse").

The Magic Carpets of Aladdin
Overall Rating: ✪
Attraction Debut: 2001

Years ago we managed to get a great picture during Gay Days of us and a few other queers with a very startled-looking Aladdin. This ride is not as fun as taking that picture was. It's an Arabian Dumbo without the elephant. The major difference between Dumbo and the carpets is that you can change the pitch (forward and backward tilt) of the car using a control in the second row—giving a whole new meaning to "backseat driver." For those of you unfamiliar with the Dumbo attraction, turn to 88 for a description.

Fairy Fact: After watching the movie, we decided that you don't have to worry about your hat falling off on this ride. After all, Aladdin zips around on his carpet and his fez never so much as catches a breeze.

Pirates of the Caribbean
Overall Rating: ✪✪✪✪✪
Attraction Debut: 1973

Still a must-see attraction, even though it's briefer than its Disneyland Resort counterpart. And we always welcome swarthy sailors. Go on the left line. It's 250 feet shorter than the right. Since the ride is essentially the same in both parks, set sail to page 74 for a description.

Fairy Fact: Looking for a hidden Mickey? In the last room, look at the base of the lanterns. They make that infamous tri-circular shape.

Frontierland

Mmm...cowboys. Oops. Sorry, we're back. In Frontierland, Disney re-creates the picturesque Wild West (minus the dust and tumbleweeds) along the Rivers of America. While the feel is authentic, we do not advise you breaking out those chaps you like to wear with nothing else. If you're feeling violent, you can shoot 'em up at the shooting gallery.

Country Bear Jamboree
Overall Rating: ✪✪✪
Attraction Debut: 1971

Ah, the country bears. Now before all you furry types in flannel get excited, these are Audio-Animatronics singing bears in a cute if slightly dull hoedown. Jeffrey admits he has a crush on a deer named Max, one of three talking heads mounted on a wall (the other two are a buffalo and a moose) who provide commentary throughout. There's a special edition at Christmas, but no matter which you see, it's still singing bears.

Fairy Fact: Along with The Hall of Presidents, the Jamboree was the first attraction to be exclusive to Walt Disney World Resort. That changed with the opening of the Disneyland version in 1972 (which closed in 2001).

Splash Mountain
Overall Rating: ✪✪✪✪✪
Attraction Debut: 1992
⚡

While this ride is excellent in both parks, Walt Disney World Resort has the advantage with a more sophisticated ride and better Audio-Animatronics. See page 78 for the details.

Fairy Fact: You go as fast as 40 mph on your fall down into the briar patch. That's faster than Space Mountain.

Big Thunder Mountain Railroad
Overall Rating: ✪✪✪✪
Attraction Debut: 1980

Identically rocking in both parks. See page 79 for the lowdown.

Fairy Fact: While Thunder Mountain first appeared in Disneyland Resort, it was originally conceived as an attraction for Walt Disney World Resort where Pirates of the Caribbean now stands.

Raft to Tom Sawyer Island
Overall Rating: ✪✪✪
Attraction Debut: 1973

Remember summer camp—complete with rafts and obstacle courses and trees to climb and caves to explore? Well, this is nothing like that. But that doesn't mean it's not fun. So hop on a log raft and head over. First off, the trees provide great shade from the Florida sunshine. There are even rocking chairs on a quiet side of the island which old-timers like us take advantage of. There's Aunt Polly's Dockside Inn, which has sandwiches (which we don't recommend) and pie and ice cream (which we do). The two islands offer rope bridges, a mill, and numerous paths to explore. And when we meet that certain someone, we love those long, dark caves.

Fairy Fact: Contrary to popular belief, the rafts that bring you over are not on tracks.

Liberty Square

Liberty Square evokes colonial America during the Revolutionary War. Flags abound as fife and drum music is piped in from all sides. While most people don't think of this period as particularly gay, consider that all of the men wore wigs and showed off their calves. Then there's the stockade. Just a thought.

The Hall of Presidents
Overall Rating: ✪✪
Attraction Debut: 1971

Although it's perhaps the most maligned of Disney attractions, we heartily recommend The Hall of Presidents. No, not for the footage depicting great moments in American history, and no, not for the Audio-Animatronics finale in which all of our nation's presidents share a stage without a single bitchy remark between them. No, we like this show because it's dark, air-conditioned, 23 minutes long, and always half empty. In short, this, ladies and gentlemen, is the closest thing Disney has to a tunnel of love (if, that is, you can get past the extreme nausea induced by the proximity of a lifelike Ronald Reagan or George W., who recorded a brand-new speech just for the attraction. Lucky us). But if you do have the attention span to listen to the show, Abe Lincoln's words about equality and human rights will strike a particularly loud and inspiring chord with gay and lesbian visitors.

☀ **Fairy Fact:** All of the presidents' costumes are hand-made using the appropriate sewing methods of the time. George Washington's is authentic down to the watch. And that's real hair on those presidents. Yep, real human hair. Kinda icky, huh?

The Haunted Mansion
Overall Rating: ✪✪✪✪✪
Attraction Debut: 1971
⚡

While the exterior in Walt Disney World Resort is more of a traditional haunted manse than the one at Disneyland Resort,

the spooky innards are essentially the same (though this ride is a little bit longer). See page 75 for a ghoulish description.

Fairy Fact: If you look closely, you'll see the top of the home is adorned with chess pieces. And while there are pawns and queens, there are no knights. Why? Because it's always "knight" *inside* the house. (No, we're not kidding.)

Liberty Belle Riverboat
Overall Rating: ✪✪
Attraction Debut: 1975

Liberty Belle is the sweet sister of the *Mark Twain* at Disneyland Park. Climb aboard page 81 for the details.

Fairy Fact: The boat was originally called the *Richard F. Irvine Steamboat,* after one of Disney's designers. Bet he was steamed when they changed the name.

⑪ The Liberty Tree Restaurant
Price: Moderate

A decent eatery featuring American fare (prime rib, roast turkey, etc). Though the food is good and the atmosphere fun (if Betsy Ross lights your fire) the restaurant, in keeping with colonial style, is low-ceilinged and a bit dark. Service is, however, excellent.

Fantasyland

Fantasyland is perhaps the gayest land of them all because it's based on complete fiction and incorporates fairies and queens. The pageantry theme at the attraction entrances, incorporating flags and banners in the style of an Arthurian fair, in Orlando pales in comparison to "new Fantasyland" in Anaheim, where the rides feel like an extension of the castle. But they're lovely nonetheless. Yes, you can shop (not only does Tinker Bell's Treasures have cute items, but the special effects that send the fairy around the shop are charming). But it's more fun to just revel in all the fantastical things around you. From Ariel's Grotto where the Little Mermaid herself greets guests to the well-manicured walkways, it's nice to be in a place where fairy dust is in the air.

Cinderella Castle
Overall Rating: ✪✪✪
Attraction Debut: 1971

Cinderella's spectacular castle towers 189 feet over the Magic Kingdom. The five mosaic panels in the foyer are each 15 feet tall and took more than a million chips and two years to complete. Inside, contrary to popular belief, the late Walt is not frozen. Instead, there's a restaurant. Out back, there's a fountain that features a lovely statue by legendary Disney sculptor Blane Gibson. At first glance, the statue seems to depict Cinderella during her housecleaning days, but from the right perspective (that is, a child's point of view) she becomes a princess against a majestic background. Drink from the fountain and you, too, will find yourself bowing to the princess (just stay off your knees).

Fairy Fact: Are you curious as to how many stones there are in the castle? None. It's all a fiberglass shell.

Cinderella's Golden Carrousel
Overall Rating: ✪
Attraction Debut: 1971

No, it's not a thrill ride. And yes, you will probably be surrounded by dozens of children. But if you feel like taking a whirl on a merry-go-round, it's great for a whiff of nostalgia.

Fairy Fact: The carrousel is actually the oldest attraction in the park. The horses were built in 1917 for the Detroit Palace Garden Park. They were later moved to Maplewood Olympic Park in New Jersey, where the Disney design team found them. Who says the Garden State has nothing to offer but toxic waste?

Mickey's PhilharMagic

Overall Rating: N/A
Attraction Debut: 2003

Hoping to take the fun of Honey, I Shrunk the Audience and It's Tough to Be a Bug! to the next level, Disney Feature Animation and Walt Disney Imagineering are teaming up to create a wild 3-D film integrating many of Disney's best-loved characters from Mickey Mouse to Ariel. The action takes place in the PhilharMagic Concert Hall. Our pal Lindsay is already insisting Ariel's clamshell top in three dimensions will beat Aladdin's pecs hands down on the 150-foot-wide screen. We're just hoping Tarzan swings into our laps.

Fairy Fact: While this will be the first time any Disney character has appeared in a 3-D film in the park (with the exception of a faux Mickey in MuppetVision 3-D), it is not the first time the Disney troop has entered the genre. Most well known is the 1953 short *Working for Peanuts*, which featured Donald Duck with Chip and Dale.

Snow White's Scary Adventures

Overall Rating: ✪✪✪
Attraction Debut: 1971

The Magic Kingdom version beats Disneyland Park's hands down. It's longer, more detailed, and it explains the story better without ending prematurely—and everyone hates a premature conclusion. But page 86 offers what you need to know.

Fairy Fact: The music on the ride was actually created from rare archival tapes which were originally used to score the film.

it's a small world

Overall Rating: ✪✪✪
Attraction Debut: 1971

While you miss the elaborate exteriors of Disneyland Park, this is essentially the same annoying, we mean, um, heartwarming ride as joyfully described on page 91. And this one's shorter!

52

Fairy Fact: That theme song that makes this ride so unforgettable is by the Sherman brothers (Richard and Robert), composers of songs for for such Disney classics as *The Jungle Book, Mary Poppins, Winnie the Pooh,* and the park's second most annoying song, The Tiki Room theme.

Peter Pan's Flight
Overall Rating: ✪✪✪✪✪
Attraction Debut: 1971

Here at Walt Disney World Resort, the flight is somewhat longer and a tad more elaborate (plus you can FASTPASS it), but soar on over to page 87 for the description.

Fairy Fact: While we always love, love, love flying over London, we have to note that there is an awful lot of vehicular traffic down there, considering that the story takes place before cars. But we're willing to forgive that lapse of accuracy since the London scene is actually built on an enlarged city map.

Dumbo the Flying Elephant
Overall Rating: ✪✪
Attraction Debut: 1971

The Dumbo attractions in both parks are nearly indistinguishable (although Disneyland Park's incorporates festive fountains), so turn to page 88 for a ride evaluation.

Fairy Fact: They're not kidding when they say hold on to your hats and glasses, people. An average of 100 pairs of sunglasses are sent over to the Lost and Found at the Magic Kingdom every day. More than 1.5 million have turned up since 1971. Don't let this be you.

Mad Tea Party
Overall Rating: ✪✪
Attraction Debut: 1971

Spinning dishes, anyone? Flip to page 91 for the facts.

The Many Adventures of Winnie the Pooh
Overall Rating: ✪✪✪
Attraction Debut: 2000

⚡

It's hard to get past the resentment we feel toward this attraction, as its installation meant the demise of Mr. Toad's Wild Ride. But we're working through it. And we do have to admit that Pooh has its charms. As the most recent of the Disney dark rides, it's the most technologically advanced with some very clever effects. There's also significant time spent on Tigger, and since we can't help identifying with a creature who spends the majority of his time bouncing on his tail and saying "ta-ta for now," we begrudgingly approve. For those of you with a more sedated, lithium mentality, there's always Jeffrey's favorite, Eeyore. And like many of you, he's constantly losing his tail. Bear in mind (and excuse the pun) that it's really popular. Go early or FASTPASS.

⓫ Cinderella's Royal Table
Price: Expensive
Meals: B, L, D

Feeling like a couple of princesses (and when don't we?), we made our way up inside Cinderella Castle for some great food. Seafood, steaks, salads, sandwiches—there's something for everyone here in this palatial setting. Stained glass windows afford you a splendid view of Fantasyland, and the vaulted ceilings are high enough to make Dumbo feel at

home. Be wary of the throne in the foyer, however. We spent an hour and a half fighting over it. And if you're lucky, Cinderella herself may pay you a visit. Make priority seating reservations if you can.

Mickey's Toontown Fair

Or, if you'd rather, the place you're most likely to get a Kodak moment with a Disney character. Created in 1988 in celebration of Mickey's 60th birthday, the Toontown Fair has stayed on as an area geared toward the smallest of the small (and no, we don't mean Tom Cruise). The land is made up primarily of interactive walk-through areas for small fry. Inexplicably, the whole thing has been given a country fair theme, so if you see Goofy, expect him in overalls.

The Toontown Hall of Fame
Overall Rating: ✪
Attraction Debut: 1996
Taking chance out of the equation, the Hall of Fame is where you can line up for character meet-and-greets. While Donald, Goofy, and company are most popular, oddly, we always seem to gravitate toward the villains line. Huh.

Mickey's Country House
Overall Rating: ✪✪
Attraction Debut: 1996
While you can get a peek at his regular home at Disneyland Park's Toontown, here you get a glimpse of where the mouse spends his weekends and vacations—call it Fire Island for the toon set. The walk through attraction is, for many, a requirement for getting to the "Judge's Tent" in the back where you can meet Mickey in person, but the detail work inside, including "mouse ears" instead of rabbit ears on his television and an awfully

redundant wardrobe (although we love his Fantasia slippers), is impressive. Out back you'll notice that even the vegetation iconifies the mouse with pumpkins, tomatoes, and a topiary all in the shape of you-know-who. All of which makes one wonder, does this mouse have a whale-size ego or what?

Fairy Fact: We hate to destroy illusions. No really, we do. But we think that our dear readers deserve to know that, due to size requirements, almost every person under a Mickey costume is, in fact, female. So ladies, remember that the next time you see Mickey and Minnie holding hands or kissing, you know a secret.

Minnie's Country House
Overall Rating: ✪✪
Attraction Debut: 1996

Martha Stewart, watch out. Minnie is vying for your title of homemaker of the year, what with her impressive cookie jar collection and all. We couldn't tell whether the quilting room was supposed to be camp or if somehow sexist Imagineers were suggesting the little lady be put in her place. Haven't these people heard of Gloria Steinem?

Fairy Fact: While her man-mouse isn't around, he's left his effigy (hidden Mickeys) in two places: in the craft room, check out the border of the portrait of Clarabelle Cow; in the kitchen, three pots are in a certain arrangement.

Donald's Boat
Overall Rating: ✪
Attraction Debut: 1996

This faux boat is pretty much just for kids, but it does have some clever water gimmicks that could cool you down on a hot day.

Fairy Fact: Donald has thoughtfully named the boat after his true love, Miss Daisy (won't Goofy be distraught).

The Barnstormer at Goofy's Wiseacre Farm

Overall Rating: ✪

Attraction Debut: 1996

Remarkably similar to Gadget's Go Coaster in Disneyland Park, this kiddie coaster sends you crashing into Goofy's barn. It sounds much more exciting than it is. The coaster cars are supposed to resemble a 1920s crop-dusting biplane. A biplane, huh? We always suspected there was something AC/DC about the Goofster.

Fairy Fact: Of the 52 seconds this ride lasts, about 30 are spent climbing up the first hill. You do the math.

Tomorrowland

Designed to be Epcot before there was an Epcot, Tomorrowland was meant to be a peek into the future. But like the version at Disneyland Park, once Tomorrowland started to look like Yesterdayland, it got a major overhaul. Now it's kind of a *Jetsons* meets *Buck Rogers* and *Logan's Run* environment. Why, by the way, does everyone's notion of the future involve outer space? Because to us, the future's great promise is a world without polyester.

The ExtraTERRORestrial Alien Encounter

Overall Rating: ✪✪✪✪

Attraction Debut: 1995

If you're looking for a great hand-holding attraction, this is it. But those with easily-frightened partners may have their manual circulation cut off. Replacing the ancient Mission to Mars, this sensory overload attraction sets you in a future where X-S Tech (X-S, excess—get it?) has discovered a way to beam people from planet to planet. First you see a demonstration involving one of Jeffrey's favorite characters, a cute and furry alien named Skippy. Skippy's fate is so awful, however, that Jeffrey is typically removed sobbing from the building. But the real thrills begin when you get strapped in and…well, we don't want to ruin it for you. But safe to say, you won't be saying, "Beam me up, Scotty," anytime soon. The ride is chock full of celebrities who lend their voices (and sometimes make-up-laden selves) to this attraction. Supermodel Tyra Banks introduces you to the world of X-S, while our favorite sweet transvestite Tim Curry (as the voice of a robot named—get this—S.I.R.) experiments on poor Skippy. Gay fave Kathy Najimy and Kevin Pollak play stressed out aliens, and Jeffrey Jones (from *Beetlejuice* and *Ferris Bueller's Day Off*) is their nasty boss.

Fairy Fact: When Michael Eisner first saw this $60 million attraction, he had it closed for more work. Reason: not scary enough.

Buzz Lightyear's Space Ranger Spin
Overall Rating: ✪✪✪✪
Attraction Debut: 1998

⚡

Looking to get out a little aggression? Grab a gun. Well, grab a toy gun on this shooting-gallery-in-motion ride based on the *Toy Story* movies. You're helping Buzz defeat the evil Emperor Zurg by shooting all the targets in your path. As in an arcade game, you rack up points against the person next to you. Of course there's a twist—a literal one as each ride vehicle is equipped with a joystick used to spin the car around for better aim (or to make yourself ill). Eddie doesn't like the ride, but that's just because Jeffrey kicks his ass every time. After you pass the orange robot in the first room, twirl your car around and shoot at the target on its hand. You'll get an additional 10,000 points. (But don't tell Eddie.)

Fairy Fact: Curious as to what the evil Emperor Zurg is after? Why, he wants the universe's crystollic fusion cell supply! Better known as all the batteries from toys.

Tomorrowland Transit Authority

Overall Rating: ✪✪✪

Attraction Debut: 1975 (originally called the WEDway People Mover)

To quote the Talking Heads, "We're on a road to nowhere" on this winding tour on an elevated platform through the attractions of Tomorrowland. But the ride is smooth, the views are great (particularly of the castle), and there are numerous dark caverns. Need we say more? If you're hunting for hidden Mickeys, when you get to the set with a woman in a beauty shop, look at the three circles on her belt buckle.

Fairy Fact: The ride is actually run by magnets that propel the cars. Don't ask us how they do this. They just do.

Astro Orbiter

Overall Rating: ✪✪

Attraction Debut: 1974 (originally called the Star Jets)

This Dumboesque ride is similar to its twin in Disneyland Park, so blast off to page 97 for the details.

Fairy Fact: At Disneyland Resort this attraction is called the Astro Orbitor, not Orbiter. Why did they do this? To confuse us, of course.

Space Mountain

Overall Rating: ✪✪✪✪✪

Attraction Debut: 1975

Though thematically the same as at Disneyland Park, this Space Mountain has its own characteristics. While it lacks the element of a musical score, this coaster is little wilder. It also seats passengers front to back as opposed to side by side, giving the sensation of being alone in space, familiar to anyone who's spent time in a gay dance club.

Fairy Fact: While it may seem wild, at its fastest this coaster's only doing 28 mph.

Walt Disney's Carousel of Progress
Overall Rating: ✪✪✪
Attraction Debut: 1972

OK, OK, we know it's tired and old. We won't make any-one ride it. But what can we say? We still like it. The kid in us still finds novelty in a theater that rotates. And yeah, the con-tent, which follows a never-aging family through a century of technology, is lame and sexist. (Uh-oh! Dad's cooking dinner in the newfangled microwave! Gosh, he burned it.) But it's kinda quaint.

Fairy Fact: Cousin Orville (sitting in the tub) is voiced by legendary Warner Bros. voice-over artist, Mel Blanc, responsi-ble for the voices of Bugs Bunny and almost all of the male Looney Tunes characters. This was his only Disney gig.

The Indy Speedway
Overall Rating: ✪✪
Attraction Debut: 1971 (as Grand Prix Raceway)

There was a time when we were excited by the speedway. Then we got our driver's licenses. Oddly, the thought of driv-ing on a track in a gas-powered car at seven miles per hour somehow lost its magic. And with no backseat to mess around in, we have to say this one is not worth the lengthy wait. Or any wait. On the upside, no designated driver required.

Fairy Fact: This ride represents one of the park's great logic gaffes. The Speedway is a snoozefest for all but the very small who are enamored of the sleek little cars. And yet there is a height requirement for drivers of 4 feet 4 inches, making the ride inac-cessible to those who would enjoy it most. Sure, that makes sense.

The Timekeeper
Overall Rating: ✪✪✪✪
Attraction Debut: 1995

It's sad that Disney opens and closes this film more than Shelley Winters does her refrigerator door. But crowds haven't

been flocking since it opened as part of the new Tomorrowland in 1995. Frankly, we don't get it. Because we think this is a fabulous attraction, by far the best of the Circle-Vision films. The Timekeeper is a robot (Robin Williams at his most mincing), who, with the help of 9-eye, his butch assistant (voiced by Rhea Perlman), takes us on a fabulous journey through time. After visits with the likes of Da Vinci and Mozart, we hook up with Jules Verne and H.G. Wells (Disney stalwart Jeremy Irons) for a whirlwind tour. The footage is sumptuous, and the comedy fun. If it's open, make it a priority.

Fairy Fact: This attraction is notable for its firsts. It was the first (and so far only) attraction to open at Disneyland Paris Park before transferring to the states. And it marks the first time that a Circle-Vision film featured staged footage and actors (not counting the noninteracting narrator in Epcot's *Wonders of China*) as opposed to the usual majestic sweeps of scenery. It's also the first one Jeffrey stayed awake through.

Chapter Eleven
Epcot

"Nobody speaks of pavilions anymore," Sandra Bernhard lamented once. "And that truly saddens me." Well, Sandra, have we got a park for you. Epcot, a pavilion paradise, which opened in 1982, was actually on Walt's plate for many years preceding his death. His fascination with the future, evident in Tomorrowland, led him to dream even bigger. E.P.C.O.T.—the Experimental Prototype Community Of Tomorrow—was to have been an ever-changing World's Fair environment, where the future's innovations came to life. "E.P.C.O.T. is the heart of everything we're doing," said Walt in the '60s. "It will never be completed but will always be introducing and testing and demonstrating new materials and systems."

Unfortunately, technology moved faster than the Imagineers ever could, and they realized that being on the edge of tomorrow would be a lot harder than first envisioned. Now, instead of E.P.C.O.T., it's just the much more user-friendly Epcot. The park is divided into two sections, Future World and World Showcase. Each is made up of a series of pavilions. While Future World (featuring pavilions such as The Land and The Wonders of Life) features the aforementioned possibilities of tomorrow, World Showcase (boasting pavilions representing 11 different countries) shows us where our ancestors came from and where we'd go if we had the dough.

How to get there: If you're staying at Disney's Beach Club Resort, Disney's Yacht Club Resort, or the Disney's BoardWalk Resort, it's an easy walk to Epcot's International Gateway—a back door, if you will, to the parks, which conveniently places you

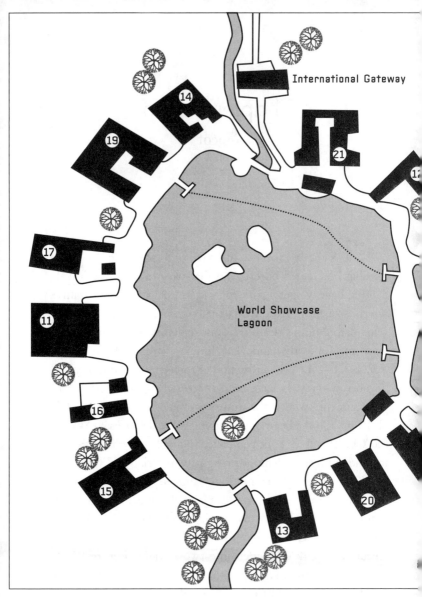

International Gateway

World Showcase Lagoon

World Showcase Pavilions

11. American Adventure
12. Canada
13. China
14. France
15. Germany
16. Italy
17. Japan
18. Mexico
19. Morocco
20. Norway
21. United Kingdom

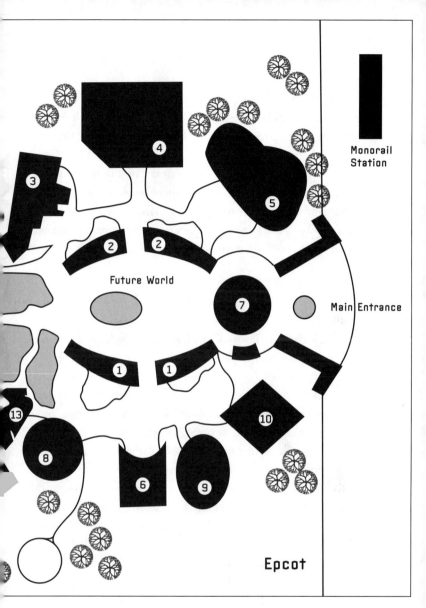

Future World Pavilions

1. Innoventions East
2. Innoventions West
3. Journey Into Imagination
4. The Land
5. The Living Seas
6. Mission: Space
7. Spaceship Earth
8. Test Track
9. Wonders of Life
10. Universe of Energy

between the France and United Kingdom pavilions. There's also a boat that travels between Disney-MGM Studios, Walt Disney World Dolphin and Swan Resorts, Disney's Beach Club, Disney's Yacht Club, Disney's BoardWalk, and the International Gate. Guests can also take the very popular monorail from the Transportation and Ticket Center (where buses are also available to Epcot and all resort areas) or take a bus from any Disney resort. If you've rented a car and are staying at a Disney resort, you can also park at Epcot for free (nonresort guests pay a fee).

Future World

Smack-dab in the middle of Future World is Spaceship Earth, a 180-foot-tall geosphere that also serves as the centerpiece of Epcot. It inspires the kind of awe we reserve for things scary and unknown, like the future—or Eddie's latest boyfriend. While over the years Future World has come to seem a little more like "present world," Spaceship Earth keeps the park looking like it's on the brink of tomorrow. Still, the new, shimmering "Epcot" sign on top of the sphere (complete with Mickey's gloved hand holding a magic wand) looks a little, well, cheap and dorky—as if people wouldn't know what park it was. That said, the place ain't all that gay; in other words, it doesn't have the obvious homo appeal of the other parks. (Fantasy! Hollywood! Animals! OK, scratch that last one.) But if you peek below the surface, there's a lot of fun (yes, some of it gay-friendly) to be had.

Future World generally opens earlier than World Showcase, so plan to hit that section first. Our listings, like the park itself, are broken down by pavilion.

Spaceship Earth

The bulk of this pavilion is the ride through the 16-million-pound geosphere, which lets you off in the adjacent Global Neighborhood.

Spaceship Earth

Overall Rating: ✪✪✪✪

Attraction Debut: 1982

This 14-minute excursion through a gigantic globe, sponsored by AT&T, takes you through the history of communication, from the drawings of the cavemen to the wide-screen televisions and World Wide Web of today to the possibilities (and probabilities) of tomorrow. And yes, the ride, narrated by Jeremy Irons, is actually inside that big golf ball. Not only does

Spaceship Earth stands at the entrance to Epcot

© Disney Enterprises, Inc.

your tour include some impressively detailed Audio-Animatronics, but Disney employs olfactory enhancers so you actually get a whiff of Rome burning. Marshmallows, anyone? If none of this sounds particularly gay, remember just how important the Internet has been in connecting gay folk to one another (in more than one way). The wait time is usually minimal, as this is one of the park's continuously loading rides.

Fairy Fact: That aforementioned golf ball is a whopping 165 feet in diameter and weighs 8,000 tons. Its outer shell is made of 11,324 aluminum and plastic-alloy triangles. And if the sphere were a real golf ball, the golfer would have to be 1.2 miles tall—or the size of the average women's basketball player.

Global Neighborhood
Overall Rating: ✪
Attraction Debut: 1982

As you disembark from your vehicle, you enter AT&T's Global Neighborhood, which has some amusing kiosks to play with—including a booth where you can call someone and incorporate sound effects so they think you're in the jungle or a haunted house. If they're stupid.

Innoventions

Enclosed in buildings to either side and just beyond Spaceship Earth, Innoventions West and Innoventions East are probably the most true to the idea of a modern-day World's Fair. Why? Because at the same time they try to teach you something, they try to sell you something. Not that this is always a bad thing.

Innoventions East and Innoventions West
Overall Rating: ✪
Attraction Debut: 1982

For those of you tired of keeping your hands and arms inside the boat at all times, Innoventions is a place where you

can get your hands on something. (Get your mind out of the gutter!) Interactive displays on topics ranging from home entertainment to health and the environment are presented at different stations. Both pavilions, hosted by Tom Morrow (get it?), feature multiple sponsors who've paid a lot of money for this particular commercial. Kids may find the numerous computerized kiosks entertaining, but we think it's a yawn. Plus it's not gay at all. But it is air-conditioned.

Dining

The **Electric Umbrella** on the east side serves basic American fare, breakfast, lunch, and dinner. All of it inexpensive by Disney standards, none of it particularly great. There are so many different cuisines to try in Epcot, we suggest you move along. **The Fountain View Espresso and Bakery** on the west side is our choice for giving the big kiss-off to Dr. Atkins.

Shopping

East side features **Mouse Gear**, an enormous gift store with all sorts of Disney items. West side has the more sophisticated Art of Disney with cels, sculptures, and collectibles. In addition, there's **Ice Station Cool,** a short walk-through and cool-off area by Coca-Cola featuring samples from around the world of some frosty beverages in startling and unusual flavors and colors.

Universe of Energy

There's no gayer pavilion than the Universe of Energy. First of all, the ride is called Ellen's [DeGeneres] Energy Adventure. Second, the building itself features colored panels on the side that create a gigantic rainbow—making it look like a gay pride float on steroids. In keeping with Future World's theme, the top of the building is covered with two acres of photovoltaic cells (solar panels to you and me) that help power the ride within.

Ellen's Energy Adventure

Overall Rating: ✪✪✪✪

Attraction Debut: 1996

Ellen's Energy Adventure is the chewy gay center of the Universe of Energy. Why? Because it's hosted by out and proud actor-comic Ellen DeGeneres (oh, yeah, and Bill Nye the Science Guy too). Exxon Mobil opened the ride back when Ms. DeGeneres had her own show on ABC (and long before she came out of the closet). Guests first see a short movie in which Ellen, at her finest, explains how she never cared about energy—that is, until she had a horrible dream that she was on the game show *Jeopardy!* facing off against her college roommate Judy (Jamie Lee Curtis), and all the questions were about energy. Yipes! Lucky for Ellen, her neighbor, Bill Nye, appears and agrees to give her a crash course in energy. Once you're seated in the immense ride vehicles, the movie continues with the big bang—no, not the Falcon video kind: creation. Suddenly, with a lurch, the cars begin to move and you enter the age of the dinosaurs (where many of the fossil fuels we use today were first created—see, we paid attention!). The amazingly lifelike dinos are all impressive, but most hysterical is watching an Audi-Animatronics Ellen fight off a large snake-like beastie. You go, girl! Once you're through with the big lizards, the movie continues, and while it's educational, Ellen manages to keep the whole thing entertaining as well. In the end she goes back to *Jeopardy!* and…well, we're not going to ruin it for you. But hey, it was *her* dream.

 **Fairy Fact:** Not only does this ride feature Ellen, Bill, Jamie, and Alex Trebek, but if you pay attention, you'll see Michael Richards discover fire, watch *Saturday Night Live* alum Ellen Cleghorne work as a production assistant, and hear Willard Scott's voice reporting the impending Ice Age.

Wonders of Life

Despite our feverish attempts, neither of us could isolate the gay gene encoded on the immense sculpted strand of DNA outside this pavilion (at 5.5 million times its actual size). Inside Wonders of Life, however, there is an abundance to be learned about health, fitness, and the body. Aside from its three main attractions listed below, the building also features some exhibits on medicine, sports, and anatomy (woo hoo!).

Body Wars

Overall Rating: ✪✪✪✪
Attraction Debut: 1989

Somewhere between making *Adventures in Babysitting* and getting nominated for an Academy Award for her performance in *Leaving Las Vegas,* Elisabeth Shue found time to costar (along with the dreamy Tim Matheson and a bevy of internal organs) in this thrilling flight-simulator ride. The time is the future, and scientists have found a way to reduce people to microscopic size (see: Honey, I Shrunk the Audience over at the Imagination pavilion), enabling them to enter the human body to do some hands-on medical work. Guests are members of a civilian crew being shrunk down and injected into a human; the object is to pick up Dr. Cynthia Lair (Shue), who has been investigating a splinter. (Yes, you read that right.) Of course, trouble arises when Dr. Lair is swept into the bloodstream and your captain (Matheson) has to go fetch her. Off you dart through the heart, lungs, and brain. Will you make it out alive? Of course you will. But you'll never look at a splinter the same way again.

Fairy Fact: The film was directed by Leonard Nimoy.

Cranium Command

Overall Rating: ✪✪✪
Attraction Debut: 1989

We must confess, we skipped this attraction on any number of visits to the park. We had no idea what we were missing. An adorable animated preshow film sets the stage; our brains are all run by little pilots who sit in our heads and tell all the body parts what to do. Little Buzzy is a newbie who's terrified he's going to screw up his human. His harsh commander warns him he'd better not or he'll be put inside the brain of a chicken (and really, that's more of an auto-pilot kind of job). The main show begins, and it's more star-studded than the Academy Awards (well, maybe not *that* glamorous). An Audio-Animatronics Buzzy, who's been placed inside the body of an adolescent boy (there are so many comments we could make, but we'll demur) calls up all of the systems of the body on screen. And who should appear but Charles Grodin, George Wendt, Dana Carvey, Kevin Nealon, Jon Lovitz, Bobcat Goldthwait, and more—all representing innards from the left brain to the stomach. Naturally, things go wrong. (Hey, it *is* a teenage boy—they're hard to control. Oops, we let that slip.) Don't be like us. See this your first time out.

Fairy Fact: The little girl our hero gets all hormonal over is Natalie Gregory, who voiced Jenny, the simpering heroine in Disney's *Oliver & Company*. Before puberty destroyed her career, she also played Alice in the all-star *Alice in Wonderland* miniseries that featured a Carol Channing–Ann Jillian duet.

The Making of Me
Overall Rating: ✪✪✪
Attraction Debut: 1989

The Making of Me is a well-done 14-minute film in which Martin Short explains reproduction by flashing back to his own conception and birth. It's cute and well-handled, with some actual fetal footage. But the question of "Why?" comes into play. If parents want to educate their kids on this subject, a 14-minute film followed by ensuing conversation at Walt Disney World Resort probably isn't the best way. And for the rest of us who don't really need the primer (or don't particularly care to be reminded) the film is superfluous.

Fairy Fact: This film runs 14 minutes. From what we've heard about breeder mating and conception, that seems about right.

Dining

You can pick up a (dubiously) healthy snack at the inexpensive **Pure and Simple.**

Mission: SPACE

Ever wonder what it's like to be in space? Us too.

Mission: SPACE

Overall Rating: N/A
Attraction Debut: 2003

This new attraction is so darn sophisticated, it's taken four years to build. Sponsored by Compaq Computer Corp. and created in association with former NASA advisers (and opened after our book was due, sorry), this ride promises to send visitors into sensory overload by blasting guests off into space and actually letting them experience the weightlessness of zero gravity. Set years in the future, visitors are transported to an International Space Station where they will experience simulated challenges faced by real astronauts. Sounds cool to us.

Fairy Fact: OK, so it's only a rumor, but we hear that Disney had to install a floor that it could "power clean" because they anticipate the zero-gravity simulation may cause some people to produce, uh, protein spills.

Test Track

The entire Test Track pavilion is the ride, which is housed in an 150,000-square-foot, circular building.

Test Track

Overall Rating: ✪✪✪✪
Attraction Debut: 1998

⚡

Let's start by saying that *anything* is more interesting than the stagnant World of Motion ride that once existed where Test Track stands today. General Motors puts you in the shoes and seat of a crash test dummy—something like Jeffrey's dating life. And afterward you can look at all the shiny new cars GM would like you to buy. The lines can be lo-o-ong, so we recommend either getting a FAST-PASS or taking advantage of their "single rider" line just off to the left of the entrance. You might not ride with your friends, but you also don't have to wait in line. (Unless, of course, the ride breaks down, which it is prone to do. On a recent trip, the ride system went down twice while Jeffrey was in line. Of course, if your car breaks down and you're with our friend Claire, she can have the auto up and running in 45 seconds flat.) Anyway, you've seen all those ads on TV where they show you how vigorously car companies test their vehicles before they hand over the keys to you. Now you get to be part of the final exam. In "cars," guests endure bumpy roads, extreme temperatures, sharp curves, and an exhilarating acceleration up to 65 mph—to name a few things. We recommend, however, that they replace the Plexiglas windshields, which were getting pretty cloudy the last time we looked through them. "It's thrilling," deadpans Michael from New York City, "if your only mode of transportation has been a horse and buggy." Adds Keith from Orlando: "You can experience your own test track every day in your car on the way to work." While we admit the most exciting part of the ride is the thrilling last moment whipping around the track, it's still worth a spin. We don't, however, recommend making out in the backseat.

Fairy Fact: In one year the Test Track vehicles travel more than 2 million miles. The cars are powered by three onboard computers, which together have more processing power than the Space Shuttle. Yeah, but can they do windows?

Imagination!

The two stunning glass pyramids highlighting this building, along with playful dancing fountains, do the namesake of this pavilion proud.

Journey Into Imagination With Figment
Overall Rating: ✪✪✪
Attraction Debut: 2002

When Epcot opened, the Imagination pavilion featured the attraction, Journey into the Imagination, starring the flamboyant Dreamfinder and an adorable purple dragon, Figment (as in "of your imagination"). The ride was a bit dated but it was a pleasant enough diversion until 2000, when the whole thing was revamped in favor of a disastrous ride we called Lack of Imagination. We loathed it with passion unbridled. Apparently we weren't alone because in 2002, it was revamped again and Figment, who was reduced to a cameo in version 2.0, now dominates. The new ride is, in fact, all Figment all the time. And while it's still not all that great at engaging the imagination, i'¹s back to being pleasant and it does include some cool effects. Also back from version 1.0 is the catchy song "One Little Spark." From 2.0, host Dr. Nigel Channing is back but he's infinitely more effective this time around as Figment's straight man (so to speak). At the end of the ride, you can get out and play at the ImageWorks, which has some hands-on activities such as sounds that are activated by stepping on lights. The whole pavilion is sponsored by Kodak and if we were them, we'd insist on a cut of all of that Figment merchandise to make up for those two years of darkness and blight.

Fairy Fact: Your host, Dr. Nigel Channing, also of Honey, I Shrunk the Audience, is none other than legendary Monty Python member Eric Idle.

Honey, I Shrunk the Audience
Overall Rating: ✪✪✪
Attraction Debut: 1994

It's identical to the attraction that's in Tomorrowland at Disneyland Park, so flip over to page 101 for a description.

Fairy Fact: Notice a missing Szalinski? Nick and Adam have a sister (Amy O'Neill), who's MIA. Guess she was too busy making that huge hit *Attack of the 5-foot 2-inch Woman*.

The Land

Spread out over six acres, this enormous pavilion, sponsored by Nestlé, deals with (duh) the land. Not just the land itself, but people's relationship with the land and agriculture. And we're not just talking about you people who have an interesting use for cucumbers. The entryway mosaics feature 150,000 individually shaped pieces of marble, granite, slate, glass, and gold, representing the layers of the Earth. And if you go down one layer farther, just below the dinosaurs you can find the year when Eddie was born.

Living With the Land
Overall Rating: ✪✪✪
Attraction Debut: 1982 (as Listen to the Land), renovated in 1994

⊘

To help bring out the Martha Stewart in all of us, Nestlé presents this ride, which displays technological advancements in growing things (plants, fish—you know, things). While the original boat ride boasted a catchier theme song, its absence doesn't take away from the basic coolness of seeing plants grown in zero gravity. Be forewarned, however, this is one of those rides whose success is 100% contingent on the affability of your guide. We have been on boats where we wanted to slit our wrists. The host may as well have been reciting the phone book. But we've also been on boats where the hosts were so darn effusive, it was like hearing all the information again for the very first time. Your 14-minute trip takes you through some rather realistic ecosystems (desert, rain forest, etc.) to see how plants have adapted to nature. Then science takes over as you enter several different chambers to learn about intercropping, crop rotation, and integrated pest management. We assure you, this is much more fascinating with the right guide. Without, just try to make sense of it.

Fairy Fact: Many of the crops you see being grown are used in food prepared at The Land's Garden Grill Restaurant and throughout the park.

Food Rocks
Overall Rating: ✪✪
Attraction Debut: 1994

This lightweight cabaret offers information most of you probably already know about food. Veggies and fruits are good. Eating protein is good. Eating grain is good. And even eating junk food once in a while can be OK. (Who's sponsoring this ride again? Oh yeah, Nestlé.) Your host Füd Wrapper (based on flash-in-the-pan rapper Tone Loc) introduces a myriad of different performers based on popular singers. Pita Gabriel, the Peach Boys, and Chubby Cheddar serenade while preaching the values of good eating. Gay folk will be particularly enamored of a fish who looks suspiciously like Cher and sings a new version of "The Shoop Shoop Song," a piano-playing pineapple who takes after Little Richard, and the house band, the Utensils, a group of kitchen, uh, utensils based on the rock group Queen. Pass me a Crunch bar. We're not saying the Imagineers for this attraction were gay. But Cher? Little Richard? Queen? You do the math.

Fairy Fact: When this show replaced Kitchen Kabaret, it wasn't because the older show wasn't working but because both conventional wisdom and the public's consciousness about nutrition had changed dramatically during the 10-year run of the earlier show, making the Kabaret's emphasis on the four food groups (remember those?) obsolete.

The Circle of Life
Overall Rating: ❂❂❂
Attraction Debut: 1994

This excellent film about humanity's relationship to the environment is hosted by *The Lion King*'s Simba, Pumbaa, and Timon (and while we'd never go so far as to call them a couple, Timon *is* Disney's first character to don drag). Though the movie borders on depressing (after all, humans aren't doing the Earth a whole lot of good), it's not dogmatic and it is highly educational.

Fairy Fact: This attraction, like the film itself, features the vocal talents of Matthew Broderick and Nathan Lane before they were paired in Broadway's mega-hit *The Producers*.

⑪ The Garden Grill Restaurant
Price: Moderate
Meals: B, L, D, 🕐

Fun for children and adults alike, this restaurant is on a giant turntable that overlooks several of the elaborate ecosystems from the Living with the Land attraction. Along with an eclectic and healthy menu (some of the veggies served are grown in the greenhouses in The Land pavilion), the Grill also serves up Disney characters who will pay you visits throughout your meal.

❶ Sunshine Season Food Fair
Price: Inexpensive
Meals: B, L, D

Got a big group with a diverse palate? You may want to take a look at this elaborate food court. With everything from

soups, salads, and sandwiches to baked goods and barbecue, there's something here to tempt everyone's taste buds. None of it is extremely memorable, but it's all just fine.

The Living Seas

This pavilion deals with, you guessed it, the oceans—both the life within them and the way we can use the seas to our advantage in the future. The front of the building simulates a natural coastline, complete with waves crashing on the man-made shore but sadly missing nude sunbathers.

The Living Seas

Overall Rating: ✪✪

Attraction Debut: 1986

We admit, this is not our favorite attraction. But we both grew up in urban environments with easy access to high-tech aquariums, so this is nothing new for us. The Living Seas takes you on a journey inside what Disney calls the world's "sixth-largest ocean"—a man-made tank that holds more than 5.7 million gallons of salt water, 65 different kinds of marine life, and 4,000 sea creatures. Following a seven-minute film (zzzzzz), guests take elevators to "the ocean floor" (cue: *The Little Mermaid*). With sharks and sea turtles, rays and dolphins, these view makes the dull movie completely worth sitting (or sleeping) through.

Fairy Fact: The tank at The Living Seas is so big that Spaceship Earth could fit inside with room to spare. And the descent into Sea Base Alpha, which seems to be about 50 feet down, is only, in fact, a few inches.

⓫ Coral Reef Restaurant

Price: Expensive

Meals: L, D

This is one restaurant where you can actually see what

you're eating—and we don't mean what's on your plate. As you dine on any number of scrumptious seafood delights (yes, they have things other than fish), you can look into the giant tank that houses hundreds of fish—which blissfully swim by as you eat their relatives.

World Showcase

Epcot's World Showcase is a frustrated traveler's wet dream. Sitting on a 1.2-mile stretch around a 40-acre lagoon are 11 pavilions representing nations around the world. Each pavilion is architecturally designed to exude the flavor of the hosting country. Since this is Disney (and a small world, after all) everything's pristine as can be, giving each land a sort of mythic, fairy-tale quality. And since the World Showcase isn't a favorite among children, crowds are fairly manageable. The pavilions are also notable for their imports: international food (which Disney waters down), international shopping (which Disney marks up), and international hotties (which Disney can't really tamper with). Each pavilion is staffed with cast members on exchange from the country in question. We find the men of World Showcase (like most of the Disney staff we encountered) to be disproportionately gay. So for those of you with a hankering for a taste of Norway, now might be your chance. But lesbians need to be mindful of the fact that stereotypical signs in America don't always translate (i.e., many European women don't shave their legs). So fine-tune your gaydar. While it's true that several of the attractions found within the pavilions are little more than commercials for "the beauty and majesty of (your country here)" they're still worth a visit. And if you do have small fry in tow, each country has a kid zone with activities (and stickers) to minimize the whining and boredom. Says Bob from Buffalo: "I've always

said that World Showcase is designed for people who want to travel but don't like foreigners."

Going clockwise around the lagoon:

Mexico
Pavilion Debut: 1982

The Mexican pavilion is unlike the others in that it is almost wholly contained within a single structure. An ancient pyramid houses a small exhibit of artifacts that (here's where we admit to being the classless heathens we are) we tend to ignore on our way to the plaza, a beautiful village marketplace under a starry sky. A quick stroll through the village to soak up the atmosphere is all that's required if shopping or eating aren't on the agenda. While the shops feature the crap you'd expect fresh from Tijuana (piñatas, sombreros, etc.), there are also some truly lovely crystal and glass to be found.

El Rio del Tiempo
Overall Rating: ✪

We highly recommend that you move on in your touring. If, however, you are a completist, a glutton, or simply enamored of boat rides, there's this. But don't say you weren't warned. "The River of Time should be named The River of Wasted Time," quips Keith from Orlando. The attraction, a boat trip through Mexico's history via film clips and bad Audio-Animatronics, is a true siestafest. It's also cheap and almost insulting to the culture of the country. (We have corn! And beans! And we dance! Ugh.) Of course, if you visit the margarita bar prior to riding, El Rio's quality may improve dramatically.

Fairy Fact: This attraction was originally conceived to be as elaborate as Pirates of the Caribbean. But cost overruns during Epcot's construction forced this attraction's budget to be halved. What was the original budget, $10?

Dining

Mexico's sit-down restaurant, the **San Angel Inn**, is modeled after the real thing in Mexico City and is quite lovely. We go for the mole because any dish that features chocolate as a main course is all right with us. It is, however, hard to justify the inn's high prices, since much of the food is standard Mexican fare and can be readily found elsewhere. There's also a fast-food **Cantina** with tacos, burritos, and, of course, margaritas. There are, in fact, individuals who, upon discovering the libations in Mexico, get no farther in their World Showcase touring. Claire from Santa Barbara, Calif., remarked, "Mexico? I lost four hours there."

Norway
Pavilion Debut: 1988

The walk-through portion of the Norwegian pavilion is one of the most diverse, featuring a Viking sailing ship, a replica of a Scandinavian castle, a 13th-century wooden stave church (containing Scandinavian art), and a charming village. The shops specialize in warm, woolly, wildly expensive sweaters (and kudos to anyone who can even imagine shopping for one in Florida heat). "Norway is great for anyone who's into blonds," observes Keith from Orlando. "Just walk around the shops and cruise the cast members." Norway also qualifies as the only place you'll find us actually shopping for trolls—there's a whole store devoted to them.

Maelstrom
Overall Rating: ✪✪

Norway's attraction, the Maelstrom, is a boat ride far superior to Mexico's. The story, told with Audio-Animatronics, tells the history of Viking explorers while mixing in the lore of trolls and squalls of the sea. The ride

is short and ends at a sweet fishing village facade where guests are led into a room for a "Norway's greatest hits" film. Those who like fjord scenery should enjoy it, but for those with less patience (read: Jeffrey), you can walk straight through the theater, following guests exiting the preceding show.

Fairy Fact: As you board, look carefully at the Vikings on the mural. One of them is accessorizing with mouse ears.

Dining

Norway's **Restaurant Akershus** features a sit-down Norwegian smorgasbord. By now you know that we're both massive fans of all-you-can-gorge-yourself-on buffets. Trying to walk around Epcot after that kind of indulgence is an impossibility tantamount to keeping a straight face through *Showgirls*. If, however, eating's your priority, this is an excellent way to do it. The food, most of which is fairly exotic, includes herring and other fish as well as stews and cheeses. It's all quite good and very well priced. All around, one of Epcot's better eating venues.

China
Pavilion Debut: 1982

The architecture of the Chinese pavilion is some of the park's most memorable, with Beijing's Temple of Heaven beautifully re-created (at about half the size of the original) and surrounded by gardens and reflecting ponds complete with lotus blossoms. Once again, for the high-minded, there are art and artifact displays. Shopping in China has a bit less character than in the other pavilions, with most of the merchandise crammed into a single department store as opposed to smaller boutiques. Silk is abundant. The question of whether wearing it is cool or absurd is strictly subjective (although Eddie looked just a bit too *Karate Kid* in the outfit he tried on).

Wonders of China
Overall Rating: ✪✪

China's attraction is the 19-minute film *Wonders of China*, shown in the always exciting, Disney-pioneered Circle-Vision 360. Eddie thinks the film is excellent, although it doesn't receive raves from everyone. "It's boring and doesn't really make you want to book a trip to Beijing anytime soon," notes Keith from Orlando. Oddly, they manage to leave out minor details like communism. Hmm.

Fairy Fact: When Wonders of China was filmed, its crew members were among the very first Western filmmakers to be granted permission to shoot in Beijing's Forbidden City. Chi Chi LaRue was next in line.

Dining

Food is available in either the sit-down **Nine Dragons Restaurant** or at the egg-rolls-to-go **Lotus Blossom Café.** Nine Dragons is beautiful but massively overpriced for food comparable to what you'd get at your airport's Panda Express. Poke your head in for the view, but there's no good reason to stay.

Germany
Pavilion Debut: 1982

While the Germany pavilion is adorable, with a village scene looking like something right out of Pinocchio, there's not much going on here. Shops feature Hummel collectible china at its absolute kitchiest and Steiff toys. Just beyond the village is a sweet model railroad for those of you who can't get enough of all things miniature. And if you happen to be in Germany on the hour, you can see the glockenspiel in action.

Dining

Germany's restaurant is **Biergarten,** for those looking to cap off Mexico's margaritas with a little beer. This one is

another stuff-your-gullet buffet, and as you'd expect, there are sausages aplenty. (Go ahead, insert your joke here.) There's also an oompah band that just about sent Jeffrey over the edge. But if you want all you can eat, Norway's a better bet and doesn't subject you to the polka.

Italy
Pavilion Debut: 1982

Italy is another pavilion without a whole lot of action (unless, of course, you create some), but it's well worth a visit for the shopping and food. Leather, anyone? Armani? Perugina chocolate? The design of the Italian pavilion is striking and among Epcot's most accurate (although people familiar with the actual Venetian landmarks will notice that their positions have been flipped). There's also a waterfront area where gondolas are moored. Unfortunately, there aren't any gondoliers to be had, and Jeffrey is usually unwilling to play dress-up.

Dining

Then there's the restaurant, **L'Originale Alfredo di Roma,** where you can watch them make pasta. Lots of it. Which they'll pile on your plate in heavy cream sauces. Then they'll charge you a *lot* of money before you stumble out onto the streets, too bloated to do much but waddle over to the nearest shady bench.

The American Adventure
Pavilion Debut: 1982

The United States gets away without actually having a pavilion. Instead it has a building to house its attraction, The American Adventure. Bookended by a burger restaurant (thank God, since there's absolutely nothing exotic to eat at Epcot!) and a gift shop selling Americana (where you can finally find that apron featuring portraits of all the presidents), the structure is something out of colonial Williamsburg, crying out for a fife and drum corps to play in front (and every hour or so, they do). Also playing live are the Voices of Liberty, an a capella octet who sing Americana in the lobby of The American Adventure. (We know it sounds corny, but they're really fabulous. Plus the guys wear those colonial pants that show off their calves!).

The American Adventure
Overall Rating: ✪✪✪✪✪
Attraction Debut: 1982

The American Adventure is a half-hour Audio-Animatronics and multimedia show hosted by Ben Franklin (Disney's first walking Audio-Animatronics figure) and Mark Twain. Although the scenes played out are a little pat, they accurately recall major historical milestones using the actual words of the characters in a culturally inclusive chronology. Lincoln, Jefferson, and Washington say the stuff you'd expect, but then we get the likes of Frederick Douglass and Susan B. Anthony talking about equal rights. Even Rosie the Riveter gets play here. Capping the show is a film montage that we've yet to see without crying. An inspiring song about the American dream backs a litany of images that puts JFK, Martin Luther King Jr., and the moon landing alongside Billie Jean King, Rock Hudson, and Ryan White. If you are unmoved by this, you are a jaded and bitter individual who should go back to your circuit party hedonism.

Fairy Fact: In the Civil War song "Two Brothers," the siblings in the Matthew Brady–style family portrait are actually Imagineers, John Olsen and Jeff Burke. And that stage the action takes place on? It isn't really there. Since there are no live people walking on the stage, there isn't one. Just a hole from which the animatronics rise and recede.

Dining

The **Liberty Tree Tavern**, America's fast-food joint, is a travesty at odds with World Showcase's very existence. If all you want to eat is burgers and dogs, stay at the Magic Kingdom. But if you must, here it is.

Japan
Pavilion Debut: 1982

The Japan pavilion is probably Epcot's biggest tease (a certain cast member in France notwithstanding). While the design, which includes an Imperial Palace, a rocky, waterfront shore with a torii gate, serene gardens, and a five-story pagoda (representing sky, wind, earth, fire, and water, the five elements from which the Buddhists believe all things are created) is striking, there's very little beyond the elaborate exteriors. The art exhibit is among the park's least interesting, while the food and shopping areas are contained in flavorless surroundings. Still, the shopping arcade has some beautiful, if pricey, china and some lovely kimonos (the short silk one Eddie bought there 10 years ago as a summer bathrobe never fails to elicit compliments from, er, guests).

Dining

Japan's full-service restaurant, **The Teppanyaki Grill,** is quite good, with food prepared on teppan grills at your table by men with very sharp knives. As is the case with teppan grills everywhere, unless your party is huge you'll be sharing a table with other diners. For faster food, there's a **yakitori house** on the other side of the pavilion. It's ridiculously priced, but the teriyaki skewers are good and make excellent weapons for later in the day.

Morocco
Pavilion Debut: 1984

The Moroccan pavilion is striking in its vibrant detail. Stucco arches and gorgeous turquoise tile mosaics are everywhere. There is (you guessed it) a museum as well as both a sit-down and a fast-food restaurant. Shopping features rugs and pottery. Disney drops the verisimilitude ball here, however, since the merchants don't actually chase you down the street offering you bargains as they do in Marrakesh. However, cracks Billy from Maynard, Mass., "I think you could buy a young Moroccan boy at the bazaar."

Dining

Since Moroccan food is probably the most exotic and hard-to-come-by cuisine Epcot has to offer, we recommend **Restaurant Marrakesh**, although the fare can be a bit spicy. The prices are reasonable, and the sumptuous setting is to die for. And who can resist the charms of those belly dancers in the *I Dream of Jeannie* outfits? Not Eddie, that's for sure.

France
Pavilion Debut: 1982

Welcome to France, Disney-style: no smoking, no attitude, and no sex on the Champs-Elyseés. Probably Epcot's prettiest pavilion, France attempts to re-create the period between 1870 and 1910, known as La Belle Epoque (or "the beautiful era" for those who don't *parlez* French). A manicured and usually quiet garden sits alongside a château while the winding village side street contrasts with the formality of the Parisian central artery, crowned by an Eiffel Tower replica (at 10% the original's size—doncha hate that?) built from the original's blueprints. Shopping includes wine (*naturalmente*), French provincial housewares (because country French is still all the rage in Greenwich), perfume, and one or

two Chanel scarves. There's also a terrific patisserie for a little sinning (certain authors, who shall remain nameless, have been known to make several trips to France on a single day for this particular attraction).

Impressions de France
Overall Rating: ✪✪✪

The France pavilion forgoes a museum exhibit (thank God!) in favor of the lush 18-minute film *Impressions de France*. Unlike the park's other movies, this one doesn't attempt to educate with lame tourist-brochure dialogue. *Impressions* is simply sumptuous footage on five screens, underscored by French classical music. It may bore the hell out of kids, but it is gorgeous.

Fairy Fact: A well-tuned ear might notice that the opening music by Camillle Saint-Saëns was inspiration for the opening bars of Alan Menken's score for *Beauty and the Beast*.

Dining

Since the word *cuisine* comes from France, the food has a reputation to uphold. The gourmet (and exorbitant) **Bistro de Paris** and the moderate sidewalk café **Chefs de France** are both excellent, with the latter Eddie's pick for an Epcot lunch. The atmosphere at Chefs, named for the three French masters who supervise the cooking—Paul Bocuse, Roger Verge and Gaston LeNotre—includes a glass room fronting the park's sidewalk. It's perfect for people-watching over buttery escargot or a chevre salad. The Bistro is directly above and features some of the best (and richest) food in Epcot.

United Kingdom
Pavilion Debut: 1982

The U.K. pavilion is a favorite for the sheer variety of its design. (And who can resist those cute accents?) There's

Tudor, pre-Georgian, thatched roofs from the Cotswolds, a slice of Hyde Park with town-house facades, a palace garden maze, cobblestones, and more. But it all blends beautifully. Since Hyde Park is almost always quiet, it's a good area in which to steal some private time (members of Parliament romping with rent boys not included). The British shops feature tea, tartan, and Pooh.

Dining

The Rose & Crown Pub is a fine choice for an ale to chase down that German beer you followed Mexico's margaritas with, and it offers the World Showcase's only waterside dining. The atmosphere is what makes it, with the wait staff right out of *Oliver!* The only problem is that you have to like British food (fish and chips, kidney pie). Or you could just go for the beer.

Canada

Pavilion Debut: 1982

If there's a pavilion in the bunch that doesn't quite work, it's Canada. Though imposing and pretty, the pavilion lacks flow, making it easy to walk right by design highlights without noticing them. Influences from the varying regions breed a wilderness lodge flanked by totem poles and tall trees, a classic French-Canadian hotel, a winding garden from Victoria, and stone buildings from Niagara. The shopping is unremarkable, although everything you need to outfit yourself as a country bear is available. And ladies, there's a lot of flannel.

O Canada!

Overall Rating: ✪✪✪
Attraction Debut: 1982

This attraction, another Circle-Vision 360 travelogue, isn't up to Disney's best, although the nine-screen technology remains breathtaking. The film's finale, though, is an

irresistible anthem that will stick in your head for weeks.

Fairy Fact: On your way into the movie, beyond the cascading waterfall, mixed in with the rocks, is a small stone with a hinge. If you lift it up, you'll find the valve to turn off the entire waterworks. You can bet that you'll also find yourself ejected from the park if you touch said valve.

Dining

Canada's restaurant, **Le Cellier Steakhouse,** is aptly named: It's in a dark, underground establishment for those gothic types who need an escape from the sun and cheer. For the rest of us, it makes sense only as a last resort or for those protein whores who require a fat steak. Prices are moderate.

Epcot Entertainment

Street entertainment at World Showcase has recently been beefed up and adds a truly fabulous cultural element to each land. While all of the countries have bands playing music of the motherland (from mariachi in Mexico to Canadian bagpipes), some of the entertainment is truly extraordinary. In China, amazing child acrobats share the stage with plate spinners. The shows are excellent as well as empowering to kids who watch other children perform. In Italy the Mysteries of Venice street show is like Carnaval, with traditional harlequin characters deliciously interacting with the crowd. In the United States the fabulous Voices of Liberty sing a capella Americana while you wait to enter The American Adventure. France has excellent living-statue art that shouldn't be missed. At the United Kingdom there's cute but corny street theater featuring Arthurian tales. And in Canada the kilt-clad band Off Kilter gets a lot of attention (particularly from a certain element who gather around waiting for a stiff wind).

The Tapestry of Dreams
Overall Rating: ✪✪✪
Attraction Debut: 1999

Originally called The Tapestry of Nations when it premiered as part of Epcot's millennium celebration, this popular, character-free parade has endured. One hundred twenty 20-foot puppets ride on the shoulders of cast members while 32 drummers beat out rhythms on 720 drums in this colorful pageant celebrating culture from around the world. This is probably Disney's most adult parade, with nothing cutesy or cartoonlike. The puppets owe more to Julie Taymor than Jim Henson. Jeffrey finds it dull, but Eddie, who always likes a good puppet, is a fan. There are two shows nightly, but the second one is immediately before Illuminations (see page 225). You'll never get good seating for both, so we recommend seeing the first Tapestry before staking out a spot for Illuminations.

Characters in World Showcase

While there are no specific "character areas" at Epcot as there are in the other parks, the World Showcase offers meeting opportunities with characters indigenous to specific countries. Look for Mary Poppins and the Pooh characters in the United Kingdom; Belle and the Beast in France; Aladdin and Jasmine in Morocco (granted, a bit of a stretch); Mulan in China, Pinocchio, Geppetto, and Snow White in Italy (which explains her cooking as well as her ability to juggle multiple men). There's also a double-decker bus that transports Mickey and crew around the world, with stops in China, Italy, and Japan.

Chapter Twelve
Disney-MGM Studios

At the opening of Disney-MGM Studios in 1989, Disney CEO Michael Eisner called it "the Hollywood that never was and always will be." It was, in fact, Disney's answer to the popularity of Hollywood's Universal Studios. Their notion was to mix typical Disney entertainment with a working film production site, educating and delighting in equal measure. There's less actual shooting visible to the guests than there used to be, but the environment is distinctly Hollywood and nothing like anything Disney had done in the past. Upon entering the park's turquoise art deco–style gates, guests are transported to a shiny version of Hollywood in the 1930s. Designed like Main Street in the Magic Kingdoms, Hollywood Boulevard serves as the park's central artery. The handsome street features shops and restaurants designed in chrome and neon, evoking a fantasy version of Hollywood (picture *I Love Lucy*'s California episodes and you get an idea). Crowning the avenue as the castle does Main Street is a gorgeous replica of Grauman's Chinese Theatre, complete with hand and footprints of the stars (although at this version you're more likely to see Betty White than Bette Davis). Adding to the ambiance is a troupe of Disney performers who roams the street as typical Hollywood types (the cigar-smoking producer, the blond and buxom starlet, etc.). You can make their day by being a little sassy (Eddie told one he was Rock Hudson's pool boy). There's also Disney's version of the classic Los Angeles landmark The Brown Derby Restaurant and a dinosaur-shaped ice cream stand, a tribute to Gertie the

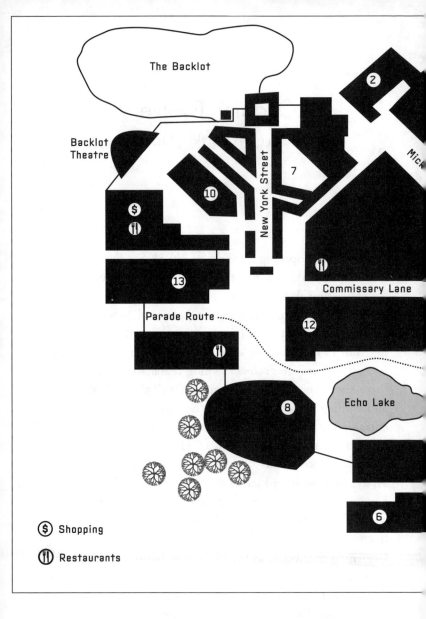

The Backlot

Backlot
Theatre

Mick[...]

New York Street

7

$ Shopping

🍴 Restaurants

10

13

Parade Route

12

8

Echo Lake

2

Commissary Lane

6

($) Shopping

🍴 Restaurants

1. Beauty and the Beast
   Live on Stage
2. Backstage Studio Tour
3. Backstage Pass
4. Fantasmic!
5. The Great Movie Ride
6. Guest Services

7. Honey, I Shrunk the Kids
   Movie Set Adventure
8. Indiana Jones Stunt
   Spectacular
9. The Magic of Disney Animation
10. Muppetvision 3-D
11. Rock 'n' Roller Coaster

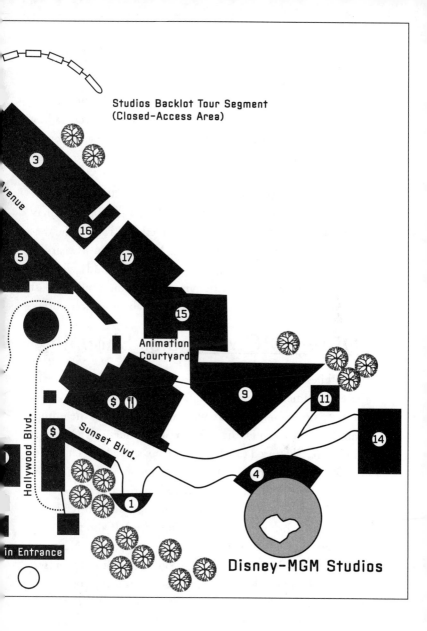

Studios Backlot Tour Segment
(Closed–Access Area)

③

⑯

⑤

⑰

⑮

Animation
Courtyard

Avenue

⑨

⑪

$ ⑪

$

Sunset Blvd.

Hollywood Blvd.

① ④

⑭

in Entrance

Disney–MGM Studios

12. Sounds Dangerous
13. Star Tours
14. The Twilight Zone™ Tower of Terror
15. Voyage of the Little Mermaid
16. Walt Disney: One Man's Dream
17. Who Wants to Be a Millionaire—Play It!

Dinosaur, the world's first animated character. Directly off Hollywood Boulevard is Sunset Boulevard, the street leading to newer attractions, The Twilight Zone™ Tower of Terror, Rock 'n' Roller Coaster starring Aerosmith, and Fantasmic! The Chinese Theatre, which houses The Great Movie Ride, was Disney-MGM Studios' centerpiece until 2001 when some classless human decided the park needed a more instantly recognizable icon as its symbol. Now directly in front of the theater is a massive replica of the hat Mickey Mouse wears in Fantasia. Aside from being an eye-sore, it's at odds with the rest of the otherwise perfect environment. And that's the last time you'll hear these gay men complain about an accessory.

Disney-MGM Studios Shopping

While many of the shops at Disney-MGM Studios carry the exact same merchandise found in the other parks, a few specialty stores on the lot are well worth a visit. To the immediate left as you enter the park is **Sid Cahuenga's One of a Kind** store. Sid's used to sell a lot of truly special merchandise, like Audrey Hepburn earrings or Jaclyn Smith pumps. Unfortunately, eBay sort of cornered that market, and Sid's has been reduced mainly to an autograph and poster store. Still, it's a fun browse for the occasional find. It also features a great selection of Disney posters and lobby cards. Near the intersection of Sunset and Hollywood is **The Beverly Sunset**, featuring Disney Villain merchandise, perfect for your inner (or not-so-inner) Evil Queen. At the **Animation Gallery**, over in the Animation Courtyard are collectibles, cels, and figurines along with the park's artier cards and posters. While **The Writer's Shop** sells the same books available elsewhere throughout Walt Disney World Resort, this particular store also offers a fabulous bakery that seldom has lines. Try the chocolate-dipped Rice Krispie treats—brick-size! And of course there are stores with merchandise tie-ins to many of the

attractions: the **Indiana Jones Outpost, Tower** (of Terror) **Shops, Tatooine Traders** (*Star Wars* and Star Tours merchandise), **Rock Around the Shop** (the Aerosmith stuff Rock 'n' Roller coaster makes you crave), and **Stage 1 Company** (Muppet stuff, of which Eddie can never have too much).

Attractions

The Twilight Zone™ Tower of Terror
Overall Rating: ✪✪✪✪✪
Attraction Debut: 1994

While there's nothing overtly gay about The Tower of Terror, its faded art deco Hollywood glamour has the same appeal that makes *Sunset Boulevard* a gay classic. From the moment you pass through the ride's gates and onto the grounds of the Hollywood Tower Hotel, atmosphere rules. Guests walk through the misty, musty remains of a once-gorgeous Hollywood hotel, past its cobwebbed lobby (accented with breathtaking detail) and into a library, where Rod Sterling, via well-cut *Twilight Zone* footage, introduces the ride. In 1939, he tells us, a film star of the Lana Turner variety checked into the hotel with her entourage in tow. As they ascended to their rooms, lightning hit the hotel, sending the five of them into (doo-doo-doo-doo) The Twilight Zone. Then it's off to the hotel's service elevators for a ride offering the best special effects Disney has to offer as you live through the starlet's ill-fated journey. Holograms and light are eerily used before the finale: a snap of cable, an electrical short, and your car plunging downward in a 13-story free-fall. The thrill portion has been modified over the years, increasing the number of drops by shooting the cars upward again as soon as they hit the ground. And the drop is actually accelerated so you're moving faster than gravity. The addition of the Tower of Terror cost $95 million, an astronomical figure when you consider that the

Jeffrey and Eddie form their own Tower of Terror

entire park only cost $300 million when it opened. Though not for the faint of heart, this ride ranks as one of Disney's very best. And of course, there's a photo kiosk on the way out where you can buy a shot of yourself mid shriek. Tip for *Twilight Zone* fans: Notice anything missing? Rod Serling's omnipresent cigarette has been digitally removed. Additionally, props on the ride come right from the series, including the cookbook *To Serve Man* and the broken eyeglasses that culminate the classic Burgess Meredith episode.

Fairy Fact: The Tower stands at 199 feet tall. Why just 199? An extra foot would have required a blinking warning light for airplanes. And that would have just looked weird.

Rock 'n' Roller Coaster Starring Aerosmith
Overall Rating: ✪✪✪✪✪
Attraction Debut: 2000
⚡

A double-loop roller coaster in the dark set to Aerosmith's music may not seem like a gay fantasy, but when you throw in indie film delight Illeana Douglas (as the group's manager

in a filmed opening sequence), the numerous trendy Los Angeles landmarks that you pass on your voyage, and the band's track "Dude Looks Like a Lady" (which is one of the rotating specially recorded songs played during the ride), the whole thing smacks of queer engineering. Passing a 40-foot-tall electric guitar, you enter into the fictional G-Force Records (which features Hollywood and Lyric Street Records—both Disney labels, go figure) where Illeana and the band say hello before sending you off to their concert in a "super stretch" limo—it seats 24 guests. The only thing that's pure fantasy is how the cars go from 0 to 60 miles per hour in an amazing 2.8 seconds. Like you could ever go that fast on an L.A. freeway.

Fairy Fact: Along with "Dude," Aerosmith's Steven Tyler and Joe Perry customized four of their most popular tunes for the ride, including "Love in an Elevator," which became "Love in a Roller Coaster" and "What Kind of Love Are You On?" which became "What Kind of Ride Are You On?"

Fantasmic!

Overall Rating: ✪✪✪✪✪
Attraction Debut: 1998

This amazing spectacle, set back in a cozy 6,900-seat amphitheater, combines lasers, lights, fireworks, waterworks, animation, and live performance to create one of the most jaw-dropping experiences at any of the parks. While there are some differences in the middle section (and a couple of new moments generate a big "'huh?" like a *Pocahontas* sequence that is her dream inside Mickey's dream—got that?), the experience is similar to the one at Disneyland Park found on page 81. But like its sister show, it's often filled to capacity early, so you may want to get a dinner package from one of the park's restaurants, which includes reserved (though not the best) seating.

Fairy Fact: The island stage for the show is surrounded by a moat with 1.9 million gallons of water.

Beauty and the Beast Live on Stage
Overall Rating: ✪✪
Attraction Debut: 1991 (revamped in 2000)

In discussing Beauty and the Beast Live on Stage, it's important to remind you all that neither of us particularly likes theme park shows. In fact, we go into them primarily for a solid dose of camp. On that level, Beauty and the Beast does not disappoint, with its unfortunate chorus boys trying to emote as they prance around in mint-and-lavender tights. That said, the current restructured version of the show is infinitely better than its predecessor and actually adheres to the film's story. Also intact are many of the voices of the film's stars. And the performers onstage appreciate finding a bit of "family." "We *love* to see gay people in the audience," gushes Keith from Orlando. "We like to have something to look at too, and if we see a bunch of hot guys, you'll be getting a great show!" The preshow, an all-male doo-wop quartet, is a good warm up. So while it's not a total washout, remember that time spent there is time you could be using to augment your tan line.

Fairy Fact: While most of the park's live shows play for a maximum of two or three years before they're replaced, this one is a record holder: still going strong since 1991.

The Great Movie Ride
Overall Rating: ✪✪✪✪
Attraction Debut: 1989

Whether you're a lesbian who lusts after Sigourney Weaver's Ripley in *Alien* or a gay man who drools over the ruby slippers in *The Wizard of Oz* (which are on display in the lobby—Jeffrey had to physically restrain Eddie from trying them on), The Great Movie Ride has something for you. The Audio-Animatronics on this voyage through films of the past and present are fantastic. As you travel through this immense dark ride with a live (most of the time, anyway) host, Julie

Andrews and Dick Van Dyke glide above the chimneys in a *Mary Poppins* room. Gene Kelly sings in the rain. A hunky Tarzan soars through the air. Bogie and Bergman say goodbye in *Casablanca*. And the *Wizard of Oz* sequence (complete with munchkins, yellow brick road, and an amazing Wicked Witch of the West) is so full of color, you'd swear you were in the movie—and in a way you are. The excellent film clip montage that closes the ride will leave you craving popcorn.

Fairy Fact: This ride was initially conceived as part of an entertainment pavilion at Epcot, next door to Imagination.

The Magic of Disney Animation
Overall Rating: ✪✪✪
Attraction Debut: 1989

The Magic of Disney Animation is another attraction that has changed greatly over the years. The attraction, a 35-minute "tour," walks you through several rooms of varying interest. First up is the delightful if dated film *Back to Neverland,* in which Walter Cronkite explains the basic steps of creating animation (or at least the steps before computers came along) to Robin Williams by turning him into an animated lost boy from *Peter Pan.* Since most of us consider ourselves animated lost boys, there is at least passing familiarity. From there guests are hoarded into an "animator's workroom" where an actual human being presides. The animator sketches a few characters (projected on a screen above him) while answering questions about animation. The success of this portion of the tour is wholly dependent on the personality (or lack thereof) of the animator. Once upon a time the sketches were given to children in the audience, but someone had the brilliant idea of selling the sketches in the adjoining shop, so that particular free lunch is over. Next is a walk-through overlooking animators at work. Since animation is a slo-o-ow process, don't expect orgasmic levels of excitement here. (Don't even expect reality; those desks are so neat even the most anal of you will be impressed.) There's also plenty of stuff on display advertising whatever's next on Disney's animated slate. Finally, there are two video sequences. The first blends classic animated scenes and interviews with top Disney artists. Then it's on to a theater where great moments in Disney animation make up a fabulous clipfest. Both videos are terrific. You'll laugh. You'll cry. You'll be inspired to shop.

Fairy Fact: Don't get too excited by the Oscars on display as you wait to enter the tour—they're all reproductions.

Voyage of The Little Mermaid

Overall Rating: ✪✪✪
Attraction Debut: 1992

⚡

Based on the 1989 hit animated flick, this live show uses puppets, humans, lasers, and a little animation to retell the 70-minute film in about 25 minutes. Opening with an eye-popping rendition of "Under the Sea" that uses dozens of elaborate puppets and a lot of black light, the show gets a bit less interesting from there until a tremendous Ursula, the sea witch, comes out looking more than a little bit like Divine. (Coincidence?) The quality of the show can vary depending on the talent of the Ariel performing that day (and it doesn't hurt if she has a cute Eric to rescue). A pleasant diversion for all ages, this is also a great place to cool down.

Fairy Fact: You never know where a fish will go once she sprouts feet. One former Ariel from this attraction became Miss America in 1993: Leanza Cornett.

Backstage Studio Tour

Overall Rating: ✪✪
Attraction Debut: 1989

There's one piece of information that will make the Backstage Studio Tour absolutely required for many of you:

It features the house used for exterior shots on *The Golden Girls*. Unfortunately, it doesn't feature much else. Once an interesting drive-through of a working studio, the tram tour was revised in 1997 to be fun but completely lacking in educational value. Sure, you get to drive by some facades of homes and towns, and yes, there's a fleeting peek into the wardrobe warehouse, but mostly the guided tram ride is an excuse to be off your feet for 25 minutes. You'll also get to go through Catastrophe Canyon, where your tram is subjected to movie-style disasters like earthquakes, fire, and flash flooding. The interesting part is actually going behind the canyon for a look at the machinery needed to create those effects. What was once the best part of the tour, the New York Street, is now available to explore on your own. The facades are pretty fabulous, but finding a street hustler is harder than it should be.

Fairy Fact: A lot of the equipment used to create the effects in Catastrophe Canyon is strictly for show. So both the "onstage" and backstage are fake, while the real backstage remains out of view. This gets more layered than RuPaul's makeup.

Backstage Pass
Overall Rating: ✪✪
Attraction Debut: 1989 (revamped in 1997)

This walking tour once served as an amusing and educational look at film technique and special effects. Unfortunately, the 1997 revamp has reduced the tour to little more than advertising Disney's latest films with prop and costume displays. The tour also takes you on to sets of shows like *Home Improvement* and presents memorabilia from old movies and TV series. If you have 30 minutes to kill, the tour can be all right. And since it features different shows and movies at different times, there may actually be something interesting to see. Of course, there may not.

Walt Disney: One Man's Dream

Overall Rating: ✪✪

Attraction Debut: 2001

Created for the 100 Years of Magic celebration (honoring what would have been Walt's 100th birthday), this paean to the creator impressively documents Walt's life and work. Disney enthusiasts will be impressed by the collection, which includes the mechanical bird that inspired Walt to create Audio-Animatronics; the dancing vaudevillian (based on the tapping of Buddy Ebsen), which was the first successful Audio-Animatronics figure back in 1951; and a model of the original Peter Pan's Flight attraction. Sure, the gratuitous models of current theme park attractions just promote current Disney product, but they do it so well that we can't quibble. The walk-through is followed by a movie about Walt that Jeffrey was actually able to stay awake through. And that's saying something.

Fairy Fact: More than 400 of the items were transferred via Federal Express from California on a plane designated Spirit of Imagination.

Who Wants to Be a Millionaire—Play It!

Overall Rating: ✪✪✪✪

Attraction Debut: 2001

Yep, it's just like the show. It's also just like the version they've added at Disney's California Adventure. Turn to page 117 for the details. And yes, that's our final answer.

Fairy Fact: While the attraction makes a point of introducing a new host, there have been several special occasions for which Regis himself has presided over the game in episodes that were later broadcast on ABC.

Jim Henson's Muppetvision 3-D

Overall Rating: ✪✪✪✪✪

Attraction Debut: 1991

Identical in virtually every way (except here there's a cute

fountain with Miss Piggy out front) to its Disney's California Adventure clone, turn to page 117 for the scoop.

Fairy Fact: Waldo, the film's vivacious "spirit of 3-D" (who we think looks like a cross between a puppy, a butterfly, and a potato), is not, as many assume, a new character. He was actually created for the short-lived ABC series *The Jim Henson Hour* and was the first computer-generated puppet (which means that a puppeteer controlled his movements by wearing a glove hooked into a computer).

New York Street
Overall Rating: ✪✪✪
Attraction Debut: 1989

New York, New York—a helluva town. And here on the New York Street, Washington Square Park and the Empire State Building are conveniently just a few feet away. The area is designed to give guests a feel for what a backlot replica of New York looks like—and, in fact, Disney does occasionally close parts of the street for shooting. Photo opportunities abound—including a great *Singin' in the Rain* shot where you can hold a stuck-in-place umbrella, push a button, and bust out a tune as water showers down. We recommend "Flashdance—What a Feeling."

Fairy Fact: As on many Hollywood studio backlots, the New York Street skyline uses forced perspective. Buildings are much smaller than their real-life counterparts, making them seem much farther away from the foreground than they are. The effect makes the entire thing look longer. Don't try this at home.

Honey, I Shrunk the Kids Movie Set Adventure
Overall Rating: ✪
Attraction Debut: 1990

Unless you have kids—or have a bizarre fixation on the set of the musical *Cats*—you may want to skip this well-executed playground made up of larger-than-life objects. Younguns will get a kick out of roaming around, but the charm for adults is considerably less.

Fairy Fact: The play area features 45 stalks of steel grass, each towering 30 feet high. Each was tested in a tunnel with 80 mph gusts to make sure it could withstand the Florida weather.

Sounds Dangerous

Overall Rating: ✪
Attraction Debut: 1999

When Disney-MGM Studios first opened, its mission was largely to entertain while educating guests about the making of the movies. Sounds Dangerous is the latest incarnation of the Sound Studio portion. Once an informative look at sound effects with Chevy Chase and Martin Short, this new, lazy version featuring Drew Carey is neither educational nor entertaining. See it only if you're in love with Drew or desperately trying to get out of the rain.

Fairy Fact: To achieve the effect of 3-D sound, Drew Carey actually wore tiny microphones in his ears during shooting.

Indiana Jones™ Epic Stunt Spectacular

Overall Rating: ✪✪✪
Attraction Debut: 1989

Jeffrey still finds himself panting over Harrison Ford in *Raiders of the Lost Ark,* and this truly incredible stunt show re-creates some of Harrison's best moments (minus Harrison, unfortunately)—including the film's electrifying opening sequence. The immense sets and tremendous effects make this lengthy show worth the wait. "Let's give it up for the stunt guys who do this, like, seven times a day," crows Erin from Garden City, N.Y. "Incredible." If you want to be one of the nine or 10 volunteers chosen to participate in the show, you need to get there *early*!

Fairy Fact: The original conception for this attraction had nothing to do with Indiana Jones. It was simply planned as a stunt show. When Disney signed a deal with George Lucas to bring Star Tours to the park, however, Indy was added to the mix and the show had to be completely overhauled just before the park opened.

Star Tours

Overall Rating: ✪✪✪✪
Attraction Debut: 1990

For a description, slam on the light speed to page 98 for the details.

Fairy Fact: In the video shown just prior to boarding, all of the seated guests, with the exception of Chewbacca and a few Ewoks, are Imagineers and their families.

🍴 The Hollywood Brown Derby

Price: Moderate/Expensive
Meals: L, D

This slice right out of old Hollywood is the only physical reminder we have of what was one of the classic restaurants of the stars. While there used to be four Brown Derby restaurants in Los Angeles, none are standing today. Luckily Disney has kept the tradition alive, including caricatures of stars on the walls and the restaurant's delicious signature Cobb salad. For dessert try the grapefruit cake. Sounds weird. Tastes amazing.

🍴 Sci-Fi Dine-In Theater Restaurant

Price: Moderate
Meals: L, D

Miss those days of the science fiction double feature at your local drive-in? Or maybe you just wish you'd been able to experience them the first time around. Either way, the Sci-Fi Dine-In offers one of the strongest sensory experiences of any restaurant in the parks. Walk into this large soundstage and you'll feel like you're outside at night. You're seated in a car (which comes complete with a table) facing a large movie screen that plays trailers and clips from any number of creepy B flicks. "Eating in a Nash Rambler while watching old movie clips can't be beat," states Sue from Wayland, Mass. All seats face the screen, which will make it difficult to carry on a serious conversation if you're in a group of three or more (then again, that could be a plus). The food is better and more elaborate than you'd think. Yes, they have burgers, but there's also grilled tuna, pasta with shrimp, and salmon. But we love the rich ice cream shakes and crispy onion rings.

❶ Mama Melrose's Ristorante Italiano

Price: Moderate

Meals: L, D

Surprisingly tasty Italian food. The wood-fired specialty pizzas are great. Eddie liked his seafood pasta a little too much—the Tramp nuzzled a scallop across the red-and-white checked tablecloth to a very startled Jeffrey.

❷ Hollywood & Vine

Price: Moderate

Meals: B, L

This cafeteria-esque restaurant has a little of everything. It's fine, but nothing special. It's also kinda noisy. Erin from Garden City, questioning the place's veracity: "Where are all the transvestite hookers?"

❶ 50s Prime-Time Cafe

Price: Moderate

Meals: L, D

Remember the good old days when mother and father would gather kids around the television for a home-cooked

meal and *I Love Lucy*? Of course not. Those are notions fabricated by the right wing to fuel its "family values" campaign. Still, it's a sweet notion, and one you can dive right into as you cozy into a booth equipped with (or within eyeshot of) a black-and-white TV playing clips from your favorite old shows. A sassy waiter or waitress will help you select from "Mom's" menu. The somewhat pricey comfort food, from meat loaf to the more exotic, is great—especially the tuna sandwich. "This is the only good food at Disney-MGM," states Michael from New York City. "Perfect for the homesick mama's boy."

Chapter Thirteen
Disney's Animal Kingdom Park

W hat sets Disney's Animal Kingdom apart from all the other Disney-themed areas is that it's a living park, full of exotic animals and plants. Visiting there, you will never have the same experience twice. The newest park (it opened in 1998 at a cost of close to a billion dollars) to Walt Disney World Resort, Disney's Animal Kingdom is disappointing to some for its lack of rides (something Disney has been working to amend), although the park was not created with the intention of being a "ride park"—it was supposed to be all about the animals. And boy, are there a lot of animals (about 1,500), not to mention plants (more than 4 million). Because the park is so large (more than 500 acres, compared to the Magic Kingdom's 107), it can take a while to get around, so we recommend leaving the stilettos at home.

There's no doubt in our minds that Disney's Animal Kingdom was designed by every homo in the Disney corral. It is motif-land with splashes of Santa Fe colors on every garbage can, lamppost, and bench contained within the five "lands" of this kingdom. Whether it's the perfectly thatched roofs of Africa, the ornate designs of Asia, or the gorgeously carved Tree of Life, the attention to detail is so overwhelming, Eddie got the vapors.

With the exception of the massive Rainforest Cafe at the entry gate, there are no table-service restaurants in the park. If it's really hot, you'll probably want to go in the morning when the park opens so that by the time you're about to evaporate, you can hit the resort pools or the water parks.

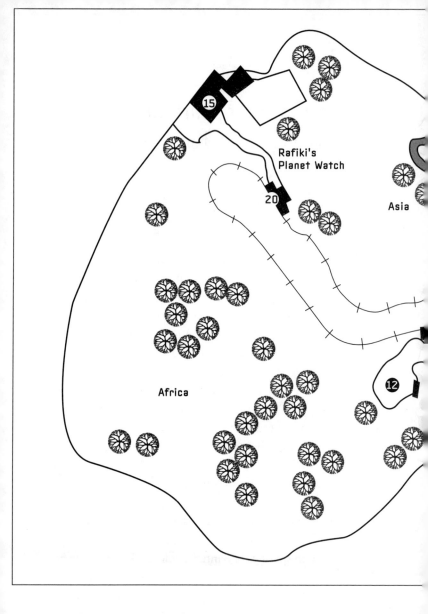

Rafiki's
Planet Watch

Asia

Africa

1. Boneyard
2. Cretaceous Trail
3. Dinosaur
4. Festival of the Lion King
5. Flights of Wonder
6. Guest Relations
7. Harambe Village
8. Kali River Rapids
9. Kilimanjaro Safaris
10. Maharajah Jungle Trek
11. Main Entrance

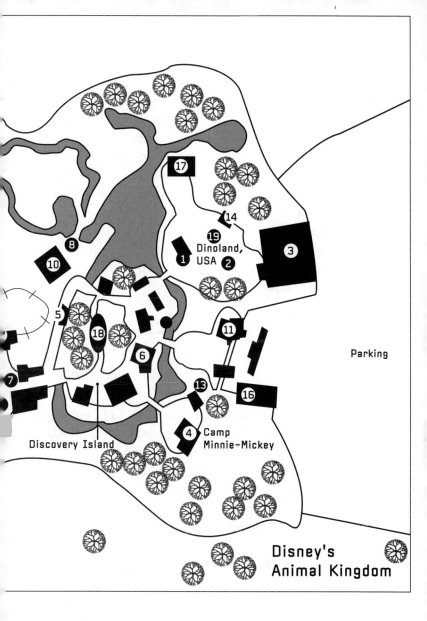

12. Pangani Forest Exploration Trail
13. Pocahontas and Her Forest Friends
14. Primeval Whirl
15. Rafiki's Planet Watch
16. Rainforest Cafe
17. Theater in the Wild
18. Tree of Life/It's Tough to Be a Bug
19. Triceratop Spin
20. Wildlife Express (Train to Rafiki's)

There have been complaints that as a theme park, others are better, and as a zoo, others are better. A combination of the two doesn't particularly help. Disney stresses that this park is something altogether different, with an emphasis on conservation and preservation (brochures on the Disney Wildlife Conservation Fund can be found everywhere). But it should be noted that Disney's Animal Kingdom is still new and hasn't yet fully grown into itself. Like all of the parks, this one needs to go through its awkward stage before it can emerge as a star.

Getting There: Disney's Animal Kingdom is reachable only by car or bus.

The Oasis

Walking into Animal Kingdom, there's the immediate sense that you're in a theme park unlike any other. While it is crowded (it is Disney, after all), the typical hustle and bustle is replaced by a majestic serenity, created by the lush landscaping and winding paths that make up the entrance area, The Oasis. Exotic birds, massive flowering trees, waterfalls, anteaters, and iguanas set the tone, which, frankly, we ignore until we leave. Sorry, but there are lines up ahead and rides to ride before the crowds hit. Catch the flowers and the birds on the way out. They ain't goin' anywhere.

Discovery Island

Discovery Island is essentially the Main Street, U.S.A. of Disney's Animal Kingdom, with bridges connecting to the four other lands in the park (which, with the exception of a path between Africa and Asia, do not interconnect). Overshadowing everything in the park (except possibly Jeffrey's ego) is The Tree of Life, which stands as the centerpiece to this land as well as to the park. The 145-foot-tall (fake) tree is adorned with thousands of green (fake) leaves

and has 325 images of different animals elaborately carved into its (fake) trunk. Did we mention the tree isn't real? Surrounding the tree in a variety of pens are (not fake) animals like Galapagos tortoises and red kangaroos, all ready for you and your camera. And inside the tree is the fantastic attraction It's Tough to Be a Bug. While the island may be light on amusements, it's definitely big on stuff to buy. Eddie often spends a lot of time (much to Jeffrey's chagrin) at Wonders of the Wild, which features unusual gifts that don't necessarily have "Disney" stamped all over them (those items you can find across the way at the Island Mercantile shop). African wood carvings and Malaysian sarongs are available at roughly the price you'd pay for a plane ticket to those places. That's not to say we didn't shop there. We just like to complain. Pizzafari has pizza, pasta, salads, and sandwiches, none of which are particularly outstanding, while the Flame Tree Barbecue offers a variety of meats and salads. Unless you're about to pass out from blood-sugar dips, we don't really recommend either of them.

It's Tough to Be a Bug
Overall Rating: ✪✪✪✪
Attraction Debut: 1998

Located inside the base of the elaborate Tree of Life, this attraction is identical to its Disney's California Adventure counterpart. Climb over to page 113 for the info.
Fairy Fact: While Dave Foley re-creates his *Bug's Life* character here, Kevin Spacey opted out. And that's the last time you'll see the words *Kevin Spacey* and *out* in the same sentence.

Camp Minnie-Mickey

While we'd like to envision this land as a work camp at which Mickey & Co. croon out "Chain Gang" and other prison hits before hooking up with Jeff Stryker in the barracks, Camp Minnie-Mickey is actually Disney's Animal Kingdom's bow to the toddlers for whom the real live furries don't cut it. Those kids are here to pose for Kodak moments with people entombed in carpeting and that's what they're gonna get! So it is here that Pooh, Pluto, and Pocahontas sign autographs (the latter even performs an animal act, but we digress). This land means one thing and one thing only to us: the best theme park show we've seen: The Festival of the Lion King. So our advice? Get there, see the show, and get the hell out before you find yourself stuck watching Pocahontas talk to birds.

The Festival of the Lion King

Overall Rating: ✪✪✪✪✪
Attraction Debut: 1998

As we've made abundantly clear, we don't like theme park shows. We'd sooner wait in line for the parking tram than sit through some of the dreck we've endured. That said, we'd have to call The Festival of the Lion King an achievement so fabulous, if it's all you saw at Disney's Animal Kingdom, it would be worth park admission. Unlike so many other shows based on the animated classics, this one makes no attempt to rehash the film's plot with bits of dialogue thrown in to link the songs. Rather, this is a truly extraordinary festival that includes impressive displays of acrobatics, fire-eating, dance, aerial tricks, and exceptional live vocals along with animatronic character floats. Keith from Orlando enjoys the "hot little tumble monkeys in unitards." Throw in the fact that the dancers are in head-to-toe spandex and, well, we're sold, hook, line, and sinker.

Fairy Fact: You like the Festival? You can catch it up to 10 times a day. There are two casts that split the day with exhaustive back-to-back performances.

The iconic Tree of Life

Pocahontas and Her Forest Friends
Overall Rating: ✪
Attraction Debut: 1998

The sassy Grandmother Willow was one of our favorite characters in Disney's film *Pocahontas,* and thank God she enlivens this otherwise innocuous live animal show in which sincere Pocahontas, wearing little more than some deerskin and an armband, introduces "her forest friends"—animals indigenous to North America—which include an armadillo, a skunk, and several rabbits (an animal whose sex life Jeffrey can relate to). While the 12-minute presentation emphasizes the importance of saving the forests and endangered species, it's basically for kids—and for people without the advantage of advice from us.

Fairy Fact: While food is permitted just about everywhere in the parks, you can't bring any into this show. It seems that Pocahontas's forest friends are even more interested in being *your* friend if you have something edible.

Africa

Designed with Swahili influence, this section of the park is remarkably beautiful, even when Jeffrey breaks into Toto's '80s pop hit of the land's name. Much of what people expect of Disney's Animal Kingdom, and much of what it delivers, is African-inspired. So it is therefore unsurprising that this section of Disney's Animal Kingdom is the park's most successful. Guests enter through Harambe village, an authentic looking Swahili marketplace with live musical performers setting the tone. Hippos and gorillas—one of whom looked suspiciously like someone Eddie had met at Pleasure Island the night before—dot the Pangani Forest Exploration Trail. Tusker House Restaurant offers a wide variety of foods, and you can pretty much guess what the Kusafiri Coffee Shop & Bakery is ready to sell ya. The Dawa Bar seemed to have cocktails flowing awfully early—woo-hoo!

Kilimanjaro Safaris

Overall Rating: ✪✪✪✪✪

Attraction Debut: 1999

At 110 acres, the Safari, the attraction for which Disney's Animal Kingdom is best known, takes up as much space as the entire Magic Kingdom. Its creation was a massive undertaking but well worth the effort. Here, guests are treated to a reasonable facsimile of a safari expedition on the African savannah, complete with rickety jeeps on dusty dirt roads. Zebras, wildebeest, ostriches, giraffes, and antelope roam freely and close to transport vehicles while the slightly more dangerous types like hippos, rhinos, and lions are securely kept at bay by unseen barriers. The 25-minute journey is truly spectacular. Of course, this being Disney, the safari was given a theme and story in which we, photo tourists, end up foiling the evil plans of some mean old elephant poachers. The story is lame and distracting, particularly when the acting skills of your guide could fit comfortably on *Baywatch Nights,* but it wouldn't be Disney without it. And with so much splendor here, it's hard to quibble.

Fairy Fact: Most of the trees on the savannah are actually made of concrete and hung with real leaves to lure the giraffes.

The Pangani Forest Exploration Trail

Overall Rating: ✪✪

Attraction Debut: 1999

Though less thrilling than the Maharajah Jungle Trek (see page 220), this one features hippos and gorillas. Or, as we like to call them, our exes.

Fairy Fact: That cool bamboo between you and the gorillas? It's made of steel.

Rafiki's Planet Watch

Blast off into outer space and get a look at Earth from miles above! Just kidding. This backstage look at how Disney cares for animals as well as the company's dedication to protecting the environment was not a highlight—despite the presence of a petting zoo (with goats!). Go once, if you must (especially if you're with Greenpeace or PETA), and see for yourself. Then go kill something to, you know, balance it out.

Asia

Disney's Animal Kingdom's Asia has very little to do with Asia as we commonly think of it. Rather, it's the Asian jungle of Nepal and Thailand. No pagodas or kimonos here. And since jungle is, by definition, bereft of architecture, it's not always so easy to distinguish Asia as Asia. The animals, however, do help. Small monkeys (gibbons, say the signs) romp on ancient temple ruins while Bengal tigers and Komodo dragons inhabit a walking tour. There's also a river rapids ride, which reminded us of our own ignorance—who knew there were whitewater rapids in Asia? We did know to expect bamboo, and there's plenty of that. Phew.

The Maharajah Jungle Trek
Overall Rating: ✪✪✪
Attraction Debut: 1999

So named because the animals are housed in the ruins of a maharajah's palace, the Trek is well worth trekking for some stunning animals. Magnificent tigers can be found here, and even though they're usually catatonic from the heat, they are breathtaking, with claws that put catty bitches like us to shame. There's a hut housing giant fruit bats, which, when they open their wings, are truly terrifying (flying rodents were never our thing). Then there are the gibbons, happily showing off their little red butts without an iota of shame. Who says we can't learn from the animal world?

Fairy Fact: Not only are the Malayan flying foxes, featured on the walk, the largest bats in the world, this is also the only place you can see them in North America.

Kali River Rapids

Overall Rating: ✪✪
Attraction Debut: 1999

There's something very sexy about water getting sprayed all over you—especially if you're in a whitewater river raft with some hotties coasting through a rainforest being doused by—oops, it's over. While it starts off with a wonderfully ominous trip up a steep hill covered with mist, this water ride doesn't live up to expectations. It *could* be great—if it were just about two minutes longer. As it is, it's good, and there are some nice effects (apparently there's some story about logging gone awry which we missed), and it's an excellent way to cool down on a steamy day. We just know that if we're going to sacrifice our coiffed hair, it oughta be better.

Fairy Fact: Inside the shrine you walk through during your wait in line, elaborate hand-painted murals on the ceiling depict a legend of Bangkok. What this legend is, we have no idea. But there you go.

Flights of Wonder

Overall Rating: ✪
Attraction Debut: 1998

Call us flighty, but we really didn't care much about the skills of birds like falcons and owls. Apparently Disney thinks you will, because the theater seats 1,000. But the chicken was amusing.

Fairy Fact: While the birds are indeed trained, they are actually just showing off their own natural skills. This means no tap-dancing turkeys.

Dinoland U.S.A.

As we've noted, the main attraction of Disney's Animal Kingdom is the presence of live animals, and Dinoland

U.S.A. is no exception. Dozens of live dinos wander around. Whoops—our mistake! Just another bus tour. Anyway, this land (sponsored by McDonald's, signs for which you can see at every turn) is actually a lot of fun, mostly because it's the one area of the park where fantasy can kick in (after all, none of us actually knew any dinosaurs—other than Eddie's ex). There are winding paths to meander featuring statues of the big lizards (if you're daring, you can climb on top of them for a cute photo) as well as some living creatures like soft-shell turtles, Chinese alligators, and other animals that survived the prehistoric world. The newly added Chester & Hester's Dino-Rama! themed fairground area offers more rides as well as carny games for which you can pay additional bucks to win a crappy stuffed animal. And for you scientific types, there's Dino-Sue, the largest, most complete Tyrannosaurus skeleton ever put together (she's still got 90% of her bones, making her more real than Cher). There's also a McDonald's, but, so help us God, if we catch you there, we will shoot and kill you.

Dinosaur

Overall Rating: ✪✪✪✪✪
Attraction Debut: 1998
⭐

While Jeffrey wishes he could go back in time to remember a particularly blurry night in Chelsea sometime in 1995, Dinosaur (originally called Countdown to Extinction) sends you back 65 million years (happy birthday, Eddie!) to bring back a living dinosaur. Observant eyes will notice that the beastie you're after is Aladar, the Iguanadon who starred in Disney's film *Dinosaur.* Of course, things go wrong, as these things do, and you find yourself racing to get back to the present without being eaten by a carnotaurus or obliterated by meteors. The ride is pretty intense, making quick and sudden movements, and may be scary for some kids (or adults), but

the Audio-Animatronics are amazing. And Jeffrey caught himself screaming like a big girl more than once.

Fairy Fact: The preshow is hosted by Phylicia Rashad (who, show queens will remember, replaced Bernadette Peters on Broadway in *Into the Woods*) and Wallace Langham, who played the is-he-or-isn't-he-gay assistant on *Veronica's Closet*.

Triceratop Spin
Overall Rating: ✪
Attraction Debut: 2001

Essentially another variation on the Dumbo ride, where passengers enter a four-person car and spin around as they control the elevation. Whee!

Fairy Fact: The opening of this ride marked the fourth *spin*-off from the Dumbo ride after Astro Orbitor at Disneyland, and the Magic Kingdom's Astro Orbiter (yeah, the spelling is different) and The Magic Carpets of Aladdin.

Primeval Whirl
Overall Rating: ✪✪✪
Attraction Debut: 2002

Take Mulholland Madness (the hairpin turn coaster at Disney's California Adventure), lengthen the track with some new curves, and throw in cars that spin around when you hit said curves, and you have a roller coaster unlike any other. (You also have a good way to lose your lunch, if you eat right before climbing aboard.) How the attraction fits into Animal Kingdom (your disc-shaped vehicle is really a space machine which sends you back to a colorful, 2-dimensional dino-world) is a bit of a stretch, but the park definitely needed a kick.

Fairy Fact: To help make the queue move more swiftly, there are actually two tracks, but thanks to some cleverly-places mirrors, you can't tell from the line.

Chapter Fourteen
The Rest of the Resort

Nighttime at
Walt Disney World Resort

Being at the Walt Disney World Resort means you have a whopping variety of stuff to do at night—and we're not talking about trolling the bathhouses—both inside the parks and inside the resort.

The Magic Kingdom, Epcot, and Disney-MGM Studios all have their own shows and parades in the evening (Disney's Animal Kingdom closes too early for after-dark events). Because many of these things can be seasonal or temporary, we suggest checking online ahead of time or consulting the complimentary brochures Disney hands out at the park gates. The Magic Kingdom has the wonderful **Fantasy in the Sky** fireworks display, which is truly jaw-dropping. (If you've already left the park and want to be able to see the fireworks, we recommend getting a reservation at the California Grill inside Disney's Contemporary Resort.) There's also the semipsychedelic **SpectroMagic**, which is kind of like a more contemporary version of Disney's Electrical Parade (but "the music isn't nearly as annoying," notes Keith from Orlando). And sometimes one of the other parades runs at night.

Epcot offers the eye-popping **IllumiNations**, which takes place in the middle of the World Showcase Lagoon and combines music, lights, lasers, water, fireworks, and projections to create an amazing celebration of the world's diverse cultures. While it's not required viewing, it's definitely worth seeing if your schedule permits. (For premium viewing you can also rent a pontoon boat by calling [407] WDW-PLAY.)

At Disney-MGM Studios, you can always catch a performance of the fantastic **Fantasmic!** (see page 199) and sometimes one of their parades runs at night as well.

If you're staying at one of the Magic Kingdom resorts on the water (which is pretty much all of 'em), you can catch Disney's longest running parade: the **Electric Water Pageant.** Started in 1971, this barrage of barges illuminated by lights floats by all the hotels nightly, chirping out synthesized versions of Disney tunes. It's a blast to watch. And Jeffrey doesn't care if the guy is made out of lights—he thinks the Triton is kinda hot.

Definitely check out our section on **Downtown Disney** for some lively nightspots. There you can twirl like you've never twirled before on the rotating dance floor at **Mannequin's Dance Palace** on Pleasure Island or catch one of your favorites bands of today (or yesterday) at **House of Blues** on West Side.

Disney's BoardWalk Resort also offers a variety of nighttime activities, including **Atlantic Dance,** where you can show off your swing skills, the piano bar **Jellyrolls,** and the everything-sports **ESPN Club.** Check out our resort reviews for details on BoardWalk.

Many of the hotel bars are open late, for that nightcap with the guy you met in line for "small world."

Orlando itself also has a pretty rocking gay nightlife scene. Please refer to our **Orlando Gay Life** section for details.

Downtown Disney

My, how you've grown. Once just a quaint little shopping area called the Village, the area has exploded into Disney's primary nightlife area. Created to compete directly with Orlando's own bars, Downtown has succeeded in luring locals

© Disney Enterprises, Inc.

A Lego dragon emerges at Downtown Disney

from miles around, while ensuring that Disney's own guests don't leave the property.

There are three sections to Downtown Disney: the Marketplace (the original "village"), Pleasure Island (with booze

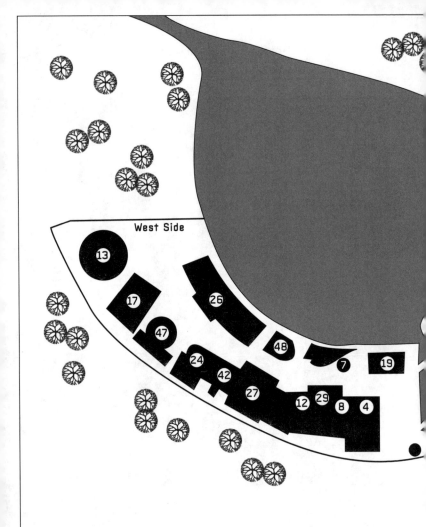

West Side

1. 2 R's Reading and Riting
2. 8 Trax
3. Adventurer's Club
4. AMC Pleasure Island 24
5. The Art of Disney
6. BET Soundstage
7. Bongo's
8. Disney's Candy Cauldron
9. Cap'n Jack's Restaurant
10. Captain's Toy Tower
11. Celebrity Eyeworks Studios
12. Changing Attitudes
13. Cirque du Soleil/La Nouba

14. Comedy Warehouse
15. Disney's Days of Christmas
16. Disney at Home
17. DisneyQuest
18. Eurospain
19. Forty Thirst Street
20. Fulton's Crab House
21. Garden Center
22. Ghirardelli
23. Gourmet Pantry
24. Guitar Gallery
25. Harrington Bay Clothiers
26. House of Blues

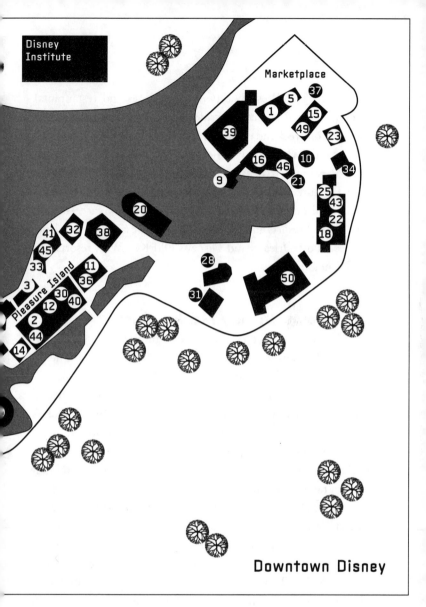

Disney Institute

Marketplace

Pleasure Island

Downtown Disney

27. Hoypoloi
28. Lego Imagination Center
29. Magnetron
30. Mannequins
31. McDonald's
32. Motion
33. Mouse House
34. Once Upon A Toy
35. Planet Hollywood
36. Pleasure Island Jazz Company
37. Pooh Corner
38. Portobello Yacht Club

39. Rainforest Café
40. Reel Finds
41. Rock 'n' Roll Beach Club
42. Sosa Family Cigars
43. Studio M
44. Superstar Studios
45. Suspended Animation
46. Team Mickey
47. Virgin Megastore
48. Wolfgang Puck's
49. Wolfgang Puck Express
50. World of Disney

and clubs), and West Side (with megastores and restaurants). Everything is nicely set alongside a large lake. The place is most crowded on weekend evenings. It's generally busy every night as well as days when the weather is crappy. It's slowest on sunny days. Parking is free, as is admission to Marketplace and West Side. Pleasure Island is free until 7 P.M., when a $19.95 (as of press time) admission must be paid. Downtown Disney is accessible by bus from all resorts and theme parks. It's accessible by boat from Disney's Port Orleans and Disney's Old Key West resorts and the Disney Institute.

Downtown Disney Marketplace

The Marketplace retains some of the intimacy of the village thanks to its low buildings and lovely lake views. There's also a small carousel and a train for kids to ride.

It's worth noting that stores like **The Art of Disney, Disney's Days of Christmas,** and **World of Disney** (the globe's largest Disney store) offer the same merchandise found in the parks, but shopping here is significantly saner. And like in the parks, packages can be delivered directly to your room if you're staying on property.

Other shops include: **2 R's Reading and Riting,** which is full of Disney books; the Pooh-filled (get your minds out of the gutter!) **Pooh Corner; Disney at Home,** which offers items for the bed, bath, and beyond; the **Gourmet Pantry; Captain's Toy Tower; Harrington Bay Clothiers,** which carries designs by Lauren and Hilfiger (but since you're in Disney, wouldn't you rather have a mouse on your polo shirt?); the brand new **Once Upon a Toy;** the sports-themed **Team Mickey;** the crystal shop **Eurospain; LEGO Imagination Center;** and **Ghirardelli** chocolatiers. Jeffrey left Eddie there for six hours once. Eddie still has no memory of where the time went. It's sad, really.

There are many places to eat in the Marketplace as well.

The chains include the immense jungle-themed **Rainforest Cafe;** the counter-service **Wolfgang Puck Express,**which features some of Wolfie's signature dishes, like his Chinese chicken salad and delicious pizzas; and **McDonald's,** for those of you who can't be without a McNugget for more than 24 hours. Two other places are noteworthy:

🍴 Cap'n Jack's Restaurant

If it's seafood you landlubbers are after, yer in the right place. Mostly good seafood is whipped up here at the sit-down eatery on the lake. Lunch and dinner are served at this moderately priced (though expensive for the pricier fishies) restaurant.

🍴 Fulton's Crab House

Located on the large ferryboat adjacent to what really is Pleasure Island (but Disney insists it's in the Marketplace, so who are we to argue?) is one of the finest restaurants on Disney property. It's so good that Jeffrey's family (his biological one) has actually spent no less than *three* Thanksgivings enjoying the expensive-but-worth-it fresh seafood. Lobster, shrimp, crab—you name it. And as mouthwatering as the entrées are, the desserts are just as good. (Priority seating recommended.)

Pleasure Island

Remember when the characters in Pinocchio went off to Pleasure Island? No school—just fun all the time! Well, welcome to Pleasure Island minus the fear of turning into a donkey and being lugged off to a salt mine (although we cannot promise that after a few cocktails you won't become an ass). We love Pleasure Island because it's the area of Walt Disney World Resort actually designed for full-grown, post-pubescent humans. Local singles converge there along with park staff who go to get off after they've gotten off. Trust us, cruising is much easier here than in the line for Dumbo.

The stores on Pleasure Island are open during the day, and Δadmission is free until 7 P.M. (the Portobello Yacht Club restaurant, while on the Island, is accessible from outside the gates). After 7 P.M. you need to be 18 or older to enter unless accompanied by a parent or legal guardian, and you need to be 21 to get into Mannequins sand BET SoundStage Club. The clubs remain open until 2 A.M. nightly, and every night at midnight it's New Years Eve. There's also some fun shopping to be done on the Island. Stores include **Reel Finds,** which is chockfull of movie and television memorabilia; the clothing store **Changing Attitudes; Suspended Animation,** which offers Disney collectibles; **Mouse House;** and **Superstar Studios,** where you can finally make your own recording of "The Wind Beneath My Wings." God help us all.

There's one noteworthy restaurant on the Island, **Portobello Yacht Club**, and while we're not quite sure how a nautical theme fits with an Italian eatery, this is a fabulous place to eat. Priority seating recommended.

And now, a-clubbing we will go. Here's how the nightspots make out.

Pleasure Island Jazz Co.

Oh, baby, won't you play me Le Jazz Hot? The music is always hot at this club. Live performances keep it humming.

Motion

Pop goes the nightclub, as this dance house plays everything from pop dance to pop alternative. The decor is a little on the minimalist side, but Jeffrey thinks the *Tiger Beat* eye candy is mighty tasty. You might wanna double-check their ID before you start plying them with liquor.

Mannequins

While some people come here for the way-out rotating dance floor, cool catwalks, and amazing light displays, we're

here because for many years Thursday nights have served as an unofficial gay night at this club. Originally Thursday was Disney cast member night on Pleasure Island, and the gay employees (we hear there are a couple) gravitated to Mannequins, which at the time was adorned with mannequins dressed as characters from Broadway shows (*Dreamgirls, Cats, Phantom*—we're not kidding). Alas, the kitsch is gone, but the gays (on Thursdays, anyway) remain.

Rock N Roll Beach Club

This three-story surfin' safari boasts music from the '50s onward. It was a little "bridge and tunnel" for our taste (we could barely see over the hair). But great for the Jersey girl in all of us. Or some of us.

8TRAX

Looking for a little retro fun? This place is always jamming with the best of the '70s and '80s. If you wanna hear "It's Raining Men," this is your best bet. But if you want them to rain on you, head back to Mannequins.

Comedy Warehouse

If you like improvisational comedy, this place can be surprisingly terrific. "Definitely worth going to," states David from Boston. "When you walk in from the back of the audience, try and sit on the right-hand side by the phone hanging on the wall—about halfway back. You'll thank me later." We have no idea what he's talking about, but we'll thank him now.

Adventurers Club

It's like the Tiki Room on acid (not that we would know what acid is like). Enter this wild and exotic hunting lodge where the characters on the walls talk to you. This was all tons of fun until Jeffrey stumped one of the creatures at Broadway trivia. They picked on us for the rest of the night. Definitely worth a stop and a fruity cocktail.

BET SoundStage Club

Love the rhythms of R&B and hip-hop? Then the SoundStage has got your groove.

West Side

Everything on the West Side feels like it's on steroids. And this isn't necessarily a bad thing. It's just a big thing. Shops include: the smoothie and coffee shop **Forty Thirst Street; Magnetron,** which features enough magnets to attract a 747; **Disney's Candy Cauldron; Sosa Family Cigars; Virgin Megastore;** the eclectic art store **Hoypoloi; Celebrity Eyeworks Studios;** and the well-stocked **Guitar Gallery,** which offers a dizzying array of custom and collector guitars.

You can also catch a flick at **AMC Pleasure Island 24** or dine at the numerous restaurants, which include the chains **Planet Hollywood** (where we love the Crunch Chicken—made with addictive Cap'n Crunch!) and the always solid **House of Blues,** where you can catch performances by a rocking array of performers from Rick Springfield to Taylor Dayne.

Other noteworthy eateries include:

🍴 Bongos

Everybody's favorite conga queen, Gloria Estefan, and her husband, Emilio, bring you this sumptuous Cuban delight. "The best and most reliable food in Downtown Disney," states Michael from Miami Beach, Fla. And who doesn't want to eat in a giant pineapple?

🍴 Wolfgang Puck

This restaurant has more tiers than a wedding cake. There are the Express section, B's Lounge & Sushi Bar, The Cafe, and the Dining Room. To be honest, we recommend going across to the Marketplace for their Express. The

Dining Room aspires to be an Orlando version of Spago, but it doesn't quite cut it. Sorry, Wolfgang, we still love your Beverly Hills flagship.

Other noteworthy entertainment includes:

DisneyQuest

West Side also has one of the country's only remaining DisneyQuest cyber gaming centers. Wanna build your own roller coaster and then ride it? How about taking a trip on Aladdin's magic carpet? Or a jungle trek? This interactive indoor theme park is pretty amazing. CyberSpace Mountain allows you to actually design your dream coaster and then get inside a tiny capsule to see what it would be like. The technology is astounding, and if you have time (or the lines aren't terribly long) it's a blast—although Eddie, who can handle any real coaster, gets nauseated here. They also have a delicious counter-service restaurant that serves up treats from the Cheesecake Factory. Admission is separate (although included on some multiday passes).

La Nouba

And last but not least, West Side is home to Cirque du Soleil and its show *La Nouba*. Cirque, which has been touring the country for years and has two permanent shows in Vegas, is a circus unlike any other. In 1998 it created another permanent spectacle, *La Nouba,* for Downtown Disney. Unlike all of Cirque's other shows, this one, in an effort to cater to the kid-friendly environment, is an intermissionless 90 minutes with a slightly heavier clown concentration. Like all of Cirque's other shows, it's a surreal animal-free circus featuring a whole lot of spandex and bare, muscular flesh. This ain't your grandma's big top, honey, but it is fabulous and wholly up to Cirque's standards. Admission is separate.

Water Parks

To Disney, even a water park is more than just a water park. It's a chance to go theme-crazy, whether it's exploring the shipwrecked setting of Typhoon Lagoon, the old-time watering hole of River Country, or the most inventive, the ski resort-themed Blizzard Beach. That said, before venturing to one of them, a couple of things must be kept in mind. First off, we'd like to remind those of you whose bathing suits are on the, um, skimpy side, that on a water slide, a Speedo becomes a thong in under three seconds. Secondly, you can't expect to visit the water parks during peak seasons without a preponderance of kids romping it up and seasoning the water as only they do. For that reason, we like to go during the dinner hour. It's not quite as hot out, but it's significantly quieter. The early hours are also much calmer, but for our money they're better spent avoiding lines in the parks than in the water.

While admission is separate (although included in some multiday passports), parking is free. You can bring your own coolers, but leave the booze in your room. (Do you really need to be drunk on a water slide? It's not pretty. We know.) Lockers and towels are available to rent. (Don't tell Disney, but we recommend you take towels from your room.) Disney swears the water temperatures are controlled, but we still think sliding's more fun in the warmer weather. Of course, the parks are also a good place to people-watch. All water parks are accessible via buses from the resorts.

River Country

This swimming hole is so authentically rustic, Jeffrey was just waiting for a hunky Tom Sawyer and a beefy Huck Finn to go swooping down the cable ride into the waters (provided that both Huck and Tom were over 18 years of age, of course). Blending into the woodsy feel of the Fort

Wilderness Resort and Campground that surrounds it, this was the first of the Disney water parks and has managed to retain its more intimate feel. Of course, intimacy has its price (story of our lives), and the park has fewer slides (read: longer lines) than its newer, bigger siblings, Blizzard Beach and Typhoon Lagoon. But the beach is fantastic and can be very relaxing. There's one tire slide and two long and winding chutes (called Whoop-'N-Holler Hollow), which are very fun, and there's an entire section devoted to tykes called Kiddie Cove. "Good for a quiet day," says David from Boston. "But not for cruising."

Typhoon Lagoon

Set in the remains of a ramshackle village that has sustained a tropical storm (picture Gilligan's Island with 7 million screaming children), Typhoon Lagoon offers nine water slides, all of them great fun. As you climb the steps to the slides, take a close look at the stern of the moored boat. Her home port is Safen Sound, Fla. There's also the Lazy River, a serene float on an inner tube, circling the park's circumference, and Shark Reef, where, if you wait in line for eight or nine hours, you can swim in a pool with some fish for five minutes. "Lots of fun water slides and rides," says Billy from Maynard, Mass. "And you usually see quite a few hot straight boys—if you're into that sorta thing." The beach areas at Typhoon Lagoon are large and good for soaking up the cancer for an hour or two. Most notable, however, is the park's surf pool featuring waves six feet high (surfing lessons are offered every morning). Since the waves are precisely calibrated, there's absolutely no spontaneity in surfing them, but they are fun nonetheless. And it was here that Jeffrey quite literally surfed into the arms of a gentleman (term used loosely) who would remain his paramour for several days. So never let it be said that only Frankie and Annette score this way.

Go surfin' at Typhoon Lagoon

Blizzard Beach

Blizzard Beach has the distinction of being the newest, largest, and weirdest of the water parks. The concept is that of a ski slope built by a not-so-clever entrepreneur who forgot that snow in Florida is about as likely as Streisand dining at McDonald's. So what you get is the dichotomy of a ski lodge, mountains, and lift (but alas, no instructors), surrounded by water gushing down the "slopes." For effect, icicles drip on you as you wait in line. There are 17 slides in all, including Summit Plummet (a 120-foot free fall) and the Run-Off Rapids, which offer an enclosed tube experience. It's dark and creepy in there, but it is different. There's also a wave pool and several areas for kids. We enjoyed taking the ski lift up, but it wasn't worth waiting 45 minutes for the privilege. The beach at Blizzard Beach is a bit crowded for comfortably lying out. While the slides here are superior to those at the other water parks, Typhoon Lagoon, with its broader beaches, offers the better overall experience.

Other Activities

What, you mean you don't want to spend every waking minute inside a theme park? Are you crazy? OK, fine. So a few of you may actually want to do other things on your vacation. Here's some of what Disney has to offer you weirdos. For more information about all of these activities, call (407) WDW-PLAY.

Tennis

Walt Disney World Resort actually has not one, not 10, but 30 courts for all you "friends of Martina" out there (hey, we mean tennis players!). Disney's Wide World of Sports Complex has the most, with 11 green clay courts. Courts can also be found at Disney's Contemporary Resort, Disney's

Grand Floridian Resort & Spa, Disney's Yacht and Beach Clubs, and Disney's Old Key West Resort. Private lessons (are there any other kind?) and clinics are also available.

Golf

We would personally rather watch *The Apple Dumpling Gang* nonstop for a hundred years than be subjected to one round of golf. But we hear it's very popular. We're told that Disney's courses are challenging as well as gorgeous, and the PGA has been using the greens for more than 30 years. With five full courses to choose from (including the well reputed Osprey Ridge), you could spend an entire vacation without ever entering a theme park (heaven forbid!). And for those of you prepping for Dinah Shore, lessons are available.

Miniature Golf

OK, this is much more our speed. Disney has two delightful courses to play on. Disney's Winter-Summerland is adjacent to Blizzard Beach and has two 18-hole courses. One boasts a snowy theme, with snowmen and ice castles (we love that movie!). The other is more summery, with sand castles and surfboards. Disney's Fantasia Gardens, a 36-hole course and by far the gayer of the greens, offers dancing hippos, leaping fountains, and marching broomsticks—all in theme with the classic Disney film.

Boats

With more than 500 different crafts to choose from, Disney boasts the largest rental fleet of boats in the world. You can rent them from most of the resorts (well, the ones on water, at least). They have everything from the "water mouse" (cute little speedboats you can zoom around in) to canoes, sailboats, and rowboats. Naturally, we prefer the water mouse as it requires exerting the least amount of energy. Eddie likes to play *Charlie's Angels* on the speedboats. Jeffrey grouses that he always has to be Kelly.

Horseback Riding

Please don't make us stoop to "hung like a horse" jokes here, people. This is a classy book. But for those of you looking to saddle up and explore your inner cowpoke (stop it!), you can enjoy a trail ride at Disney's Fort Wilderness Resort and Campground.

Fishing

Again, not something we would go to Walt Disney World Resort to do. But hey, we're not you. Maybe you've just been dying to go bass fishing for decades and this is finally your big chance. You can join an excursion on a two-hour guided tour (rods, reels, and frosty beverages provided), and believe it or not, you may actually catch a 14-pounder. But don't think you're bringing home dinner; whatever you catch, you throw back. So they can make you pay for that bass later at dinner.

Chapter Fifteen
Orlando and Other Area Parks

<u>Orlando Gay Life</u>

While we typically don't spend too much time off Disney property when we're in Orlando, there are a surprising number of gay bars and clubs to choose from, if that's your thing. Of course, we would never venture into any such establishments. But if we were to, we might tell you that **Southern Nights** at 375 S. Bumby—we don't make these names up—([407] 898-0424) is the bar and club we like best. With an expansive outdoor area, regular drag shows, an ample dance floor, and a warm overall environment, we would be perfectly happy to park it there on any given night. **Club Firestone** (578 N. Orange, [407] 872-0066) is also quite the hopping dance spot with circuit boys and circuit wanna-bes. For a calmer, more intimate setting, **The Cactus Club** at 1300 N. Mills offers a decent environment for a mixed crowd to mingle, as does the **Peacock Room,** which is conveniently located across the street. Our lesbian friends tell us that they like **Faces** at 4910 Edgewater Dr. ([407] 291-7571). Men are welcome there too, but they're the minority.

Several Web sites offer detailed and up-to-date information including **Contax,** Florida's statewide gay rag (www.contax.com); **Watermark,** Orlando's gay newspaper (www.watermarkonline.com); and www.gayorlando.com.

If you're looking for slightly more interactive diversions, there's always **Club Orlando** at 450 E. Compton St. ([407] 425-5005). Club Orlando is unlike any other bathhouse Eddie's encountered (hey, someone's gotta do the research around here). While many bathhouses have a few pieces of neglected fitness equipment available, Club Orlando functions as a legitimate gym with plenty of people coming only to work out. There's also a full-size pool, outdoor hot tub, and full tanning deck. And then there are those little rooms for when you have some time to kill after a workout...

Finally, mention must be made of the **Parliament House** (410 N. Orange Blossom Trail), Orlando's own gay hotel complex. Typically, when a place has a big pool, rooms, a bar, a dance club, a theater, and volleyball court on its grounds, the word *resort* springs to mind. Not in this case. It's not that there's anything wrong with the Parliament House, it's just that it's sort of closer to a Motel 6 than a Hilton. But it is a fascinating establishment. The bar is frequently hopping, the theatre always has some godawful but fun gay play, Sunday tea dances are always popular and, oh yeah, there's Balcony Bingo. Otherwise known as trolling the balconies to see who's left their door ajar and is looking for company. Brings the concept of amusement park to a whole new level.

Surrounding Theme Parks—Florida

Universal Orlando

We can pretty safely bet that next to Walt Disney World Resort, the most visited tourist attraction in Orlando (if you don't count Eddie's lap) is Universal. And thanks to the recent additions of Islands of Adventure and CityWalk, Universal is more of a destination. Both parks feature Universal Express, their version of the FASTPASS. Unlike at Disney, however, you can get more than one pass at a time. Call (407) 363-8000 or visit www.universalorlando.com for information.

How to Get There: Exiting Disney property, take I-4 East (toward Orlando). Go seven miles and take Exit 30A

(Universal Boulevard.). Make a left at the light at the top of the off-ramp. You can't miss it.

Universal Studios Florida

Universal's original theme park, which opened in 1990, is also the less successful of the two Universal parks. It has only a few great rides and it's laid out terribly. Unlike the smooth circle that is Islands of Adventure or the "hub" system that Disney tends to use, Universal just sprawls. Like Disney properties, the park is divided into several lands (many of which have some fab design elements): Production Central, New York, San Francisco/Amity, Hollywood, Woody Woodpecker's Kidzone, and World Expo. But the attractions don't necessarily match the areas they're located in (explain why **Twister...Ride It Out** is in New York or why the **Wild Wild Wild West Stunt Show** is in San Francisco). And can we just note that there's a whole section devoted to San Francisco and the Castro is nowhere to be found? Who designed this place?

That's not to say a trip to Universal Studios is a wasted trip. There are some great attractions. The most recent addition (at press time) was the amazing **Men in Black Alien Attack** ride, which puts you on the streets, armed with a laser gun to blast as many wayward aliens (for points) as possible. **Back to the Future the Ride,** a flight simulator attraction based on the film, and **Terminator 2: 3-D Battle Across Time**, a 3-D film that plunges you into *T2,* are both great.

Some of the special effects attractions like the aforementioned Twister (where you stand around and witness the effects of a major tornado), **Kongfrontation** (where a ride through New York goes terribly, terribly wrong!), and **Earthquake** (do we really need to explain?) are good. But the boat ride **Jaws** is a little one-note for our taste (oh look, it's a shark). It's a little more fun on the backlot tour at the Los Angeles park, which incorporates Earthquake, Jaws, etc. on one long ride. We did find it amusing, however, that on the Jaws ride, near a half-eaten boat floats a pair of mouse ears.

And after all the hard-core action, for those of you looking for the softer side, there's **Lucy: A Tribute,** a walk-through honoring America's favorite henna-rinsed redhead. Included in the display are costume pieces. You can't get close enough to try them on, but you can certainly imagine.

Universal's Islands of Adventure

As much as we hate to admit this, Islands is probably the best designed theme park going. It may not be as magical as the Magic Kingdom, but we have to hand it to Universal's design team—the place is spectacular. Not only are the rides all superbly executed, but the attention to the detail in the park's design is incredible. If you can work an extra day into your trip, Islands is a must-see.

Unlike the Studios, Islands is broken down much more successfully into lands, which surround a giant lagoon. You enter at the Port of Entry (makes sense), which has some sort of Middle Eastern theme to it. Going clockwise you hit Marvel Super Hero Island, where numerous cute men (and women) in tights are to be found. The section boasts several amazing thrill rides, including the incredible **Incredible Hulk Coaster** (which Eddie rode with glee while Jeffrey hid) and **Doctor Doom's Freefall,** which again sent Jeffrey running. But the most outstanding ride on the island (and the park—or any park) is **The Amazing Adventures of Spider-Man,** which ingeniously combines 3-D technology with a thrilling ride as you're caught in the middle of a battle between Spidey and the baddies.

Next you hit the Toon Lagoon, where all your Sunday funnies faves come to life. If you like getting wet, you'll love **Dudley Do-Right's Ripshaw Falls,** a stellar log flume ride, and **Popeye & Bluto's Bilge-Rat Barges,** a soaks-you-to-the-bone raft voyage (where Popeye and Bluto pretend to care more

about Olive Oyl than each other), both of which feature great animatronics as well as great splashes.

As you walk through the gates of Jurassic Park, you can't help feeling like you're in the movie (too bad Laura Dern isn't here for the ladies). And the **Jurassic Park River Adventure,** where dinos dine on you (or try to), rocks. Next up is The Lost Continent and the amazing **Dueling Dragons,** a pair of inverted roller coasters that intertwine and race each other, sending you on more loops and corkscrews than Eddie's last relationship. The walk-through attraction **Poseidon's Fury: Escape From the Lost City** features some incredible special effects, if a weak plot.

Finally you arrive in Seuss Landing (or you may get here first, depending on which way you go around the lagoon). If you ever wanted to venture inside a Dr. Seuss storybook, this is your chance. From the enchanting creatures on the **Caro-Seuss-el** to the flying fish (think the Dumbo ride with trout) of **One Fish, Two Fish, Red Fish, Blue Fish** to the dark ride **The Cat in the Hat** (which reenacts the classic kid's book), it's a feast for the eyes and the senses. It even has a restaurant where you can get green eggs and ham.

The shopping is the only thing that sort of lacks. Not because they don't have some cute stuff—they do. It's just that everything from T-shirt to mug is emblazoned with "Universal's Islands of Adventure," which is annoying for someone who just wants a Cat in the Hat tank top and doesn't want to be a walking billboard for the theme park.

Although it's somewhat sacrilegious to admit this in print, we love this park. We don't come to Orlando without a visit.

CityWalk

CityWalk is very similar to Downtown Disney, although more blatantly commercial because you have to walk through CityWalk in order to get from the parking structures to the theme parks. Very clever. But we're not buying it.

Still, they do have some good restaurants, and the place is laid out much better than its claustrophobic sister in Los Angeles. Eateries include **Pastamoré,** which serves up great Italian; **Emeril's,** from chef Emeril Lagasse; and **Jimmy Buffett's Margaritaville,** which features great margaritas and beach chairs on the sidewalk to watch the passing crowd. The **Hard Rock Cafe** is always good for a solid meal, and **Hard Rock Live** often draws in top entertainment.

There's a wide variety of stores, more restaurants, and entertainment. But since you'll have to walk past it all to get to the parks, you don't need us to tell you about it.

SeaWorld

Presumably because of its proximity to the ride-heavy Disney and Universal theme parks, SeaWorld in Florida has beefed up the number of attractions it offers, which are mingled in with the numerous shows and exhibits about sea life. While Eddie can't get enough of their new roller-coaster, **Kraken** (named after some spooky sea monster), the seven turns upside down nearly made Jeffrey lose his lunch. He enjoyed the water thrill ride **Journey to Atlantis** much more. As in San Diego, visitors can see the **Shamu Experience** (we're guessing Shamu is kind of like Mickey Mouse, who manages to exist in several places at the same time). And their Cirque du Soleil-esque **Cirque de la Mer** is very amusing. While Jeffrey thought **Terrors of the Deep** was named for the girls who used to pick on him in grade school, the exhibit features some very cool toothy monsters like sharks, eels, and (ooh) barracuda.

How to get there: It's just a few miles north of Walt Disney World Resort. Take Interstate 4 east to Exit 28 and head east. For details visit www.seaworld.com or call (800) 327-2424.

Busch Gardens

While Islands of Adventure has the Hulk coaster, Busch Gardens boasts the **Gwazi,** the **Kumba,** the **Montu,** and a vari-

ety of other coasters with names that sound like fruity tropical drinks. The Gwazi may be the coolest, as it's really two intertwining wooden coasters with completely different tracks (Jeffrey prefers the smoother "Tiger" side of the ride, while Eddie revels in the spirals of the "Lion" track). Along with a great number of rides, the park also boasts live animals (think Disney's Animal Kingdom before Disney's Animal Kingdom) with some shows which we, um, skipped. But the flume ride **Stanley Falls** is a must on a hot day, as is the **Tanganyika Tidal Wave** if you really just want to get soaked to the bone.

How to get there: Busch Gardens is about 70 miles southwest of Walt Disney World Resort. From Walt Disney World Resort, get on I-4 to I-75. Go north on I-75 to the Fowler Avenue exit (Exit 54). Bear left on the exit ramp, and proceed west on Fowler Avenue to McKinley Avenue. Turn left on McKinley. Proceed south on McKinley to parking and the main entrance to the park. For details visit www.buschgardens.com or call (813) 987-5082.

The Holy Land Experience

Holy crap! In 2001 this park dedicated to "Christ-honoring Christian" values opened to fanfare of biblical proportions. But heathens that we are, we haven't yet heard His word. Although we've promised to go as soon as we figure out how to smuggle in a big enough flask. This 15-acre "living, biblical history museum" boasts things that make queer-as-a-$3-bill Jewish fags from the Northeast like us cringe. They have a Wilderness Tabernacle where you find yourself among the 12 tribes of Israel before a 20-minute, sit-down, fully automated multimedia presentation looking at Israel's ancient priesthood and its sacrificial(!) system, and there's also a replica of Calvary's Garden Tomb where visitors can "pray, read the Scriptures, and reflect on the stirring events surrounding them." We assume, by that, they mean Space Mountain. We are tempted to go, but we have yet to set our Manolo Blahniks in the place because we're afraid we'll burst into flames upon arriving at the parking lot.

How to Get There: Don't say we didn't warn you, but from Walt Disney World Resort you take the I-4 East to Exit 31A. Turn left on Conroy Rd. to Vineland Rd. Turn right and enter on the right. For more information (or just for a hoot) visit www.theholylandexperience.com or call (866) USA-HOLYLAND (but all you really need to dial is 866-USA-HOLY).

Part Four
Odds 'n' Ends

Chapter Sixteen
Lists and Charts and Ratings—Oh, My!

Compare and Contrast

As you read through our wise and insightful attraction descriptions, you may notice that we occasionally refer you to a description of the same ride at another park. Primarily we do this to save paper (environmentalists that we are) and so you don't have to schlep around a book the size of your hope chest. In most cases, however, while the descriptions apply to both versions of the rides, the attractions often do have variation. Here's how they stack up:

DLR = Disneyland Resort
WDW = Walt Disney World Resort

Attraction: Disneyland/Walt Disney World Railroads
Where It Is: DLR Disneyland, WDW Magic Kingdom
Differences: DLR's features four stops and a trip to the Grand Canyon and Primeval World. WDW's is longer but has only three stops.
Who Wins? DLR

Attraction: Splash Mountain
Where It Is: DLR Disneyland, WDW Magic Kingdom
Differences: WDW's version came second, so the Audio-Animatronics are more sophisticated, the story is told more clearly, and the ride system works more efficiently.
Who Wins? WDW

Attraction: Jungle Cruise
Where It Is: DLR Disneyland, WDW Magic Kingdom
Differences: Because they had to make way for Indiana Jones Adventure, DLR's Jungle Cruise lost a few feet of waterway, making Disney World's a longer ride.
Who Wins? WDW

Attraction: Big Thunder Mountain
Where It Is: DLR Disneyland, WDW Magic Kingdom
Differences: virtually none
Who Wins? tie

Attraction: Fantasmic!
Where It Is: DLR Disneyland, WDW Disney-MGM Studios
Differences: At DLR the spectacle essentially rises out of nowhere on Tom Sawyer's Island and the walkway surrounding the Rivers of America, while WDW's is in its own arena. The show at DLR only incorporates Disney's animated films made through *Beauty and the Beast,* while WDW's goes through *Mulan.* The plot at WDW is a bit more confusing.
Who Wins? The two are different, but it's still a tie.

Attraction: Tom Sawyer Island
Where It Is: DLR Disneyland, WDW Magic Kingdom
Differences: WDW's island is bigger with more winding caves, but DLR's tends to be less crowded.
Who Wins? tie

Attraction: Mark Twain/Liberty Belle Riverboats
Where It Is: DLR Disneyland, WDW Magic Kingdom
Differences: They're about the same.
Who Wins? tie

Attraction: Dumbo the Flying Elephant
Where It Is: DLR Disneyland, WDW Magic Kingdom
Differences: virtually none (but we think Disneyland's is prettier)
Who Wins? tie

Attraction: "it's a small world"
Where It Is: DLR Disneyland, WDW Magic Kingdom
Differences: The attraction at Disneyland is housed in a gorgeous, ornate structure and is a longer, more elaborate journey. Of course, people may prefer the more compact Orlando edition.
Who Wins? DLR

Attraction: King Arthur Carrousel
Where It Is: DLR Disneyland, WDW Magic Kingdom
Differences: Um, none. A merry-go-round is a merry-go-round, right?
Who Wins? tie

Attraction: Peter Pan's Flight
Where It Is: DLR Disneyland, WDW Magic Kingdom
Differences: Florida's ride is slightly bigger, and the buildings of London are more three-dimensional.
Who Wins? WDW

Attraction: Snow White's Scary Adventures
Where It Is: DLR Disneyland, WDW Magic Kingdom
Differences: At WDW you get the whole story, whereas at DLR, after a particularly harrowing moment, you get a nonsensical "and they lived happily ever after."
Who Wins? WDW

Attraction: Mad Tea Party
Where It Is: DLR Disneyland, WDW Magic Kingdom
Differences: none, except the attraction at DLR is covered to protect it from rain
Who Wins? tie

Attraction: Star Tours
Where It Is: DLR Disneyland, WDW Disney-MGM Studios
Differences: none except for the differently designed exteriors.
Who Wins? tie

Attraction: Astro Orbiter/Astro Orbitor
Where It Is: DLR Disneyland, WDW Magic Kingdom
Differences: a vowel
Who Wins? tie

Attraction: Autopia/Tomorrowland Speedway
Where It Is: DLR Disneyland, WDW Magic Kingdom
Differences: DLR's cars and track were recently refurbished, and the landscape is scenic.
Who Wins? DLR

Attraction: Space Mountain
Where It Is: DLR Disneyland, WDW Magic Kingdom
Differences: DLR's more recently refurbished ride boasts speakers blaring intense music in your ears for more thrilling space travel.
Who Wins? DLR

Attraction: Honey, I Shrunk the Audience
Where It Is: DLR Disneyland, WDW Epcot
Differences: none
Who Wins? tie

Attraction: Pirates of the Caribbean
Where It Is: DLR Disneyland, WDW Magic Kingdom
Differences: Disneyland's version is significantly longer and more elaborate. And you get the gorgeous Louisiana bayou.
Who Wins? DLR

Attraction: Haunted Mansion
Where It Is: DLR Disneyland, WDW Magic Kingdom
Differences: There's less of an inside queue at WDW, so you get on your doom buggy sooner. But you see the same things.
Who Wins? tie

Attraction: Who Wants to Be a Millionaire—Play It!
Where It Is: DLR Disney's California Adventure, WDW Disney-MGM Studios
Differences: none
Who Wins? tie

Attraction: Muppets 3-D
Where It Is: DLR Disney's California Adventure, WDW Disney-MGM Studios
Differences: none
Who Wins? tie

Attraction: It's Tough to Be a Bug
Where It Is: DLR Disney's California Adventure, WDW Disney's Animal Kingdom
Differences: The queue for the ride at Disney's Animal Kingdom goes in and around the immense Tree of Life, giving it the edge.
Who Wins? WDW

Top Fives

Disneyland Resort

Jeffrey
1. Splash Mountain
2. Indiana Jones Adventure
3. Roger Rabbit's Car Toon Spin
4. Matterhorn Bobsleds
5. Haunted Mansion

Eddie
1. Splash Mountain
2. Haunted Mansion
3. Space Mountain
4. Pirates of the Caribbean
5. Alice in Wonderland

Readers' Poll
1. Space Mountain
2. Indiana Jones Adventure
3. Haunted Mansion
4. Pirates of the Caribbean
5. Splash Mountain

Where to Eat
1. Redd Rocket's Pizza Port
2. Storytellers Cafe (inside Disney's Grand Californian Resort)
3. Rancho del Zocalo Restaurante
4. House of Blues (Downtown Disney)
5. Ralph Brennan's Jazz Kitchen (Downtown Disney)

Disney's California Adventure

Jeffrey
1. Soarin' Over California
2. Mulholland Madness
3. California Screamin'
4. It's Tough to Be a Bug
5. Golden Dreams

Eddie
1. California Screamin'
2. Soarin' Over California
3. Golden Dreams
4. Muppets 3-D
5. Animation

Readers' Poll
1. Soarin' Over California
2. California Screamin'
3. Maliboomer
4. Grizzly River Rapids
5. It's Tough to Be a Bug

Where to Eat
1. Golden Vine Winery
2. MaliBurritos
3. Chips, Strips, and Dips
4. Storyteller's Cafe (inside Disney's Grand Californian Resort)
5. House of Blues (Downtown Disney)

Walt Disney World Resort

Magic Kingdom

Jeffrey
1. Splash Mountain
2. Tomorrowland Transit Authority
3. Buzz Lightyear's Space Ranger Spin
4. Alien Encounter
5. Haunted Mansion

Eddie
1. Splash Mountain
2. Haunted Mansion
3. Space Mountain
4. Pirates of the Caribbean
5. Peter Pan

Readers' Poll
1. Space Mountain
2. Splash Mountain
3. Alien Encounter
4. Haunted Mansion
5. Pirates of the Caribbean

Where to Eat
1. Cinderella's Royal Table
2. Tomorrowland Terrace
3. Tony's Town Square Restaurant

Epcot

Jeffrey
1. Ellen's Energy Adventure
2. American Adventure
3. Spaceship Earth
4. Test Track
5. Body Wars

Eddie
1. American Adventure
2. Spaceship Earth
3. Ellen's Energy Adventure
4. Impressions de France
5. Test Track

Readers' Poll
1. O Canada! (we're not kidding)
2. Test Track
3. Spaceship Earth
4. Ellen's Energy Adventure
5. Living Seas

Where to Eat
1. Coral Reef (Living Seas)
2. Chefs de France (France)
3. San Angel Inn (Mexico)
4. Teppanyaki Dining Room (Japan)

Disney-MGM Studios

Jeffrey
1. Twilight Zone™ Tower of Terror
2. Rock 'n' Roller Coaster Starring Aerosmith
3. Fantasmic!
4. Voyage of The Little Mermaid
5. The Great Movie Ride

Eddie
1. Twilight Zone™ Tower of Terror
2. Rock 'n' Roller Coaster Starring Aerosmith
3. The Great Movie Ride
4. Fantasmic!
5. Muppets 3-D

Readers' Poll
1. Twilight Zone™ Tower of Terror
2. Rock 'n' Roller Coaster Starring Aerosmith

Where to eat
1. Brown Derby
2. '50s Prime-Time Cafe
3. Mama Melrose's Ristorante Italiano
4. Sci-Fi Dine-In Theater Restaurant

Disney's Animal Kingdom

Jeffrey
1. Dinosaur
2. Festival of the Lion King
3. Kilimanjaro Safaris
4. Kali River Rapids
5. It's Tough to Be a Bug

Eddie
1. Kilimanjaro Safaris
2. Dinosaur
3. Festival of the Lion King
4. It's Tough to Be a Bug
5. Kali River Rapids

Readers' Poll
1. Kilimanjaro Safaris
2. Festival of the Lion King
3. It's Tough to Be a Bug
4. Kali River Rapids
5. Dinosaur

Where to Eat
We suggest you dine outside the confines of this park, but if you must, Rainforest Cafe is at the park entrance.

The Disney Parks' Top 10 Spots to Share a Gay Moment
(i.e. hold hands or kiss without encountering glares)

Eddie happens to be one of those people who's perfectly content to hold hands with dates anywhere within the parks. However, since there are families who aren't always particularly evolved around and since being the standard-bearers of political correctness can occasionally grow wearisome, we offer this list not as the top spots to be closeted but as a guide to a few private nooks for those who want to take a break from the fishbowl.

Haunted Mansion (DLR or WDW)

Tom Sawyer Island (DLR or WDW)

Sun Wheel (Disney's California Adventure)

The Hall of Presidents (WDW)

The Disney Gallery Terrace (DLR)

Peter Pan's Flight (DLR or WDW)

The park behind Epcot's Rose and Crown Pub (Epcot)

Tomorrowland Transit Authority (WDW)

Spaceship Earth (Epcot)

Maharajah Jungle Trek (Disney's Animal Kingdom)

Ride Ratings Chart

Want to know which are the best rides in the park without having to read through every description? Here's our easy, clip-n-save chart to help you assess what's must-see and what's must-miss.

✪ Cruella De Vil
✪✪ Give a Little Whistle
✪✪✪ Zip-A-Dee-Doo-Dah
✪✪✪✪ You Can Fly! You Can Fly! You Can Fly!
✪✪✪✪✪ Supercalifragilisticexpialidocious

Disneyland

Disneyland Railroad
Overall Rating: ✪✪✪

Great Moments With Mr. Lincoln
Overall Rating: ✪✪✪

The Enchanted Tiki Room
Overall Rating: ✪✪

The Jungle Cruise
Overall Rating: ✪✪✪✪

Indiana Jones Adventure
Overall Rating: ✪✪✪✪✪

Tarzan's Treehouse
Overall Rating: ✪✪

Big Thunder Mountain Railroad
Overall Rating: ✪✪✪✪

Tom Sawyer Island
Overall Rating: ✪✪✪

Mark Twain Riverboat and
Sailing Ship Columbia
Overall Rating: ✪✪

Fantasmic!
Overall Rating: ✪✪✪✪✪

Pirates of the Caribbean
Overall Rating: ✪✪✪✪✪

The Haunted Mansion
Overall Rating: ✪✪✪✪✪

Roger Rabbit's Car Toon Spin
Overall Rating: ✪✪✪✪

Chip 'n' Dale Treehouse
Overall Rating: ✪

Goofy's Bounce House
Overall Rating: ✪

Gadget's Go Coaster
Overall Rating: ✪

Minnie's House
Overall Rating: ✪✪

Mickey's House
Overall Rating: ✪✪

Davy Crockett's Explorer Canoes
Overall Rating: ✪✪✪

Splash Mountain
Overall Rating: ✪✪✪✪✪

Sleeping Beauty Castle
Overall Rating: ✪

Snow White's Scary Adventures
Overall Rating: ✪✪✪

Pinocchio's Daring Journey
Overall Rating: ✪✪

Peter Pan's Flight
Overall Rating: ✪✪✪✪

King Arthur Carrousel
Overall Rating: ✪

Mr. Toad's Wild Ride
Overall Rating: ✪

Dumbo the Flying Elephant
Overall Rating: ✪✪

Casey Jr. Circus Train and
Storybook Land Canal Boats
Overall Rating: ✪

it's a small world
Overall Rating: ✪✪✪✪

Mad Tea Party
Overall Rating: ✪✪

Alice in Wonderland
Overall Rating: ✪✪✪✪

Matterhorn Bobsleds
Overall Rating: ✪✪✪✪

Astro Orbitor
Overall Rating: ✪

Star Tours
Overall Rating: ✪✪✪✪

Disneyland Monorail
Overall Rating: ✪✪✪

Autopia
Overall Rating: ✪✪

Innoventions
Overall Rating: ✪

Space Mountain
Overall Rating: ✪✪✪✪✪

Honey, I Shrunk the Audience
Overall Rating: ✪✪✪

Disney's California Adventure

Soarin' Over California
Overall Rating: ✪✪✪✪✪

Grizzly River Run
Overall Rating: ✪✪

Redwood Creek Challenge Trail
Overall Rating: ✪

Golden Dreams
Overall Rating: ✪✪✪✪✪

Boudin Bakery
Overall Rating: ✪

Mission Tortilla Factory
Overall Rating: ✪

It's Tough to Be a Bug
Overall Rating: ✪✪✪✪

Golden Vine Winery
Overall Rating: ✪✪

Disney Animation
Overall Rating: ✪✪✪✪

Jim Henson's Muppetvision 3-D
Overall Rating: ✪✪✪✪✪

Who Wants to Be a Millionaire—Play It!
Overall Rating: ✪✪✪✪

Superstar Limo
Overall Rating: ✪

California Screamin'
Overall Rating: ✪✪✪✪✪

King Triton's Carousel
Overall Rating: ✪

Sunwheel
Overall Rating: ✪✪✪

Maliboomer
Overall Rating: ✪✪✪

Orange Stinger
Overall Rating: ✪✪

Jumpin' Jellyfish
Overall Rating: ✪

Mulholland Madness
Overall Rating: ✪✪✪

Golden Zephyr
Overall Rating: ✪

Magic Kingdom

Walt Disney World Railroad
Overall Rating: ✪✪✪

Swiss Family Treehouse
Overall Rating: ✪

The Enchanted Tiki Room, Under New Management
Overall Rating: ✪✪✪
Jungle Cruise
Overall Rating: ✪✪✪✪

The Magic Carpets of Aladdin
Overall Rating: ✪

Pirates of the Caribbean
Overall Rating: ✪✪✪✪✪

Country Bear Jamboree
Overall Rating: ✪✪✪

Splash Mountain
Overall Rating: ✪✪✪✪✪

Big Thunder MountainRailroad
Overall Rating: ✪✪✪✪

Raft to Tom Sawyer Island
Overall Rating: ✪✪✪

The Hall of Presidents
Overall Rating: ✪✪

The Haunted Mansion
Overall Rating: ✪✪✪✪✪

Liberty Belle Riverboat
Overall Rating: ✪✪

Cinderella's Golden Carrousel
Overall Rating: ✪

Snow White's Scary Adventures
Overall Rating: ✪✪✪

it's a small world
Overall Rating: ✪✪✪

Peter Pan's Flight
Overall Rating: ✪✪✪✪✪

Dumbo the Flying Elephant
Overall Rating: ✪✪

Mad Tea Party
Overall Rating: ✪✪

The Adventures of Winnie the Pooh
Overall Rating: ✪✪✪

Mickey's Country House
Overall Rating: ✪✪

Minnie's Country House
Overall Rating: ✪✪

Donald's Boat
Overall Rating: ✪

The Barnstormer at Goofy's Wiseacre Farm
Overall Rating: ✪

The ExtraTERRORestrail Alien Encounter
Overall Rating: ✪✪✪✪

Buzz Lightyear's Space Ranger Spin
Overall Rating: ✪✪✪✪

Tomorrowland Transit Authority
Overall Rating: ✪✪✪

Astro Orbiter
Overall Rating: ✪✪

Space Mountain
Overall Rating: ✪✪✪✪✪

Walt Disney's Carousel of Progress
Overall Rating: ✪✪✪

The Indy Speedway
Overall Rating: ✪✪

The Timekeeper
Overall Rating: ✪✪✪✪

Epcot

Spaceship Earth
Overall Rating: ✪✪✪✪

Global Neighborhood
Overall Rating: ✪

Innoventions East and Innoventions West
Overall Rating: ✪

Ellen's Energy Adventure
Overall Rating: ✪✪✪✪

Body Wars
Overall Rating: ✪✪✪✪

Cranium Command
Overall Rating: ✪✪✪

The Making of Me
Overall Rating: ✪✪✪

Test Track
Overall Rating: ✪✪✪✪

Journey Into Imagination With Figment
Overall Rating: ✪✪✪

Honey, I Shrunk the Audience
Overall Rating: ✪✪✪

Living With the Land
Overall Rating: ✪✪✪

Food Rocks
Overall Rating: ✪✪

The Circle of Life
Overall Rating: ✪✪✪

The Living Seas
Overall Rating: ✪✪

El Rio del Tiempo
Overall Rating: ✪

Maelstrom
Overall Rating: ✪✪

Wonders of China
Overall Rating: ✪✪

The American Adventure
Overall Rating: ✪✪✪✪✪

Impressions de France
Overall Rating: ✪✪✪

O Canada!
Overall Rating: ✪✪✪

Disney-MGM Studios

The Twilight Zone™ Tower of Terror
Overall Rating: ✪✪✪✪✪

Rock 'n' Roller Coaster Starring Aerosmith
Overall Rating: ✪✪✪✪✪

Fantasmic!
Overall Rating: ✪✪✪✪✪

Beauty and the Beast Live on Stage
Overall Rating: ✪✪

The Great Movie Ride
Overall Rating: ✪✪✪✪

The Magic of Disney Animation
Overall Rating: ✪✪✪

Voyage of The Little Mermaid
Overall Rating: ✪✪✪

Backstage Studio Tour
Overall Rating: ✪✪

Backstage Pass
Overall Rating: ✪✪

Walt Disney: One Man's Dream
Overall Rating: ✪✪

Who Wants to Be a Millionaire—Play It!
Overall Rating: ✪✪✪✪

Jim Henson's Muppetvision 3-D
Overall Rating: ✪✪✪✪✪

New York Street
Overall Rating: ✪✪✪

Honey, I Shrunk the Kids Movie Set Adventure
Overall Rating: ✪

Sounds Dangerous
Overall Rating: ✪

Indiana Jones™ Epic Stunt Spectacular
Overall Rating: ✪✪✪

Star Tours
Overall Rating: ✪✪✪✪

Disney's Animal Kingdom

It's Tough to Be a Bug
Overall Rating: ✪✪✪✪

The Festival of the Lion King
Overall Rating: ✪✪✪✪✪

Pocahontas and Her Forest Friends
Overall Rating: ✪

Kilimanjaro Safaris
Overall Rating: ✪✪✪✪✪

The Pangani Forest Exploration Trail
Overall Rating: ✪✪

The Maharajah Jungle Trek
Overall Rating: ✪✪✪

Kali River Rapids
Overall Rating: ✪✪

Flights of Wonder
Overall Rating: ✪

Dinosaur
Overall Rating: ✪✪✪✪✪

Triceratop Spin
Overall Rating: ✪

Primeval Whirl
Overall Rating: ✪✪✪

Glossary

Attraction: What Disney likes to call all its rides, shows, walk-through exhibits, and parades.

Audio-Animatronics: Disney's version of a robot, combining robotics and sound to create an animated, life-like character.

Cast Member: A Disney employee.

Character Dining: A restaurant where Disney characters will come and harass you at your table.

Circle-Vision 360: A film shown in a round auditorium with screens encircling the perimeter, creating a 360-degree image.

Dark Ride: An indoor attraction, where a vehicle moves through a diorama setting.

Fast Loader: An attraction that loads guests continuously or quickly, creating a speedy line.

FASTPASS: A ticket available at a kiosk on a number of popular rides that enables you to come back later and cut to the front of the line. See page 32 for details.

Hidden Mickey: When creating the park, in lieu of signing their names on attractions they completed, Disney designers would create a "hidden Mickey" as a signature to their work. These are figurative images of the mouse planted on a ride, building, or landscape.

Host/Guide: A cast member who actually participates on an attraction, like the captains on the Jungle Cruise or the tour leaders on The Great Movie Ride.

Imagineer: In Disney-speak, a designer/architect/engineer who is involved in the creative process of developing the resorts.

Priority Seating: Disney doesn't offer restaurant reservations. Instead there's priority seating, where you can book a dining time in advance. You'll probably still have to wait—but not as long as the people who just walked up.

Slow Loader: An attraction whose design limitations mean guests load slowly.

Bibliography

Bacon, M. *No Strings Attached.* New York: Macmillan, 1997.

Birnbaum, S. and Safro, J. *Birnbaum's Walt Disney World 2002: Expert Advice from the Inside.* New York: Hyperion, 2001.

Finch, C. *The Art of Walt Disney.* New York: Harry N. Abrams, Inc., 1995.

Gordon, B. and Mumford, D. *The Nickel Tour.* Santa Clarita, Calif.: Camphor Tree Publishers, 2000.

Koenig, D. *Mouse Under Glass.* Irvine: Bonaventure Press, 1997.

Koenig, D. *Mouse Tales: A Behind-the-Ears Look at Disneyland.* Irvine: Bonaventure Press, 1994.

Lainsbury, A. *Once Upon an American Dream: The Story of EuroDisneyland.* Lawrence: University Press of Kansas, 2000.

Lefkon, W. (ed). *Walt Disney World Resort: A Magical Year-By-Year Journey.* New York: Hyperion, 1998.

Marling, K.A. (ed). *Designing Disney's Theme Parks.* New York: Flammarion, 1997.

Peterson, M. *The Little Big Book of Disney.* New York: Disney Editions, 2001.

Philips, I., (ed). *Damron Men's Travel Guide.* San Francisco: Damron, 1999.

Rafferty, K. with Gordon, B. *Walt Disney Imagineering.* New York: Disney Editions, 1996.

Sehlinger, B. *The Unofficial Guide to Disneyland.* New York: Macmillan Travel, 1999.

Sehlinger, B. *The Unofficial Guide to Walt Disney World.* New York: Macmillan Travel, 1998.

Sherman, R.B., and Sherman, R.E.. *Walt's Time.* Santa Clarita, Calif.: Camper Tree Publishers, 1998.

Smith, D., (ed). *The Quotable Walt Disney.* New York: Disney Editions, 2001.

Zibert, E. *Inside Disney.* Foster City, Calif.: IDG Books, 2000.

Index

Adventureland

    Disneyland 70

    Walt Disney World Resort.... 143

Africa

    Disney's Animal Kingdom 218

Alice in Wonderland 92

American Adventure, The 185

Asia

    Disney's Animal Kingdom....220

Astro Orbiter 159

Astro Orbitor 97

Audio-Animatronics....68, 69, 71,
    72, 74, 78, 86, 91, 117, 144, 146,
    148, 166, 172, 181, 182, 186, 200,
    204, 223

Autopia 99

Backstage Pass 203

Backstage Studio Tour 202

Barnstormer at Goofy's Wiseacre
    Farm, The 157

Beauty and the Beast Live
    on Stage 200

Big Thunder Mountain Railroad

    Disneyland 79

    Walt Disney World Resort 147

Blizzard Beach 236

Body Wars..................................171

Boudin Bakery 112

Busch Gardens 248

Buzz Lightyear's Space

    Ranger Spin 158

Camp Minnie-Mickey 215

California Screamin' 119

Casey Jr. Circus Train 89

Character Dining 27

Chip 'n' Dale Treehouse 94

Cinderella's Golden

    Carrousel 150

Circle of Life, The 178

Circle-Vision 360 ....161, 184, 190

Columbia (Sailing Ship) 81

Country Bear Jamboree..........146

Cranium Command................171

Critter Country..........................77

Dark Ride 278

Davy Crockett's

    Explorer Canoes 77

Dinoland U.S.A.......................221

Dinosaur 222

Discovery Island 214

Disney-MGM Studios 193-210

Disneyland Monorail 98

Disneyland Park 65-103

Disneyland Railroad 68

DisneyQuest 235

Disney's Animal

    Kingdom Park 212-223

Disney's California

    Adventure Park 105-124

Donald's Boat 156

80

Downtown Disney
  Disneyland 126
  Walt Disney World Resort....226
Dumbo the Flying Elephant
  Disneyland 88
  Walt Disney World Resort 153
El Rio del Tiempo 181
Ellen's Energy Adventure......170
Enchanted Tiki Room, The
  Disneyland 71
  Walt Disney World Resort 144
Epcot.....................................163-192
ExtraTERRORestrial Alien
  Encounter, The 157
Fantasmic!
  Disneyland 81
  Walt Disney World Resort 199
Fantasyland
  Disneyland 83
  Walt Disney World Resort 149
Fast Loader 31
FASTPASS 32
Festival of the Lion King 216
Flights of Wonder 221
Food Rocks 172
Frontierland
  Disneyland 79
  Walt Disney World Resort 146
Future World 166
Gadget's Go Coaster 95
Global Neighborhood 169
Golden Dreams 111
Golden State 109
Golden Vine Winery 114
Golden Zephyr 123

Goofy's Bounce House..............95
Great Moments With
  Mr. Lincoln 69
Great Movie Ride, The 200
Grizzly River Run 109
Hall of Presidents, The 148
Haunted Mansion, The
  Disneyland 75
  Walt Disney World Resort 148
Hidden Mickey........145, 156, 159
Hollywood Pictures Backlot....115
Honey, I Shrunk the Audience
  Disneyland 101
  Walt Disney World Resort 176
Honey, I Shrunk the Kids
  Movie Set Adventure 205
Impressions de France............189
Indiana Jones Adventure 72
Indiana Jones Epic Stunt
  Spectacular 206
Indy Speedway, The 161
Innoventions
  Disneyland 100
  Walt Disney World Resort 168
it's a small world
  Disneyland 91
  Walt Disney World Resort 152
It's Tough to Be a Bug
  Disneyland 113
  Walt Disney World Resort 215
Jim Henson's Muppetvision 3-D
  Disneyland 116
  Walt Disney World Resort 204
Journey Into Imagination
  With Figment 175

Jumpin' Jellyfish 122
Jungle Cruise
    Disneyland 71
    Walt Disney World Resort 144
Kali River Rapids 221
King Arthur Carrousel 87
King Triton's Carousel 120
Kilimanjaro Safaris 219
Knott's Berry Farm 128
Legoland 129
Liberty Belle Riverboat 149
Liberty Square 147
Living Seas, The......................179
Living With the Land 176
Lost Children 26
Mad Tea Party
    Disneyland 91
    Walt Disney World Resort 152
Magic Kingdom 139-161
Magic of Disney
    Animation, The..................201
Maharajah Jungle Trek, The 222
Main Street, U.S.A.
    Disneyland 65
    Walt Disney World Resort 139
Making of Me, The 172
Maelstrom 182
Maliboomer 120
Many Adventures of Winnie the
    Pooh, The
    Disneyland 79
    Walt Disney World Resort 154
Mark Twain Riverboat 81
Matterhorn Bobsleds 92
Mickey's Country House........155

Minnie's Country House 157
Mickey's House...........................96
Minnie's House 95
Mission: SPACE 173
Mission Tortilla Factory 112
Mr. Toad's Wild Ride 88
Mulholland Madness 123
New Orleans Square 74
New York Street 205
O Canada! 190
Oasis, The 214
Orange Stinger 122
Pangani Forest
    Exploration Trail................220
Paradise Pier 119
Peter Pan's Flight
    Disneyland 87
    Walt Disney World Resort 153
Pinocchio's Daring Journey 86
Pirates of the Caribbean
    Disneyland 74
    Walt Disney World Resort 145
Pocahontas and Her
    Forest Friends 218
Primeval Whirl........................223
Priority Seating.........................19
Redwood Creek
    Challenge Trail 111
River Country 236
Rock 'n' Roller Coaster
    Starring Aerosmith............198
Roger Rabbit's Car
    Toon Spin 93
San Diego Wild
    Animal Park 130

San Diego Zoo 130

SeaWorld

    Orlando..................................248

    San Diego 129

Sleeping Beauty Castle 84

Slow Loader 31

Snow White's Scary Adventures

    Disneyland 86

    Walt Disney World Resort 152

Soarin' Over California 109

Sounds Dangerous 206

Space Mountain

    Disneyland 78

    Walt Disney World Resort 146

Spaceship Earth 166

Splash Mountain

    Disneyland 78

    Walt Disney World Resort 146

Star Tours

    Disneyland 98

    Walt Disney World Resort 207

Storybook Land Canal Boats 88

Sunshine Plaza 108

Sunwheel 120

Superstar Limo 118

Swiss Family Treehouse 143

Tarzan's Treehouse 73

Test Track 173

Timekeeper, The 160

Tom Sawyer Island (Raft to)

    Disneyland 80

    Walt Disney World Resort 147

Tomorrowland

    Disneyland 97

    Walt Disney World Resort 157

Tomorrowland Transit

    Authority 159

Toontown

    Disneyland 93

    Mickey's Toontown Fair ..155

Triceratop Spin 223

Twilight Zone™ Tower of

    Terror, The

    Disneyland 118

    Walt Disney World Resort 197

Typhoon Lagoon 237

Universal

    Islands of Adventure 246

    Studios, Florida 245

    Studios, Hollywood 131

Voyage of The

    Little Mermaid 202

Walt Disney:

    One Man's Dream 204

Walt Disney Railroad 143

Walt Disney

    World Resort 132-241

Walt Disney's Carousel of

    Progress 160

Who Wants to Be a

    Millionaire—Play It!

    Disneyland 117

    Walt Disney World Resort 204

Wonders of China 184

World Showcase 180

Contact Us!

Hey, we want to know what you're thinking too! We'd love to hear your own reviews of attractions, restaurants, hotels—everything. Remember, we're not just looking for what's great; we want to know what's *gay*.

You can E-mail us at GayDLand@aol.com, or you can snail mail us at:

Jeffrey & Eddie
Queens in the Kingdom
c/o Alyson Books
6922 Hollywood Boulevard, Suite 1000
Los Angeles, CA 90028

If we like what you write, you may end up in the next edition of the guide. If we don't, we'll set your letter on fire and laugh at you behind your back. But hey, no pressure.

About the Authors

Jeffrey Epstein is a native of Newton, Mass. After attending Northfield Mount Hermon prep school, he headed to the Tisch School of the Arts at New York University (where he met Eddie) to pursue drama—the theatrical, not emotional, kind. And for a few years he tried acting...and event planning and gym management. After none of those panned out, he settled on the nice stable life of a freelance writer, mainly covering soap operas—a genre in which he never had any particular interest. After moving to Los Angeles, he began writing for such publications as *InStyle, Cosmopolitan, Movieline,* and *Teen People.* He is currently the senior editor at *Out* magazine. He enjoys movies, television, theater, and, oh right, Disney theme parks.

Though **Eddie Shapiro**'s writing and theater criticism have been published in periodicals across the country, he has spent much of his life as an actor, performing off-Broadway and regionally, and touring the country in five separate one-man musicals for children. He has, in fact, done more children's theater than he can remember, but chances are he's scarred your kid. For several years Eddie has been working for AIDS Walk in both Los Angeles and New York, most recently serving as event manager. He is a graduate of Phillips Academy, Andover, NYU's Tisch School of the Arts (where he met Jeffrey), and Circle in the Square Theatre School. He is also the coauthor of *The Actor's Encyclopedia of Casting Directors,* but his royalty percentage is tiny, so you don't have to buy that one.